★DEBOLT'S DICTIONARY OF★

AMERICAN POTTERY MARKS

★WHITEWARE & PORCELAIN★

COLLECTOR BOOKS
A Division of Schroeder Publishing Co., Inc.

Searching for A Publisher?

We are always looking for knowledgeable people considered to be experts within their fields. If you feel that there is a real need for a book on your collectible subject and have a large comprehensive collection, contact us.

COLLECTOR BOOKS
P.O. Box 3009
Paducah, Kentucky 42002-3009

Cover photography by Kern F. Little – LENSWORK.
Cover designed by Beth Summers.

Additional copies of this book may be ordered from:

COLLECTOR BOOKS
P.O. Box 3009
Paducah, Kentucky 42002-3009

@$17.95. Add $2.00 for postage and handling.

Copyright: C. Gerald DeBolt, 1994

Printed by IMAGE GRAPHICS, INC., Paducah, Kentucky

Table of Contents

Preface

This book represents a doubling of the marks and a more than doubling of the information provided in my *Dictionary of American Pottery Marks: Whiteware and Porcelain* published by Charles E. Tuttle Company in 1988 (now out of print). It represents three more years of rather intensive field research. Virtually all of the one thousand additional marks given in this new edition are marks I have seen at flea markets, antique shows, auctions, etc. throughout the eastern United States. Hundreds of these marks are found in no other book.

Two very important discoveries were made in the last several years. First, Edwin AtLee Barber missed many, particularly early, marks in his 1904 marks book. He missed most of the marks from the 1860s, 1870s, and early 1880s. I continue to find previously unknown marks from these early years and I am sure there are many more to be discovered. Second, I've been able to decode most of the dating systems used by American whiteware manufacturers from the early 1900s to the 1960s. See "American Pottery Dating Systems" on p. 208.

Some other important discoveries made in the last few years are:

1. The quality of American whiteware made before the 1890s is superior to what I had previously believed. I had believed that American whiteware made before 1890 was far inferior to the British ware from the same time. Although Britain exported much superior ware to this country, the majority of these imports was of about the same quality as domestic whiteware.

2. American whiteware from the 1870s and early 1880s is not particularly rare at such venues as flea markets. Only whiteware from the 1860s or earlier would be considered rare.

3. W. Percival Jervis, an important potter, artist, and writer, produced a pottery marks book in 1897, seven years before Barber's landmark book. Its 24 pages of American pottery marks are the earliest attempt to document American marks I'm yet aware of. I came upon the book by accident; I wasn't aware it existed. I've not seen it listed in any bibliography; consequently, I believe it is generally unknown today. Since it is probably extremely difficult to find, I've reprinted these pages in the back of this book. See p. 243.

I believe early American whiteware has the potential for becoming an important collectible. First, there is enough of it around to make it possible to collect, yet it is scarce enough to make the search for it a bit of a challenge. Second, many of the early pieces qualify as genuine antiques, now being 100 or more years old.

A third factor making early American whiteware attractive to collectors is the price. Dealers and collectors do not yet know very much about American whiteware. They are usually unaware of the age of much old and even rare early ware. Consequently there is an excellent chance you can find some really nice old pieces for very reasonable prices. This is destined to change. Recent research and resultant publications will inevitably attract the attention of the general antique collecting public. That may well cause prices to soar. Now is the time to collect early American whiteware.

Another factor is the diversity of styling. Comparable British whiteware usually followed tried and true conventional styles. Pieces tend to be tasteful but predictable. With American whiteware, the opposite is often true. There is considerable variety and innovation. Some styling is awfully good; some is merely awful! Seldom is it boring, and that is the fun of it.

A final consideration for the prospective collector is that reproductions are not and probably will not become a serious problem. Only if prices become excessive is the problem likely to appear. Even then, convincing reproductions will be difficult to make.

Acknowledgments

First, I would like to thank the friends and family members who have supported me through the years of researching and writing.

Second, I would like to recognize the many hundreds of antique dealers throughout the eastern United States who have helped me in one way or another.

Finally, I would like to thank the following for giving me special help: the Jamisons of Corning, NY; Marie Reiter of Pittsburgh, PA; Roma Holloway of Pittsburgh, PA; Jane Crane of Uniontown, PA; the staff of the Uniontown Public Library, Uniontown, PA; Bud Franks of Fayette Printing Co., Uniontown, PA; Ronald L. Michael, editor of the Society for Historical Archaeology, California University, California, PA; Florence Corder and Ethel Fox of New Geneva, PA; Lee and Adam Sedlock of Perryopolis, PA; Hessie Lint of South Connellsville, PA; Leonard A. Elby of Connellsville, PA; Joanna Miller and Bill Maust of Casselman Antiques, Grantsville, MD; Rhonda Mandeville of Moyers, WV; Joyce Miller of Bridgewater, VA; and Rocky and the dealers of Rocky's Antique Mall, Rt. 11, north of Staunton, VA; Faith Fearer of Uniontown, PA; Tom Bloom of Wellsburg, WV; Jack Crislip of Connellsville, PA; Don Folweiler of Staunton, VA; Olin King of Cleveland Heights, OH; Rosemarie Tomasek of Uniontown, PA; the William Diedrichs; Bob and Juanita Hawley of Mt. Storm, WV; Paul Christie of Pittsburgh, PA; Dwayne and Billie Bastian of Clarksville, PA; Jacqueline Sage of Connellsville, PA; Betty McManus of Fairchance, PA; Louise Shell-Skala of Uniontown, PA; Dale Abrams of Columbus, OH; the Kopps of York New Salem, PA, James R. Newman of Uniontown, PA, and Leota DeBolt of Uniontown, PA.

Introduction

Whiteware is any pottery that has been refined to the extent that, in its natural state, it is white or nearly white. It includes all pottery from cream-colored ware (Queen's Ware) to porcelain. Porcelain is the most highly refined whiteware. Ironstone (stone granite), semi-porcelain and most American majolica are included in the whiteware category.

The purpose of this book is to help identify the manufacturer, the place of manufacture, and the approximate age of old American whiteware or porcelain from its mark, if it has one. It is designed to help the serious collector of old American whiteware as well as the novice trying to identify that fancy old Victorian tureen aunt Alice gave you before she moved to her condo in Florida. A thoughtfully and carefully constructed index is the key to this book. It is designed to help you identify a mark with minimum information and effort. To save time and needless frustration, you should read the following seven steps before attempting to use the index.

Step I. Country of Manufacture

The first thing to look for on a mark is the name of a foreign country. It is usually below the mark, infrequently above. If it is marked England, France, Germany, etc., then it is obviously not made in the U.S.A. If it is marked Nippon or Silesia, it may not be so easy to determine the country of origin. English pottery marks often include a regional mark. Staffordshire is the best known. These marks are included in the index. Also, the index includes company names, initials, and words commonly found on foreign marks and identifies the country of manufacture. Many, particularly old, European marks include no words. The index is designed to help you identify these marks as being of foreign origin.

If you now have concluded that your mark is not foreign, go on to Step II.

Step II. Company Name or Initials

The name of a company or its initials found anywhere on a mark often makes the identification of an item very easy. If the mark has what appears to be a company name, simply look it up in the section "Principal American Marks," which is an alphabetical listing of American companies and their marks. If it is not there, then look for it in the index. There are two reasons a mark may not appear in the principal listing. First, the company may not have started until the 1960s or later. Second, what appears to be a company name may in fact not be. For example, Mellor & Co. on a mark actually indicates the Cook Pottery Company. Remember to look for these "company names" in the index.

All company initials, or apparent company initials, are listed in the index. If you are certain you're reading the initials correctly and they are not listed in the index, then that company is probably a foreign one. The index includes many foreign company names and initials, particularly from the 1800s and early 1900s; however, I am sure many later companies have been overlooked.

Be very careful about ascribing a mark that consists only of initials to any particular company. C. Jordan Thorn, who wrote a marks book in the 1940s, erroneously attributed an S.P. Co. mark to the Southern Porcelain Co. Barber in his 1904 marks book said that the only mark he could find for this old company was the one listed in this book. (See p. 133.) This was marked on telegraph insulators! He believed that other items may have been so marked. Southern Porcelain Co. products are very rare. If you have an item marked only S.P. Co. it was made by Steubenville Pottery or, possibly, Sebring Pottery. Again, be very careful about ascribing any mark that consists only of initials to any particular company. Only do so if it was listed by Barber or if you have other irrefutable evidence!

If a mark has no company name or intials, or if the name or intials are not legible, go on to Step III.

Step III. An Identifying Word

On American marks, identifying words usually indicate a pattern, a shape, or a special product of that company. Don't choose such words as *semi-porcelain, ironstone china, semi-vitreous, white granite,* or *warranted.* Such terms are very commonly used on American marks (similar terms on English marks) and are generally useless for identifying marks. However, if such a term is the only word or words on an American mark, it will be listed in the index.

If there are no identifying words on a mark or if they are not legible, go on to Step IV.

Step IV. Describing the Mark

Pick out some obvious feature that might generally describe the mark. Examples might be a globe, a wreath, a moon or crescent, an eagle, a bird (if it doesn't look like an eagle), a lion, two lions, a horse, two horses, a lion and a unicorn (the British Coat of Arms), and many more. If two different animals are on a mark the one on the left will be listed first in the index.

If the most distinguishing feature about a mark is its shape — a square, a diamond, a rectangle — look up that shape in the index. However, a circle is not listed; it is so commonly used that its inclusion would confuse the index. There is not a single American mark that needs to be described as a circle.

Step V. The British (English) Coat of Arms

The British Coat of Arms mark consists of a lion, a central shield with a crown on top, and a unicorn. One variant has a second lion instead of the unicorn. You may be surprised that the British Coat of Arms was used rather frequently to mark early American wares. It was done with the intent of making the product appear to be of British origin. The general public believed British-made wares were superior to American-made wares. Often they were. To help insure sales, American companies would resort to marking with the British Arms. Barber believed the first use of the Arms mark in America was by Rouse & Turner c.1850 at the Jersey City Pottery. There are more than sixty British Arms marks used by American companies, some using two or more variations. Fortunately, most have company names, initials, or some identifying words to tell them apart. However, there are many British Arms marks (including a two-lion variant) that are difficult to distinguish. These marks are shown on pp. 228 to 233.

Step VI. Monograms

If at all possible, try to identify a mark without using monograms. The Victorians of the late 1800s loved monograms, seemingly the more complicated the better. Many pottery marks incorporate monograms in one way or another. Some are large and obvious; others are so tiny, as on the shield of a British Arms mark, that it takes a magnifying glass to see them. Some are fairly easy to decipher. Others are very difficult, particulary regarding the intended order of the letters. If you can identify the order of the letters in a monogram, you will find them in the index. If you can't decipher a monogram, use something else to identify the mark. For example: one mark of the East Palestine Pottery Co. is just the company monogram inside a wreath with no words. In this case, look under the word *wreath* in the index.

Step VII. Nondescript Marks

In some instances a monogram may make up the entire mark, or the monogram may have a nondescript background. If you have a mark that is an unfathomable monogram or otherwise defies description, see pp. 235 to 239. Use these pages only as a last resort.

What is Early American Whiteware?

Prior to the 1980s, books dealing with American whiteware marks dealt primarily with the period before 1900. They did not try to extend their coverage beyond that of Edwin A. Barber's *Marks of American Potters,* published in 1904. This book extends that coverage to c.1970. Any whiteware made before 1920 can be considered early. This is an historical, not an arbitrary, definition. The main event for bringing about the division was World War I, with American involvement 1917 – 1918. The war changed America profoundly, and that change is reflected in the United States' pottery industry. No longer would we be content to look back to Europe. A new American patriotism brought about a pride in things made in the U.S.A. American companies, using mass-production techniques, were already gearing up to keep the domestic whiteware markets denied their European counterparts by the dislocations of war.

The 1920s was a period of transition. For many older companies that did not modernize, the 1920s proved difficult, culminating in total collapse with the coming of the Great Depression. For a small number of progressive companies, the 1920s was the springboard to the future. The next 30 years would be the era of American dominance in the domestic whiteware industry. This dominance would even extend, albeit to a lesser degree, to fine porcelain. The granting to the Lenox Co. in 1917 of the right to supply dinner service to the White House was a major event in the industry. This was the first time this honor had gone to an American company. No longer would our country's industry take a back seat to the European industry.

From c.1930 to c.1960 America's whiteware industry was generally robust; however, by the early 1950s the handwriting was already on the wall. The 1950s saw the virtual collapse of the American industry. Cheap foreign, particularly Asian, imports flooded the country. By the 1960s the American whiteware industry was essentially dead. Only Lenox and a handful of companies that specialized in hotel and institutional ware survived.

In summary:

Prior to the 1920s—
1. The American public generally favored European whiteware, particularly fine porcelain.
2. The industry often used marks that concealed their U.S. identity.
3. The industry looked to Europe for innovation.
4. The industry was not geared for mass-production.

After the 1920s to c.1960—
1. Those U.S. companies that retooled for mass-production generally prospered.
2. Americans began to look to their own countrymen for innovation.
3. MADE IN U.S.A. was proudly proclaimed on marks.

How To Recognize Early American Whiteware and Its Marks

Distinguishing Characteristics of Early American Whiteware

It is a good idea to learn something about what early (before 1920) American whiteware looks like before you begin searching for early American marks. While not necessary for using this book, a little knowledge about early whiteware will save you some time and effort. Some study of books on the subject and a few visits to antique shops or shows will help you develop a sense of what to look for. Once you have developed a sense for the "Victorian" or "turn-of-the-century" look, you might want to try determining if the ware is American or imported. While early American potters often copied European styles, there are differences.

Some differences came about because of the technical problems encountered by the early American potters. Since most workers in the early American industry were English themselves, some having prior experience in the English industry or the help of English experts to get them started, they naturally attempted to make their whiteware as it had been made in England. Using American clays and other raw materials, however, caused English methods to not always work as planned. Some companies failed completely. Others had limited success. Even then, the resulting whiteware was often not as good as its English counterpart. One example of this is the problem of crazing.

Crazing is a fine web of tiny cracks in the glaze of whiteware caused by the improper matching of the glaze to the whiteware body. Experience had helped the English to minimize the problem. However, English solutions to the problem often failed when dealing with American raw materials. While not all early American whiteware is subject to crazing, much of it is. Some American whiteware made after 1920 can also have crazing. Due to their vitrified state, imported European wares of this period will generally not have crazing. English whiteware from the early and middle 1800s, however, is subject to crazing as is some later English Staffordshire ware. The crazing on British Staffordshire tends to be delicate with the lines smaller and closer together than on most American whiteware.

Distinguishing Early American Marks from Foreign Marks

Foreign Marks in General

The McKinley Tariff Act required that from 1891 on, all wares imported into the United States had to have the country of origin marked on them. With the exception of England, the vast majority of whiteware imported before the 1950s came into the U.S. during the late 1800s and early 1900s. As a result, nearly all early wares from foreign countries, except England, will have the country name as part of their mark. That name, however, may not be the modern or English language version. Also, some country marks are really regional or provincial marks. These various names are listed in the index. In any case, most early foreign whiteware imports, except those from England, will be a hard, translucent porcelain that is not likely to be confused with early American whiteware.

Items made to be sold within a foreign country, not for export to the United States, did not need the country's name on the mark. By any number of means, these items can have found their way into the United States. This is particularly true regarding whiteware made in England. Britain had a vast empire with colonies including Canada. British wares sent to Canada could easily find their way to the U.S. These wares would not necessarily have *England* on their marks. Also, vast amounts of British whiteware were imported into the U.S. before 1891. Very little of this was marked with the word *England*.

Some much later foreign wares, usually imported into the United States after Word War II, were and are marked with paper labels containing the name of the country of origin. See p. 13 for more on this fairly recent problem.

In conclusion:

1. Most foreign whiteware found in the United States today that has a country of origin as part of its mark was made after 1891.

2. However, it can't be said that the lack of the country of origin on the mark indicates an American item or a foreign item made before 1891.

English Marks

Large amounts of British whiteware were imported into the United States in the 1800s. Most of that imported before 1891 will not have *England* on the mark. The following information will help you identify British whiteware and its marks.

1. This book's index has a fairly comprehensive listing of company names, initials, regions, cities and towns found on English marks.

2. In addition to the index, the following general rules for British marks will be helpful.

a. British marks of the 1800s tend to be complex. The elaborate cartouches used by early Staffordshire potters are particularly distinctive:

Nothing like this was used on American whiteware.

b. The Staffordshire knot was never used on early American marks.

Besides two nearly undetectable exceptions (see pp. 45 and 98), I have never seen an American mark from any period that incorporated the Staffordshire knot.

The Staffordshire knot was used alone or incorporated into a more complex mark. When used alone, the Staffordshire knot often had letters in the open spaces of the knot representing the initials of the company. Either the left or the middle initial will be the first letter of the company's initials. Usually it is the left one.

c. The names of towns and cities are often used on British marks.

All of these names are listed in the index. Most of these towns are located in the Staffordshire district of England. Often the initial of the town was used in conjunction with the company's initials. If the letter is an *L* it can cause confusion with French Limoges porcelain since some Limoges was marked in a similar way. However, Limoges ware will be translucent porcelain; the English ware will usually be simple opaque whiteware.

A.B.C.
―――――
L

d. The use of *Ltd.* (for Limited) is distinctive to British marks.

However, for some reason, two American companies did use *Ltd.* as part of their marks. See pp. 33 and 202. *Ltd.* really had no meaning in this country. All other marks using *Ltd.* will be British.

e. Both American and British companies used the British Royal Coat of Arms to mark whiteware. See pp. 228 to 233.

f. Initials and monograms are frequently used on British marks.

Often they are the only thing you can use to distinguish the mark. Those used in the 19th century are often in an elaborate script difficult to read. *Js* look like *Is*. Many other letters are hard to make out. This is almost never true with American marks. However, complex monograms were used in both countries. American monograms are discussed elsewhere in this book. See p. 7.

g. Other points about British marks:
1. Lions, not just as a part of the Royal Coat of Arms, are common on British marks but are fairly rare on American marks.
2. Crowns, though used by some American companies, are far more common on British marks, particularly after WWI.
3. BONE CHINA is often used on later English marks; I don't think the term was ever used on American marks. Oxford Bone China introduced by Lenox in 1962 is an exception.
4. The eagle, common on American marks, is rare on British marks. When used on British marks, the eagles are usually copied from eagles found on American coins of the period.
5. TRADE MARK is far more frequently used on British marks than on American marks.
6. Some British marks included the word *England* for 10 or more years before 1891.

How to Tell an Early American Mark from a Late American Mark

A Barber Mark

In 1904 Edwin AtLee Barber published his *Marks of American Potters*. This book remains an important research tool today. An item that has a mark shown in Barber's book can be irrefutably called an early piece. For those companies that continued production well past the 1920s, these early Barber marks are sometimes the only ones that can be considered unquestionably early. In this book I often refer to a Barber mark as a pre-1904 mark: a mark found in Barber's book that was in current use in 1904 could have been used for some time after that but seldom were they used beyond c.1910. The Edwin M. Knowles vase mark was a major exception. In any case, nearly all the companies listed in Barber's book had ceased production by the time of the Great Depression. Many had ceased production long before that.

Characteristics That Early (before c.1920) Marks Will Not Have
1. Early marks will not include U.S.A. or MADE IN U.S.A.

There are a few exceptions to this. Barber listed a few marks with U.S.A. added to the location of manufacture, for example: East Liverpool, Ohio, U.S.A. Only two Barber marks had U.S.A. set apart as commonly found on later marks. These were for the East Liverpool Potteries Co. and the Thomas China Co. of Lisbon, Ohio. With these and a few other exceptions, U.S.A. found on a mark will indicate it was from the 1920s or later. See p. 199.

2. An early mark will not say 18 or 22 karat gold. This practice seems to have started in the 1920s. See p. 199.

3. Early marks will seldom have numbers or a combination of numbers and letters under the mark. The numbers and letters usually indicate a dating system. See p. 208 for the chapter titled "American Pottery Dating Systems."

4. Early marks will never say *by* and the company name, for example: Ivory Porc. by Sebring (the Sebring Pottery Co). This type of mark indicates some special pattern or new whiteware (Ivory Porcelain in this case) made by a particular company (Sebring in this case). Early marks were never so designed. A few did use *made by* and the company's name, but even this was very rare.

5. Early marks will never say *fine china*. Just as *bone china* is a late term on British marks, *fine china* is a late term used on American marks. It was probably not used until after World War II. *Fine china* is also found on "fake" marks used on modern Asian imports. See p. 12.

6. The name Russel Wright appears on whiteware made in the 1940s and 1950s.

Characteristics That Early (before c. 1920) Marks Will Include
1. A British Royal Coat of Arms. See pp. 228 to 233.
2. Monograms — some quite complex. See pp. 235 to 239 for some monogram marks that are difficult to identify.
3. Fancy "Victorian gingerbread" decoration. This is particularly true of late 19th century marks.
4. Garter marks:

These are similar to British garter marks. American garter marks date from the 1870s to c. 1902.

5. Plain marks with company initials:

E.L.P.Co.   N.C.Co.   ADMIRAL
WACO CHINA   E.L.O.   V.P.Co.

KT&K   C.P.Co.
CHINA   ROYAL

These plain marks were used all through the early years to at least c.1920. They seem to have been used most commonly in the first decade of the twentieth century. Marks used in the 1920s were usually simple, but this particular style was infrequently used.

Fake Marks

Fake marks are not yet a problem for collectors of early American whiteware. First, whiteware marks are still generally unknown to the collecting public; therefore, reproducing them would be meaningless. Second, early American whiteware seldom commands a monetary premium meriting the reproduction of marks. Third, since much early American whiteware has no marks, a fake mark stamped on an old piece, if at all suspect, might actually lower its value. The potential buyer might now believe the whiteware itself is a reproduction.

The aforementioned notwithstanding, I have recently come across some Victorian-looking whiteware complete with old-style marks. Both the whiteware and the marks were new. The marks were not reproductions of old marks, just marks made in an early style. However, it must be kept in mind that when or if early whiteware takes its place with other American antiques, reproductions are sure to follow.

The real problem with fake marks is late American whiteware made after World War II. Japan and other Asian nations produced and continue to produce whiteware with paper labels marked with the country of origin. Some of these wares have no other marks. Others have marks made to simulate American or European marks. I have a plate marked NORCREST FINE CHINA. It also has a paper label with JAPAN on it. Once the paper label is removed there will be no indication as to the country of origin. Many of these imports use the term *fine china*. This term is also quite common on the marks of late American whiteware made after World War II. Some of the imported wares are of good quality, others are not. These products are not likely to be confused with early American whiteware, but they are going to cause problems for collectors in the future.

Unmarked Ware

Perhaps a book dealing with marks should not discuss unmarked ware; however, since much early American whiteware was not marked, I felt a few points are in order. Only those with considerable experience should try to determine if an unmarked piece is early American. Unmarked items come from all periods from the earliest whiteware made in this country to ware made today. Some will be imports, even modern imports. Imported ware with the country name on just a paper label and no other mark will become unmarked whiteware once the label is removed. American dinnerware sold in sets from at least the 1890s onward that were marked will frequently have some items in the set that will not be marked. Once that item is separated from the rest, it becomes just another unmarked piece of whiteware. It is fine to collect unmarked, apparently early whiteware. The price is often right. However, collect for aesthetic pleasure, not for investment potential.

Principal American Marks

1. Acme Pottery (Porcelain) Co.
Crooksville, OH
1903 – 1905

(1903 – 1905)

---

2. Akron China Co.
Akron, OH
1894 – 1908

See p. 229 for more about the first mark below.

(c.1895)

(c.1898 – c.1905)

(after 1905)

---

3. Akron Queensware Co.
Akron, OH
1890 – 1894

1890 – 1894

---

4. Albright China Co.
Carrollton, OH
1910 – c.1930

Their mark includes ALBRIGHT CHINA. See p. 166.

---

5. Alliance Vitreous China Co.
Alliance, OH
c.1910 – c.1930

One AVCO CHINA mark was found with U.S.A. 1930.

(c.1920)

(1929)

(1920s)

6. American Art China Works

(Rittenhouse, Evans & Co.)
Trenton, NJ
1891 – c.1899

They made a thin, translucent, belleek type of china. R.E. & Co. stands for Rittenhouse, Evans and Company.

7. American China Co.

Toronto, OH
1897 – c.1910

The first five marks date from 1897 to c. 1904.

See p. 229.

MADE BY
THE
AMERICAN CHINA CO.
TORONTO, OHIO

EUGENIA

BILTMORE

(c.1905 – c.1910)

(c.1905 – c.1910)

The two American China Co. marks at left are among the earliest to incorporate U.S.A. as an integral part of a pottery mark. See p. 199 for more discussion about this.

8. American Chinaware Corporation

East Liverpool, OH, et al.
1929 – c.1931

The American Chinaware Corporation was formed in 1929 from eight companies trying to avoid dissolution. Chief among these was Knowles, Taylor and Knowles, a giant of the East Liverpool, Ohio, industry. Others were the Carrollton Pottery Co.; National China Co.; Pope-Gosser China Co.; E.H. Sebring China Co.; Smith-Phillips China Co. and two lesser companies. This combination failed after about two years. The Pope-Gosser Co., however, survived as a separate and reorganized company until the 1950s.

Marks for this company are on the next page.

8. American Chinaware Corporation (continued)

The mark at the left is poly-chrome as is the AMERCÉ mark at the far right — at least sometimes.

---

9. American Crockery Co.
Trenton, NJ
1876 – 1890s

(c.1880)

AMERICAN CHINA
A. C. Co.

(c.1890)

---

10. American Porcelain Manufacturing Co.
Gloucester, NJ
1854 – 1857

A.P.M.Cº

---

11. American Pottery Co.

See Jersey City Pottery on p. 66.

---

12. American Pottery Works or Sebring Pottery Co.
East Liverpool, Ohio 1887 – c.1902
Sebring, Ohio c.1902 – c.1940
1887 – 1940 (1948)*

STONE CHINA
SEBRING BROS. & CO.

(1887 – c.1895)

SEBRINGS
SEMI-VITREOUS
PORCELAIN
(c.1895 – c.1905)

The Sebring Porcelain

(c.1895 – c.1905)

SEBRING POTTERY CO.
CHINA

(c.1890 – c.1900)

* See p. 189 in "Miscellaneous American Marks" for marks from the 1940 – 1948 period.

12. American Pottery Works or Sebring Pottery Co. (continued)

The following four marks are for Sebring's KOKUS CHINA. KOKUS STONE CHINA was an iron-stone ware. KOKUS CHINA after 1900 was a semi-vitreous china sometimes of quite good quality.

(c.1900 – c.1905)

(c.1895)

The mark at the left is from Gates and Ormerod. This mark is reprinted from *Historical Archaeology* Vol. 16, Numbers 1 & 2, p. 233.* See p. 269.

KOKUS
CHINA

(after 1904)

Kokus
CHINA

(c.1905 – c.1915)

(c.1905 – c.1920)

THE S.P. CO.
———————
PORCELAIN

(c.1905 – c.1915)

S.P. CO.
S.——V.
SEBRING, O.

(c.1914 – c.1918)

S. P. CO.
S—V
SEBRING, O.

H 30 (1930)

E 19 (1919)

(c.1919 – c.1930)

THE SEBRING POTTERY CO.

(1920s)

JADE WARE
BY
SEBRING
U. S. A.

(c.1925 – c.1935)

Ivory Porcelain by Sebring
Reg. U.S. Pat Off
Pat 2-24-1925

Sebring's IVORY PORCELAIN was one of many "IVORY" marked wares produced by nearly every American whiteware manufacturer in the late 1920s. Sebring's IVORY PORCELAIN was possibly the first, being patented in early 1925 and produced through the 1930s. See also p. 200.

*This is one of 27 marks reprinted from *Historical Archaeology*, Volume 16, Numbers 1 & 2 (1982) by permission of the Society for Historical Archaeology, P.O. Box 231033, Pleasant Hill, CA 94523-1033.

12. American Pottery Works or Sebring Pottery Co. (continued)

WARRANTED
22 K GOLD
HAND DECORATED

Ivory Porcelain by Sebring

REG. U.S PAT. OFF.
PAT. 2-24-1925

CUNNINGHAM
PICKETT DIV.
TROPIC

(late 1930s)

" *The Jasmine* "
Golden Maize
—— BY ——
THE SEBRING POTTERY CO.
SEBRING, OHIO
Reg U.S Pat. Off. No.230442

(c.1930)

Sebring patented GOLDEN MAIZE July 19, 1927. There are a number of GOLDEN MAIZE marks including one headed "The Nile Daisy" instead of "The Jasmine."

The earliest of these marks was just GOLDEN MAIZE BY SEBRING with the patent number and date under the mark.

The history of the Sebring family in Sebring, Ohio and other places is extremely complex. The family had control of, or an interest in, many companies. Also, there were constant changes in the ownership of their various companies. The Crescent China Co. and Leigh Potteries, Inc., both of Alliance, Ohio, were two such companies. See p. 37 for a discussion of these companies and their marks.

---

13. Anchor Pottery Co.
Trenton, NJ
1894 – mid 1920s.

J.E. Norris founded the Anchor Pottery Company. His initials can be found on marks used both before and after 1904.

The first 8 marks are Barber (pre-1904) marks.

IRON STONE CHINA

WARRANTED

(c.1894)

(Note the A.P. monogram on the above mark.)

(c.1894)

(c.1898)

J.E.N.

(c.1900)

(c.1898)   (c.1898)

(See next page for more Anchor Pottery marks)

13. Anchor Pottery Co. (continued)

(c.1900)   (c.1904 – c.1912)

Berlin
ANCHOR POTTERY   (c.1900)
J.E.N.

Various forms of the mark at left were used after c.1904 to 1910 or a bit later. After WWI the Anchor Pottery was owned by the Grand Union Tea Co. In 1926 Anchor was acquired by the Fulper Pottery.

---

14. Arsenal Pottery
Trenton, NJ
c.1869 – 1890s

This company was also called the Mayer Pottery Manufacturing Company. I have seen no marks for this company.

---

15. Atlas China Co.
Niles, OH
c.1922 – c.1927

This company was called the Crescent China Co. for a short time in 1921. The Globe China Co. was started in 1925 by the same people who started the Atlas China Co. In 1927 the Atlas China Co. was joined with the Globe Pottery of Cambridge, Ohio, forming the Atlas-Globe China Co. The Atlas-Globe China Co. lasted from c.1927 to 1934 when Universal Potteries, Inc. was organized in Cambridge, Ohio. See Atlas-Globe Co. below. See Universal Potteries, Inc. on p. 154.

18 CARAT COIN GOLD
ATLAS CHINA COMPANY

ATLAS CHINA Co.
NILES, OHIO

---

16. Atlas-Globe China Co.
Cambridge, OH
c.1927 – 1934

See Atlas China Co. for a history of the Atlas-Globe China Co.

ATLAS-GLOBE
CHINA COMPANY
D 27

(1927)

BROADWAY ROSE
A-G.C. Co.
CAMBRIDGE OHIO

MADE IN U.S.A.

17. Bailey-Walker China Co.
Walker China Company after 1943
Bedford, OH
1922 – 1943

The Bedford China Co. preceded the Bailey-Walker Co. See p. 167 in "Miscellaneous American Marks" for a possible mark. See p. 157 for Walker China Co. marks. Bailey-Walker and Walker dating systems are discussed on p. 157 as well as p. 224.

(1920s)

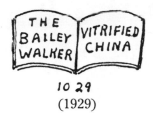

18. Barberton Pottery
Barberton, OH
1901 – 1905

See p. 167 for a possible mark.

19. J.H. Baum
Wellsville, OH
1888 – 1896

This mark is from Gates and Ormerod. It was published in *Historical Archaeology,* Volume 16, Numbers 1 & 2, p. 14.

20. L.B. Beerbower & Co.
Elizabeth, NJ
1879 – c.1904

21. Beerbower & Griffen/Phoenix Pottery
Phoenixville, PA
1877 – 1879

The center of the mark at the right is the Coat of Arms of the state of Pennsylvania.

22. Bell Pottery Co.
Findlay, OH
1888 – c.1904

The Bell Pottery moved to Columbus, Ohio, about 1904. They were out of business in about two years. I have yet to see a Bell mark with Columbus. All the following marks indicate Findlay, Ohio.

It is said that Bell made and distributed both decorated and undecorated ware; therefore, some ware will have amateur decoration. The few pieces that I have seen from this company have been true translucent porcelain, painted and artist signed. The painting looked professional to me. Bell hand painted porcelain might be mistaken for French Limoges porcelain, particularly if it has the first mark given below.

B P CO F O	THE BELL POTTERY CO. FINDLAY, OHIO	BELL CHINA B. P. CO. Findlay, Ohio
The above mark might be mistaken for a French Limoges mark.	This mark was impressed on heavier ware.	This mark was used on hotel porcelain.

23. Edwin Bennett Pottery Co.
Baltimore, MD
1846 – 1936

Based on my own observations and those of Edwin AtLee Barber some 100 years ago, the Edwin Bennett Pottery Co. of Baltimore, Maryland, would have to be regarded as one of America's premier pottery houses. Although I have seen fewer than a dozen samples of Bennett pottery over the last ten years, I remember all but one, each being distinctive in some way. This is true of both early and later ware. Among the latter was an excellent blue willow piece, not hotel type, from about 1915. Except for early Buffalo Pottery ware, most other American blue willow is a heavy hotel type of whiteware.

E&W BENNETT
CANTON AVENUE
BALTIMORE MD.

The mark at left was used from 1848 to 1856 while Edwin Bennett was partnered with his brother William. William Bennett left the company in 1856. The mark was used on majolica and other wares.

23. Edwin Bennett Pottery Co. (continued)

(c.1870 – c.1875)

The above mark is worth special mention. See p. 167 in "Miscellaneous American Marks."

(c.1873 – c.1880)

(c.1884 – c.1890)

Barber said the marks above were used on very special Parian plaques. I've seen one on an ordinary whiteware piece.

(c.1886)

This is a variant of the Michigan Coat of Arms. Note the E. B. monogram.

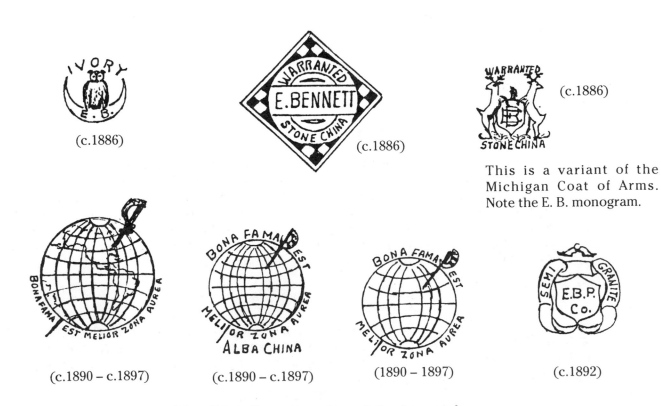

(More Edwin Bennett marks on following page.)

23. Edwin Bennett Pottery (continued)

(1894)

The above mark may have been in the form of a paper label only.

(1896)

(1896)

An E.B.P. Co. monogram is on the above mark.

Albion

WARRANTED

(1897 – c.1905)

BENNETT **S** – **V** **B**ALTIMORE

(c.1910 – c.1925)

BENNETT **B**LUE **W**ILLOW **W**ARE

(c.1915)

BENNETT **B**AKEWARE

(c.1930)

---

24. William Bloor
East Liverpool, OH
c.1860 – 1862

W BLOOR

---

25. Bonnin and Morris
Philadelphia, PA
c.1770

This very rare mark is a P in blue under the glaze.

---

26. Bradshaw China Co.
Niles, OH
c.1900 – c.1912

The Bradshaw China Co. became the Tritt China Co. about 1912. This company ended about 1921. I have not yet seen a Tritt China Co. mark. The mark below is from Barber's 1904 marks book.

TRADE SHAW MARK

27. Brewer Pottery Co.
Tiffin, OH
c.1890 – c.1892

This company made sanitary ware after 1892. The Trenton Pottery Co. and J. Hart Brewer helped organize this company. See p. 232 for a possible mark.

28. J. Hart Brewer Pottery Co.
Trenton, NJ
late 1890s – c.1902

J. Hart Brewer joined Samuel E. Thropp about 1893 as owner of the Trenton Pottery Co. The company was called Thropp & Brewer. Later Mr. Brewer got his own company. Although he died in 1900, the company continued for a while.

Before 1893 the Trenton Pottery was under Fell & Thropp. See p. 48. See also Trenton Pottery.

See p. 232 for a possible J. Hart Brewer Pottery Co. mark.

29. Brighton Pottery
Zanesville, OH
c.1905

Their mark is the company name and city in a circle.

30. Brockmann Pottery Co. et al.
Cincinnati, OH
1862 – 1912

Tempest, Brockmann & Co. (1862 – 1881)
Tempest, Brockmann & Sampson Pottery Co. (1881 – 1887)
Brockmann Pottery Company (1887 – 1912)

(before 1881)
T. B. & Co.

(1887 – 1904 or later)
B. P. Co.

B. P. Co.
(1887 – 1904 or later)

24

31. Brunt, Bloor, Martin & Co.
East Liverpool, OH
1876 – 1882

32. William Brunt, Jr. & Co.
East Liverpool, OH
1877 – 1878 (later for marks; see below)

Although this company became William Brunt, Son & Co. in 1878, I am sure their marks continued to say W.B., Jr. & Co. for a few more years. These marks are so common that it would be impossible for them to have been used only for the one year 1877 to 1878. The only other explanation is that whiteware was made before 1877. Gates and Ormerod were very clear that this was not the case. Only Rockingham and yellow wares were made before 1877.

IRONSTONE CHINA
W. B. JR. & Co.

(1877 – c.1882)

TRADE MARK
IRONSTONE CHINA
W.B. Jr. & Co.

(1877 – c.1882)

Once in a while this phoenix mark is found with W.B. & Co. instead of W.B., Jr. & Co.

The William Brunt, Jr. & Co. became William Brunt, Son & Co. from 1878 to 1892 (or 1894). The following marks date from about 1880 to 1892.

TRADE MARK
IRONSTONE CHINA
W. B. S. & Co.

(c.1880)

OHIO
WBS&Co

(c.1882 – 1892)

W.B.S.&Co
·7

(c.1882 – 1892)

33. William Brunt Pottery Co.

East Liverpool, OH
1894 (or 1892) – 1911

Barber said this company was incorporated in 1894 as two of the marks below seem to indicate; however, Gates and Ormerod say 1892. See p. 232 for a mark that may have been used by the Brunt Pottery Co. between 1892 and 1894 or even earlier.

ALPINE CHINA
94
WARRANTED
☆ W.B P.CO. ☆

(1894 – 1911)

(1892 or 1894 to 1911)

(1894 – 1911)

The following Barber (pre-1904) marks may date back as far as the 1880s when the Brunt Pottery Co. was called William Brunt, Son & Co. They date from c.1883 to c.1904.

ELECTRIC   CHICAGO

Alliance   ROCKET   Chester

The following marks date c.1900 to 1911.

NEW ERA
W.B.P. CO.

NAPOLEON
W.B.P. CO.

EAST LIVERPOOL
OHIO U.S.A.

BRUNT
ARTWARE

34. Brush Pottery
Roseville, OH
1925 – 1970s or later

This company made mostly art pottery or, perhaps more accurately, "craft" pottery. Some of the ware is similar to McCoy ware.

They made many cookie jars. Their marks usually include BRUSH and a painter's jar or palette.

---

35. Brush-McCoy Pottery
Roseville and Zanesville, OH
1911 – 1925

They made both utilitarian and art pottery; their mark usually includes the word MITUSA.

---

36. Buffalo Pottery Co.
Buffalo, NY
1903 to the present

Early Buffalo Pottery is usually marked with a buffalo, BUFFALO POTTERY and, often, the date. It is this early ware that is most collectible. Most was made before World War I; however, some vitreous dinnerware and some reintroduced Deldare ware were made as late as the mid-1920s. Later wares, made from about World War I onward, are marked with BUFFALO CHINA. This is a thick hotel (restaurant or institutional) type of pottery. This type of pottery is still being made. See p. 168 for sample BUFFALO CHINA marks.

See *The Book of Buffalo Pottery* by Seymour and Violet Altman for more about this company.

---

37. Burford Bros. Pottery Co.
East Liverpool, OH
1879 – 1904

(1880s)

IRON STONE CHINA

(1880s)

(1880s)

HOTEL

(c.1880 – 1904)

(c.1880 – c.1900)

(1880s – c.1900)

ELECTRIC

(1880s – c.1900)

37. Burford Bros. Pottery Co. (continued)

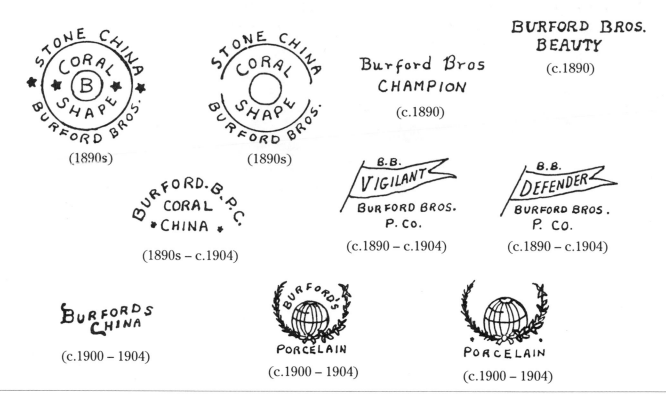

(1890s)   (1890s)

(c.1890)

(c.1890)

(1890s – c.1904)

(c.1890 – c.1904)

(c.1890 – c.1904)

(c.1900 – 1904)

(c.1900 – 1904)

(c.1900 – 1904)

---

38. Burley & Winter Pottery Co.
Crooksville, OH
1870s – c.1930

Although they made stoneware, some items such as mugs, pitchers, etc. appear to be whiteware. Their marks included the words BURLEY & WINTER.

---

39. Burroughs & Mountford Co.
Trenton, NJ
1879 – c.1895

The mark at left was found on an umbrella stand with a nice overall flow blue decoration. The mark itself was in flow blue. This mark with TRADE MARK above was also seen on an exquisite flow blue pitcher. See pp. 168 and 169 for more Burroughs & Mountford marks.

40. Cambridge Art Pottery Co. 1895 – 1909
Guernsey Earthenware Co. 1909 – c.1923
Cambridge, OH

They apparently made some ware that was not art pottery. These marks may have been used only on art pottery. They were used before 1909.

The Guernsey Earthenware Co. made ordinary whiteware. These marks were used after 1909.

   (c.1920)

41. Cameron Potteries Co.
Cameron, WV
c.1900 – 1907

See p. 172 for possible marks.

42. Canonsburg China Co.
Canonsburg, PA
1901 – c.1909

Although the mark at left is generally believed to have been used only before c.1909, I am positive it was used after 1909, probably to the mid-1920s. See Canonsburg Pottery Co. below.

43. Canonsburg Pottery Co.
Canonsburg, PA
c.1909 – 1970s

This company was a reorganized form of the Canonsburg China Co.

This mark is a carry-over from the Canonsburg China Co. See above. I have seen the mark on wares made after WWI to the early 1920s. I have also seen it accompanied by WARRANTED 18 KARAT GOLD indicating its being used to the mid-1920s, or perhaps a bit later. See p. 199.

43. Canonsburg Pottery Co. (continued)

See p. 169 for more Canonsburg Pottery Co. marks.

Canonsburg
Pottery Co.

(1920s and perhaps a
bit earlier)

AVON

(1920s; 1930s)

KEYSTONE

CANONSBURG
POTTERY CO.

(1930s; 1940s)

(1950s)

---

44. Carr China Co.
Grafton, WV
1916 – 1950s

They made a thick hotel type of ware primarily or exclusively. CARR CHINA was included as part of their mark. See also p. 170.

CARR CHINA CO.
GRAFTON, W. VA.
47   (1947)

"*Dayton*"
CARR CHINA
GRAFTON, W. VA.

---

45. Carrollton Pottery Co.
Carrollton, OH
1903 – 1929

Much of their ware is not typical Ohio pottery. Although their whiteware is often of poor quality, their designs are frequently noteworthy.

(c.1903 – c.1910)

(c.1910 – c.1920)

(1920s)

---

46. Cartwright Brothers
East Liverpool, OH
c.1880 – 1927

Gates and Ormerod say they made their first cream-colored ware and ironstone in 1887. The company was incorporated as the Cartwright Bros. Co. in 1896.

Marks on the following page.

46. Cartwright Brothers (continued)

Considering that they used so many marks and that they had a long history, one would expect to see much of their ware today. That is not the case. I do not believe this company was very prolific. I have seen very few of their marks and none more than once or twice. Gates and Ormerod show a few other Cartwright marks.

The mark at left may be quite blurred. Gates and Ormerod show it that way, and the one I saw was equally blurred. The moon and star were reasonably clear as was part of CARTWRIGHT. The mark would date c.1887.

(c.1887)

Elsmere

(1890s)

TEXAS

(c.1900)

Avalon

(c.1900)

Brooklyn

(c.1900)

Other shape marks may be CABLE, TRENT and PACIFIC.

(1887 – c.1896)

(1892 – c.1905)

A mark like the one above has GLENDORA.

The mark above and the FLORENCE mark are from Gates and Ormerod. These marks were first published in *Historical Archaeology,* Volume 16, Numbers 1 & 2, pp. 31, 32.

46. Cartwright Brothers (continued)

C. B. Co.
S. V.
CHINA

(c.1910 – c.1927)

THE CARTWRIGHT BROS.CO.

(c.1910 – c.1920)

C. B.P Co.
MADE IN U.S.A.
CHINA

(1920s)

---

47. Catalina Pottery   See A.174 on p. 204.

---

48. Ceramic Art Co.   See Lenox.

---

49. Chelsea China Co.
New Cumberland, WV
1888 – 1896

I found the mark at the left on a piece so discolored it was impossible to tell if it was whiteware. It may have been yellow ware. If so, it may date before 1888.

CHINA

(c.1888)

WHITE GRANITE

(1890s)

---

50. Chelsea Keramic Art Works 1866 – 1891
Chelsea Pottery, U.S. 1891 – 1896
Chelsea, MA

This company moved to Dedham, Massachusetts, where it was called Dedham Pottery. See p. 41. Most of the ware marked would be considered art pottery; however, some was not.

C
K A
W

(1875 – 1889)
impressed

CHELSEA KERAMIC
ART WORKS
ROBERTSON & SONS

(1875 – 1880)
impressed

(1891)

(1893+)

---

51. Chesapeake Pottery
Baltimore, MD
1880 – 1914

This Baltimore company became D.F. Haynes & Co. in 1882. From 1887 to January 1890 it was called the Chesapeake Pottery Co. From 1890 to 1895 it was Haynes, Bennett & Co. After 1895 it was called D.F. Haynes & Son.

Jervis said in his 1897 marks book that the Chesapeake Pottery used no marks in the 1890s. Barber seems to confirm this by his dating of their marks. This company was a favorite of Edwin Barber. He devoted 12 pages, including many photographs, to this company in his 1893 pottery book. I have seen very few early marks for this company. Most of what I have seen has had the mark given by Barber as being used after 1900. Although the Chesapeake Pottery items I've seen have been quite good, I would rank the company below Edwin Bennett's. See p. 167 for another Avalon Faience mark.

51. Chesapeake Pottery (continued)

(1882 – c.1884) (1882 – c.1884) (1882 – c.1884) (1882 – 1884)

Each of the four marks above has a D.F.H. or D.F.H. & Co. monogram. This is for D.F. Haynes (& Co.)

(1887 – 1890)

ARUNDEL
HOME FLOWERS DEC.

(1887 – 1890)

ARUNDEL
GLEN ROSE DEC.

(1887 – 1890+)

(1900 and later)

Note the Chesapeake Pottery Co. monogram on the above mark.

Other decoration names found on the above marks include POPPY, COREOPSIS, and possibly others.

The above mark is rather common.

52. Chester Pottery Co.
Phoenixville, PA
1894 – 1899

(1895 and 1896)

The mark at the left is the Arms of Pennsylvania.

C.P.Co. LTD

(1897)

C. P. Co.
LTD.

(after 1897)

53. Chittenango Pottery Co.
Chittenango, NY
1897 – c.1901

This company is important because it was one of the few early American companies to make true porcelain. I've seen only two pieces of their ware. One was a mug. The other was a plate made for Buffalo's Pan-American Exposition of 1901.

(continued on page 34)

53. Chittenago Pottery Co. (continued)

Both pieces were true porcelain. The plate was of excellent quality comparable to good European porcelain. Unfortunately a fire c.1901 forced them to cease porcelain production. Their ware is probably rather rare since production was for so short a time.

C. P. Co.
CHITTENANGO
CHINA

C. P. Co.
CHITTENANGO, N.Y.
CHINA

C. P. CO.

C. P. Co.
CHINA

I found the above mark impressed, but it may also be found printed.

---

54. City Pottery Co.
Trenton, NJ
1859 – c.1880

IRONSTONE CHINA
C. P. Co.
(c.1878)

Barber said their 1871 mark was Y.B.A. with the English "mark." In 1875 it was C.P.Co. with the English "mark." The English mark is undoubtedly the British Coat of Arms. The 1876 mark is the one given at lower left. The New Jersey Coat of Arms mark at left would date c.1877 to c.1880. The detail in this coat of arms is very similar to that of the New Jersey Coat of Arms mark of the Greenwood Pottery. If the mark were blurred, it might be difficult to distinguish the one from the other; however, if clear, the C. and the G. are easy to distinguish. See p. 58.

Except for the company initials, the detail of the New Jersey Coat of Arms mark of the East Trenton Pottery is identical to that of the City Pottery mark indicating a possible linking of the two. City Pottery ended c.1880. East Trenton Pottery began c.1885. See p. 47.

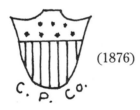
(1876)
C. P. CO.

---

55. Cleveland China Co./George H. Bowman Co.
Cleveland, Ohio
1890s – 1930s

George H. Bowman was a distributor not a manufacturer of whiteware. Pieces with the Bowman or Cleveland China marks were made by other companies. Some pieces are of foreign manufacture; however, most are American.

CLEVELAND
CHINA

(c.1910 – c.1920)

CLEVELAND
CHINA
3 22 (1922)

(1920s)

Cleveland China
G. H. B. Co.

WARRANTED
18 CARAT GOLD

(c.1925 – c.1935)

56. Colonial Company
East Liverpool, OH
1903 – c.1930

S-V CHINA
COLONIAL.

(c.1910 – c.1920)

(c.1903 – c.1915)

(c.1915 – c.1930)

COLONIAL
STERLING
CHINA
PATENTED 1919

The above mark is a
possible Colonial Co.
mark. See p. 171.

---

57. Columbia Art Pottery Co.
Trenton, NJ
1893 – c.1902

Morris and Willmore founded this company to make porcelain and ordinary whiteware. The first mark was used on ordinary whiteware. Both marks were used on porcelain.

---

58. Cook Pottery Co.
Trenton, NJ
1894 – 1920s

This company took over from the Ott & Brewer Co. Until the 1900s their mark usually included Mellor & Co. Mellor was Cook's partner. Cook's name was used on Crescent Pottery Co. marks. See p. 37.

MELLOR & CO.

(1894 – c.1900)

The mark at left may not have IRON-STONE CHINA.

MELLOR & CO.

(1894 – c.1900)

SEMI VITREOUS

MELLOR & Co.

(c.1897)

Delfc
D.C.

(1897)

The mark at left was used on Cook's "Delft." The word ETRURIA may accompany the mark. See p. 174.

(c.1905 and earlier)

This mark may be found without a company name. It is also found with CH.H.C. under the mark. See p. 170.

58. Cook Pottery Co. (continued)

(c.1895 – c.1900)

See p. 173 for more about this and a similar mark.

(c.1900 – c.1910)

The above mark is a common Cook Pottery Co. mark.

MELLOR & CO.

(c.1905)

FLORENCE COOK POTTERY CO.

(c.1910)

COOK POTTERY CO. TRENTON, N.J.

(c.1910 – c.1920)

---

59. Coors Porcelain
Golden, CO
c.1915 – 1939 (for dinnerware)

All marks include the word COORS with U.S.A. or GOLDEN, COLORADO. Don't confuse with the later H.F. Coors & Co. See Lois Lehner's *Complete Book of American Kitchen and Dinner Wares* for more about Coors.

---

60. Coxon & Co. (Empire Pottery)
Trenton, NJ
1863 – c.1880

J.F. Thompson was a partner of Charles Coxon. In the 1870s the company was called Coxon & Thompson. See p. 172 for an 1860s Coxon mark.

This mark was probably used before 1875. Marks used after that date probably had Coxon & Thompson.

---

61. Coxon Pottery
Wooster, OH
1926 – 1930

They made a fine porcelain marked COXON BELLEEK.

62. Crescent China Co. c.1920 – c.1927
Leigh Potters, Inc. c.1927 – c.1932
Alliance, Ohio

This company was so closely tied to the Sebring Pottery Co. that it could be considered a part of that company. These companies even shared marks as seen below. Leigh Potters, Inc. was just a slightly reorganized form of Crescent China. See pp. 172 and 173 for other Crescent China Co. marks.

SIENNA THE CRESCENT CHINA Co. WARE.

(c.1925)

Golden Maize
BY
THE CRESCENT CHINA CO.
ALLIANCE, OHIO
Reg. U.S. Pat. off. No. 230442

See p. 18 for an almost identical GOLDEN MAIZE mark of the Sebring Pottery Co. The above mark dates c.1927.

UMBERTONE
(c.1930)

LEIGH WARE *by Leigh Potters* inc. U.S.A.

(c.1930)

---

63. Crescent Pottery
Trenton, NJ
1881 – c.1906

This company was founded by Charles Cook & W.S. Hancock. See also the Cook Pottery Co.

IRON STONE CHINA
(1885)
Arms of New Jersey

SEMI-GRANITE COOK & HANCOCK COPYRIGHT
(1890)

PARIS WHITE CRESCENT POTTERY WARRANTED
(1890)

DAINTY COOK & HANCOCK
(1890)

MELLORIA COOK & HANCOCK
(1896)

DAINTY
(1896 – 1898)

SEVERN C.P.Co.
(1898)

DAINTY
(1898)

MELLORIA
(1896 – 1898)

CRESCENT WARRANTED
(1899 – 1902)

UTOPIA CPCo CRESCENT
(1900 – 1902)

Crescent also used ALPHA and simulated English Registry Numbers with the UTOPIA mark at left. See p. 173 for more about registry numbers. The T.P.Co. monogram in the center of the mark is explained on p. 150.

64. Cronin China Co.
Minerva, OH
1934 – 1950s

This company followed the Owen China Co. in Minerva, Ohio.

In the 1940s and probably later a circular mark with company name and potters' union name was used. These "union marks" were used by many companies from c.1940 to c.1960. See p. 173 for a sample union mark used by Cronin.

GUARANTEED

18 K GOLD

CRONIN CHINA CO.

(c.1934)

CRONIN CHINA
MINERVA,
O.

(1930s)

CRONIN CHINA
MINERVA,
O.

WARRANTED
22 KARAT GOLD

(1930s)

---

65. Crooksville China Co.
Crooksville, OH
1902 – 1959

This company used numerous marks in its more than fifty years of production. I don't think this company was very productive in its early years. Most of the ware found today dates from c.1920 to 1950.

Except for the one mark given in Barber's 1904 marks book, shown first below, the company's marks did not use the word CROOKSVILLE until the 1920s. Instead they used C.C.Co. as initials or as a monogram. Some early marks had no initials or monogram. STERLING PORCELAIN was made by Crooksville from c.1910 to c.1920. STINTHAL CHINA was made from c.1910 to c.1930. In the 1920s the word CROOKSVILLE was added to the Stinthal mark.

See p. 188 for a discussion of STERLING CHINA possibly made by Crooksville.

CROOKSVILLE CHINA CO

(c.1902 – c.1910)

STERLING
Co
PORCELAIN

(c.1910 – c.1920)

STERLING

Hiawatha

PORCELAIN

(c.1920)

STINTHAL
CHINA
C. C. Co.

(c.1910 – c.1920)

Stinthal China
Co

(c.1910 – c.1920)

STINTHAL
CHINA
CROOKSVILLE

(1920s)

65. Crooksville China Co. (continued)

Most of the marks used by Crooksville after c.1920 had numbers or two letters under the mark. The numbers indicate a very simple dating system, the last two digits indicating the year. For example: 729 is for 1929 (the earliest I've seen); 730 is for 1930; 337 for 1937; 1040 for 1940; 345 for 1945; etc.

Marks with two letters under the mark may also indicate a dating system. These letters under the mark may indicate a year — perhaps all of them dating before 1929 when numbers came into use. I've not yet determined this, and I doubt if it is true. I suspect this company was not that predictable. Marks with two letters were probably used into the 1930s.

CROOKSVILLE
U. S.A. C-U
(1920s)

IVORA
CROOKSVILLE
CHINA CO,
730   (1930)
(c.1930)

The IVORA mark at left was used at least as early as 1929.

IVO·GLO
CROOKSVILLE
CHINA CO,
(c.1930)

PANTRY
BAK-IN
by WARE
Crooksville
(1930s)

CROOKSVILLE
CHINA CO
U.S.A. A-P
(late 1920s and 1930s)

by
CROOKSVILLE
U. S. A. D-5
(c.1925 through 1930s)

Provincial Ware
(c.1930)

The above mark was used on ware made for city distribution. The ware is often in chrome frames.

CROOKSVILLE
CHINA CO.
345 (1945)
(1940s)

CROOKSVILLE
CHINA CO,
1040
MADE IN U.S.A.

The mark at left was used from c.1929 through the 1940s. The mark is also found with 2 letters, not numbers, above MADE IN U.S.A. These marks may date before 1929.

Trellis
C
(c.1930)
See p. 81 for a discussion of TRELLIS marks.

66. Crown Pottery Co.
Evansville, IN
1891 – c.1950

This first group of marks date from c.1891 to c.1904.

The above mark was used only on dinnerware

REX.

C.P. CO.
REX

Crown Porcelain

REGINA
C. P. CO.

C.P. CO.
ROYAL

JEWEL
C. P. CO.

ALMA.　HELEN.　HOBSON.　RENA.

The mark at left is a virtual copy of a Johnson Bros. c.1900 British mark.

CROWN HOTEL
WARE

The next three marks were used before World War I. The Crown Pottery (now called Crown Potteries) Co. worked for jobbers between WWI and the 1930s. Little, if any, of the wares produced during this period was marked.

SEMI
PORCELAIN

C. P. Co.

(c.1905 – c.1915)

SEMI-PORCELAIN
(c.1905 – c.1915)

SEMI-PORCELAIN
(c.1905 – c.1915)

The following four marks were used in the 1930s and 1940s. Most of the marks during this period were dated as seen below. See p. 195 for a later use of their crown on probably unrelated marks.

C.P. C⁰
12 36
(1936)

MADE IN
U.S.A.
4 46
(1946)

CROWN POTTERIES CO.
MADE
IN　　U.S.A.
EVANSVILLE, IND.

OVENWARE
2 37
(1937)

67. Croxall Pottery (& Sons) Co.
East Liverpool, OH
1888 – c.1912

Before 1888 this company was Croxall & Cartwright. Croxall was a large producer of Rockingham and yellow wares to the late 1890s, although they are said to have been making whiteware in the early 1900s. I've seen no marked examples of it. Either they made very little whiteware or never marked it; consequently, no marks are known for this company.

68. Cunningham and Pickett
Alliance, OH
c.1938 – 1960s

This company was a distributor, not a manufacturer of whiteware. See p. 200 for a sample mark. See Lois Lehner's *Complete Book of American Kitchen and Dinner Wares* for a listing of companies associated with Cunningham and Pickett in the 1950s and 60s.

69. Dedham Pottery
Dedham, MA
1896 – 1943

The word REGISTERED was added to the Dedham mark in 1929.

70. Delaware Pottery
Trenton, NJ
1884 – 1895

They became part of Trenton Potteries in 1895. See p. 150.

71. Denver China & Pottery Co.
Denver, CO
1901 – 1905

72. Derry China Co.
Derry Station, PA
1900 – c.1905

73. Dresden Pottery
East Liverpool, OH
1876 – c.1927

The marks for the Dresden Pottery can be separated into four categories:

I. 1876 – c.1882. During this period the company was called Brunt, Bloor, Martin & Co. See p. 25.

II. 1882 – c.1915. The Dresden Pottery was organized as the Potters' Cooperative Co. in 1882. For about ten years the company used several variations of the British Coat of Arms to mark their wares. These are given first below. From about 1890 to 1915 their marks nearly always included the word DRESDEN.

III. c.1916 – c.1925. During this period their marks included POTTERS CO-OPERATIVE CO. or T.P.C-O. Co. Before 1915 a few marks had T.P.C.CO. If the initials have C-O., the mark was used after 1916.

IV. c.1925 – c.1927. During this brief time DRESDEN was used again. These marks are dated.

(1880s)

(c. 1890)

(1890s)

The P.C. monogram on these two marks is for Potters' Cooperative.

The D.P.W. monogram is for Dresden Pottery Works. The 90 is for 1890. See p. 208 for a discussion on dating systems.

73. Dresden Pottery (continued)

Based on my observations of many Dresden pieces, I would say the company produced a better quality of ware in the early years. Dresden made much whiteware of good quality in the 1890s. By 1910 virtually all their whiteware was an inferior porous product subject to serious crazing; however, I recently saw an excellent c.1920 piece of their whiteware.

(1890s)

(1890s)

(1890s)

(c.1895)

DRESDEN
HOTEL CHINA

(c.1895 – c.1900)

T. P. C. Co.
E. L. O.

(1890s)

DRESDEN
HOTEL CHINA
WARRANTED

The above mark may be impressed or printed. It dates c.1900 – c.1910.

(c.1895 – c.1900)

The ribbon mark at left may say instead of DRESDEN:
1. CALIFORNIA
2. MADRID
3. PORTLAND
4. YALE

(c.1900 – c.1905)

(c.1900)

Gates and Ormerod credit this mark to Dresden Pottery. I can't confirm or deny this; however, the mark is quite different from other Dresden marks. I can confirm that the mark was used c.1900. The mark is fairly common and the whiteware it marks is of better quality than most, particularly later, Dresden ware.

73. Dresden Pottery (continued)

(c.1895 – c.1905)

(c.1905 – c.1910)

DRESDEN
CHINA

(c.1908 – c.1915)

POTTERS
Co-OPERATIVE Co.
SEMI
• VITREOUS •

(c.1915 – c.1920)

THE
POTTERS
Co-OPERATIVE Co.
• VITREOUS •

(c.1915 – c.1920)

(1923)

(c.1920 – c.1925)

T. P. C-O Co.
1 21 1   (1921)
SEMI - VIT.

(c.1920 – c.1925)

DRESDEN
CHINA
MADE IN U.S.A.
7 25

(1925)

Dresden
S.V. CHINA
MADE IN U.S.A.
3 26

(1926)

Lois Lehner recorded a Dresden China Co. operating in Salineville, Ohio, before 1910. They apparently didn't mark their ware; however, there is an outside chance the Dresden China Co. used a DRESDEN CHINA mark too. Since the correct name of Dresden Pottery, East Liverpool, Ohio, was Potters' Cooperative Co., they probably could not claim exclusive right to mark wares DRESDEN CHINA.

74. East End Pottery Co.
East Liverpool, OH
1894 – 1909

For a short time c.1909 this company was called the East End China Co.; however, one East End Pottery mark continued to be used for two more years. An inventory backlog probably accounted for this. See the third mark below. See also the Trenle Co. on p. 147.

(c.1895)

See p. 229 for a similar mark.

E. LIVERPOOL O.

(c.1900)

The marks below were used before 1901.

(c.1904 – c.1909)

This mark was found on 1910 and 1911 calendar plates. See p. 147 for a similar mark of the East End China Co.

Alaska   DEWEY
             E.E.P. CO.   *Columbus*

---

75. East Liverpool Pottery Co.
East Liverpool, OH
1894 – 1900

(c.1896)

E. L. P. CO.
WACO CHINA

Note the E.L.P. Co. monogram on the above mark.

WACO CHINA

E. L. P. Co.   E. L. P. Co.

Some WACO marked whiteware is of excellent quality. It is highly vitrified with no trace of crazing.

76. East Liverpool Potteries Co.
East Liverpool, OH
1900 – 1903 and/or 1907

The East Liverpool Potteries Co. was formed in 1900 from a combination of six smaller companies. This combination failed and in 1903 all member companies left the East Liverpool Potteries except the Globe Pottery and the United States Pottery Co. These two companies separated in 1907 and the East Liverpool Potteries Co. ended; however, the United States Pottery Co. of Wellsville, Ohio, continued to use East Liverpool Potteries Co. marks until the 1920s. See the United States Pottery Co. for these later marks.

77. East Morrisania China Works
New York, NY
c.1890 – c.1904

D. Robitzek was the owner of this company. The ironstone ware made by this company was unusual. Unlike the usual thick American ironstone, their ironstone was a thin ware more in keeping with Mason's original English ironstone.

78. East Palestine Pottery Co.
East Palestine, Ohio
1884 – 1909

(c.1885 – c.1895)

(c.1895 – c.1905)

(c.1895 – c.1905)

The wreath mark above may have under it COLUMBIA, LAFAYETTE PORCELAIN, IRIS, or others. Note the E.P.P. Co. monogram. See p. 174 for another East Palestine mark.

78. East Palestine Pottery Co. (continued)

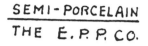

SEMI-PORCELAIN
THE E. P. P. CO.

(c.1900)

(c.1905 – c.1909)

(c.1905 – c.1909)

(c.1905 – c.1909)

The above wreath mark may have other words on it. One example is QUEEN. IRIS was used to late 1909, on a 1910 calendar plate.

---

79. East Trenton Pottery Co.
Trenton, NJ
c.1885 – c.1905

E .T. P. Co.

(1880s)

See p. 34 for a discussion of an almost identical mark.

(probably 1890s)

The monogram on the above mark seems to be incomplete. This mark is from Barber.

E. T. P. Co.

(probably 1890s)

OPAQUE CHINA
E. T. P. Co.

(after 1890)

The above mark is impressed. See p. 174 for another impressed East Trenton mark.

---

80. Empire Pottery
Trenton, NJ
1880 – 1892

The Empire Pottery had been owned by a number of people over the years. They had made cream-colored ware since the 1860s. See Coxon & Co. on p. 36. The early authors disagree as to when Alpaugh & Magowan took over the company. Barber said 1884; Ramsay said 1880. I believe Wood & Barlow owned the company between 1880 and 1884. Barber mentioned them as owners but didn't give any dates. He ascribed to them the Imperial China mark given on p. 48. Based on ware I've seen, I date it before the A. & M. ironstone china mark of the Empire Pottery. The Imperial China marks I've seen were impressed on cream-colored ware, one kind of ware made early by this company.

80. Empire Pottery (continued)

The A. & M. under the middle mark is for Alpaugh & Magowan. The T.P.Co. monogram on the third mark is for the Trenton Potteries Co. See p. 150 for an explanation.

The mark at left is an impressed mark.

(1880 – 1884)

(1885 – c.1890)

(c.1892)

---

81. Enterprise Pottery Co.
Trenton, NJ
c.1880 – 1892

The mark given here may have marked only sanitary ware.

Enterprise
Pottery Co.

---

82. Faience Manufacturing Co.
Greenpoint, NY
1880 – 1892

(c.1880)

The above mark is incised.

(c.1885)

(1886 – 1892)

---

83. Fell & Thropp Co.
Trenton, NJ
1879 – 1893

Fell & Thropp were the last owners of the old Trenton Pottery to make regular whiteware. About 1890 the company was called Fell & Brewer (J. Hart Brewer). Sanitary ware became the sole manufacture. By 1893 new owners continued the manufacture of sanitary ware. See Trenton Pottery Co. for a full history.

83. Fell & Thropp Co. (continued)

These marks date from about 1880 to about 1890.

---

84. Florentine Pottery Co.
Chillicothe, OH
early 1900s

---

85. Ford China Co.
Ford City, PA
c.1890 – c.1910

This mark would date c.1900. Instead of BRISTOL, the upper ribbon may say DERBY, LEEDS, TURIN, VICTOR or others. Ford marks are usually in soft colors and difficult to see. Note the F.C.Co. monogram.

---

86. Franklin Pottery Co.
Franklin, OH
1880 – 1884

The dates and the mark are from John Ramsay.

$$\frac{F\ P\ C}{F}$$

---

87. Fraunfelter China Co.
Zanesville, OH
1923 – 1930s

Fraunfelter made a hard-paste porcelain. Some of their ware is excellent and highly collectible. Their mark includes the word FRAUNFELTER.

87. Fraunfelter China Co. (continued)

(1920s,1930s)

(after 1930)

88. French China Co.
Sebring, OH
1898 – c.1929

The French China Co. was a major Ohio pottery. I have found numerous pieces marked by this company from the early 1900s to the late 1920s. They were probably the most prolific maker of American flow blue. Although most of their flow blue was typical American decal decorated ware with flow blue borders, they also produced some ware with "all-over" flow blue patterns. The latter is a deep cobalt blue with a genuine flowing quality.

After a brief period in East Liverpool the company moved to Sebring, Ohio, c.1900 where they made and marked ware to c.1929. The period from 1929 to c.1934 was a complex time of bankruptcies and reorganizations. About 1934 the French Saxon China Co. was founded. (See Saxon China Co. on p. 127) This company continued to the 1960s.

These first seven marks date before c.1905. The LA FRANCAISE mark is rather common. Early flow blue has this mark.

La Francaise Porcelain

LYGIA

PLUTO
F. C. Co.

Greek

Kenneth

TIGER

CUPID

fleur-de-lis

La Francaise
PORCELAIN

LA FRANCAISE
SEMI VITREOUS
A 4

The two marks at left date from c.1905 to c.1915. They are quite common. They are the marks most often found on this company's flow blue ware; however, the earlier LA FRANCAISE mark given above was also used as were possibly others. See next page for a later fleur-de-lis mark.

88. French China Co. (continued)

The French China fleur-de-lis mark shown below has two forms. The earlier mark looks more like a three plumes (Prince of Wales's Crest) mark; the later mark is a more conventional fleur-de-lis. The earlier mark was in use as early as 1907 and possibly earlier. The number and letter under this mark may indicate a date; however, I've been unable to determine this. Although I've seen the mark quite often, the number under the mark is almost always blurred. The letter always looks like an A. The blurring of the number on otherwise clear marks seems almost intentional! The later fleur-de-lis mark was used after 1915. This mark is not common. I believe it was used for just a few years, probably not after 1920.

(c.1905 – c.1915)

(c.1915 – c.1920)

This mark may also have SEMI-VITREOUS under the mark instead of MARTHA WASHINGTON.

The following plain marks date from c.1917 to c.1929. The two-digit number on each of these marks is the year the mark was used. For example: 19 is for 1919, 20 is for 1920, 26 is for 1926, etc. This is a simple dating system. Note the inconsistency in the placing of the two digit number. Note also the 6A under the one mark. This is almost certainly 1926; however, this shows the difficulties involved with dating systems that are not always consistent. See p. 208 for a discussion of dating systems.

F. C. Co.
A — 1 8
CHINA

(1918)

F. C. Co.
I — 19
CHINA

(1919)

F. C. Co.
20 3

(1920)

F. C. Co.
MARTHA
WASHINGTON
B 25

(1925)

F. C. Co.
MARTHA
WASHINGTON
6 A

(1926)

F. C. Co.
26 - 3

(1926)

F. C. Co.
1 27

(1927)

French China
Co.
F 2 8 5

(1928)

51

89. Fulper Pottery
Flemington, NJ
1860 – 1930s

They made and marked art pottery from c.1910 to c.1930. See *Art Pottery of the United States* by Paul Evans for more about the company.

---

90. Geijsbeek Pottery Co.
Denver & Golden, CO
1899 – 1904 (or later)

GEIJSBEEK POTTERY CO.

DENVER COLO.

(1899, 1900)

G. P. C.

(1899, 1900)

(1900)

This 1900 mark may have the word GOLDEN in the center.

(1901 and later)

---

91. W.S. George Pottery
Canonsburg, PA
c.1909 – 1955

W.S. George had an interest in a number of factories. His main operations were in East Palestine, Ohio; however, the Canonsburg operation was probably the first to use a George mark. See below. Some time before 1909 (as early as 1905), W.S. George opened a factory in Canonsburg with his brother. Earlier he had opened the Canonsburg China Co. See p. 29. In 1909 he left the Canonsburg China Co. and his brother became president of this company, now called the Canonsburg Pottery Co. The other company was named the W.S. George Pottery. It operated in Canonsburg, Pennsylvania, from c.1909 to 1955. There was evidently a close relationship between the W.S. George Pottery and the Canonsburg Pottery Co. I've seen sets of dishes with marks for both companies.

RAINIER

GEORGE BROS.

(before 1909)

The *N* in RAINIER may look like a *K*. See p. 175 for more about this mark.

---

92. W.S. George Pottery
East Palestine, OH
1909 – late 1950s

This company was a continuation of the East Palestine Pottery Co. W.S. George had been involved with this company for a number of years. The name was changed in 1909, about the same time the W.S. George Pottery was formed in Canonsburg, Pennsylvania. The marks given below, except for the first one, may have been used at any of the W.S. George factories. In addition to factories in Canonsburg, Pennsylvania, and East Palestine, Ohio, W.S. George had taken over the Pennsylvania China Co. of Kittanning, Pennsylvania, in 1913. See p. 111. The W.S. George name was again in use in the late 1980s on limited edition ware. This ware would have no direct connection with earlier W.S. George wares.

92. W.S. George Pottery (continued)

W. S. GEORGE
POTTERY CO.
EAST PALESTINE, OHIO

(c.1910)

W. S. George

(before 1920)

This plain signature mark was used before 1920. Signature marks were used until the 1950s; however, after c.1920 the mark would include a shape name and/or other devices. See p. 176 for an exception to this generalization.

WHITE GRANITE
W. S. GEORGE
1062

(before 1920)

W. S. GEORGE
Queen

(c.1910 – c.1920)

W. S. GEORGE
Derwood

(c.1910 – c.1920)

(Also IRIS: see p. 176)

W.S. George marks from the 1920s through the 1940s usually included: a shape name, *W.S. George*, a series of numbers under the mark, and a letter A, B, C, or D following the number series. There are a few marks that don't have a letter following the numbers. A few marks appear to have a letter other than A, B, C, or D. I believe this was caused by imprecise marking. The letter probably indicated the factory where the ware was made. MADE IN U.S.A. is on some marks but not on others. Its use might indicate a later mark.

The numbers under the mark possibly indicate a dating system. Thus far I've been unable to decipher the system. See p. 226 for a listing of W.S. George shape names with accompanying numbers and letters.

The earliest shape names I've seen are DERWOOD and ARGOSY. DERWOOD was used before 1920 (see above) and was common in the 1920s. It was less frequently used after c.1930. ARGOSY was also used in the 1920s or earlier; however, it was used much later with the addition of IVORY or PINK on the mark. See below.

ARGOSY
W.S. George
IVORY

110D

This ARGOSY mark with IVORY (or PINK) dates from c.1930 to the 1940s. A plain ARGOSY mark was used in the 1920s or earlier. Another mark with IVORY is on the next page.

92. W.S. George Pottery (continued)

DERWOOD
W.S. GEORGE
IVORY
1-27

The above W.S. George mark is unusual in that the 27 under the mark is probably for 1927. Most numbers under W.S. George marks are either coded dates or possibly not dates at all. This 27 might indicate the year in which W.S. George introduced its IVORY ware. Most American whiteware manufacturers introduced an ivory line in the late 1920s. See p. 200.

This very common mark was used in the five or six years W.S. George was in production after 1953. The 1904 on the mark proably indicates the year when W.S. George took control of the East Palestine Pottery Co. The company name was not changed until 1909.

---

93. Glasgow Pottery
Trenton, NJ
1863 – 1905

The mark below was used on semi-porcelain.

(c. 1870)

(1876)

(1878)

(1884)

GLASGOW M CHINA

(1882)

(1893)

The J.M. monogram, the M. initial, and the M. monogram on the above marks are for John Moses, who founded the company. The mark at the right was used on semi-porcelain (the S.P.) in 1880, according to Barber. A date on a mark may indicate any number of things. See p. 208 for a discussion of dating systems.

(1880)

JOHN MOSES

93. Glasgow Pottery (continued)

(c.1890 – c.1895)

(c.1890 – c.1895)

IRONSTONE CHINA
J.M. & Co.

(c.1890 – c.1895)

Note the G.P.Co. monogram on the shield of the above mark.

The following 12 marks date from 1895 to 1905. The use of J.M. & S. on the mark confirms that it was not used before 1895. The J.M. & S. Co. is John Moses and Sons Co.

Note the G.P.Co. monogram on the shields of the above marks.

GLASGOW CHINA
VITRIFIED
TRENTON, N.J.

Note the design similarities of the above mark to the earliest Glasgow mark. See p. 54.

BERKELEY
J.M. & S. CO.
TRENTON, N.J.

TRILBY
JM & S.CO.
TRENTON N.J.

SAPPHO
J.M. & S. CO.

TRILBY
J.M. & S.CO.

JIGILANT
J.M. & S. CO.

PSYCHE is the word in the center of the two marks above.

93. Glasgow Pottery (continued)

In 1899 the Glasgow Pottery made ware for the use of the National Home for Disabled Volunteer Soldiers. The date on the mark at left, March 3, 1865, is the date of the approval of the act of Congress establishing the Home. This mark is probably rare.

Q.M.D.

The Glasgow Pottery also manufactured ware for the Quartermaster's Department. The mark used is given at left.

U S.M.C.

They also made ware for the United States Marine Corps. This mark is given at left.

---

94. Globe China Co.
Cambridge, OH
c.1925 – c.1927

I've seen several marks for this company. In each case the mark included GLOBE CHINA COMPANY and CAMBRIDGE, OHIO. See the Atlas China Co. on p. 19 for a brief history.

---

95. Globe Pottery Co.
East Liverpool, OH
1888 – 1900; 1907 – 1912

This company was part of the East Liverpool Potteries Co. from 1901 to 1907. See p. 46.

(c.1890 – c.1900)

The mark at left is the most commonly seen Globe Pottery mark. Barber dated it 1896; however, I am sure it was used both before and after that date. It was possibly being used in 1903 when Globe was part of the East Liverpool Potteries Co. and presumably using no independent marks. The words FESTOON or PROGRESS may accompany this mark.

(1896)   (1897)   (1898)   (c.1895 – c.1900)

95. Globe Pottery Co. (continued)

(c.1900)

(1907 – 1912)

(1907 – 1912)

96. Godwin & Flentke 1878 – 1882
William Flentke 1882 – 1886
East Liverpool, OH

(1878 – 1882)

(1882 – 1886)

The marks at left are from Gates and Ormerod. They are two of 27 marks reprinted from *Historical Archaeology,* Vol. 10, Numbers 1 & 2, p. 46.

The *G* on the mark at far left may look like a *C*.

97. Goodwin Brothers 1876 – 1893
Goodwin Pottery Co. 1893 – 1912
East Liverpool, OH

(c.1880)

(c.1880)

(c.1890)

(c.1885)

GOODWIN'S
HOTEL CHINA

(after 1893)

97. Goodwin Pottery (continued)

GOODWIN'S

(after 1893)

GOODWIN POTTERY
SEMI-PORCELAIN

(1893 – c.1904)

THE GOODWIN POTTERY CO.
SEMI-PORCELAIN

(1893 – c.1904)

See p. 177 for an interesting story about the above mark.

PORCELAIN

(after 1893)

GOODWIN

MORENO

(c.1905 – 1912)

USONA

Goodwin.

The USONA mark at left is usually in red on decorative ware. It dates c.1905 – 1912.

---

98. Greenwood Pottery Co.
Trenton, NJ
c.1868 – 1930s (probably)

There are at least four different accounts of it the history of the Greenwood Pottery (or Potteries). For a discussion of the various accounts, see p. 177. All the marks given here, except the last one, are from Barber's 1904 marks book. The dates given are also from Barber.

IRONSTONE CHINA
G. P. Co.

(1868 – 1875)

The mark at left is the Coat of Arms of New Jersey. The details of the mark are almost identical to those of a mark for the City Pottery of Trenton, New Jersey. See p. 34. (My drawing may not accurately reflect the similarities.) Since *C*s and *G*s often look alike on marks, a blurred mark would be impossible to ascribe; however, the *G* on the Greenwood mark is usually very precise. A clear *C* would indicate the City Pottery.

G.P.
Co.

(1868 – 1875)

The mark at left may be printed or impressed.

GREENWOOD CHINA
TRENTON, N.J.

(1886)

(impressed mark)

98. Greenwood Pottery (continued)

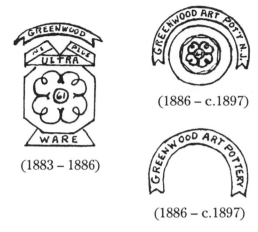

(1883 – 1886)

The above mark, dating c.1920 or 1930, is the only later Greenwood mark I've seen. It is possibly the same company discussed by Barber. See p. 177 for an explanation.

The marks at left were on porcelain art ware.

(1886 – c.1897)

(1886 – c.1897)

---

99. Grueby Faience (Pottery) Co.
Boston, MA
c.1894 – 1911

They made art pottery between 1894 and c.1910. Barber said the ware was a semi-porcelain whiteware. The marks given below were used before 1904. See Paul Evans's *Art Pottery of the United States* for more about the company.

GRUEBY POTTERY
BOSTON. U.S.A.

GRUEBY

GRUEBY
BOSTON. MASS.

---

100. Haeger Potteries, Inc.
Dundee, IL
1914 – present

They made some early art pottery; they made no early whiteware. The art pottery I've seen from the 1960s and later would be called "industrial art pottery" by Paul Evans. Some is marked ROYAL HAEGER.

---

101. Hall China Co.
East Liverpool, OH
1903 – present

Hall's later ware is what collectors are most interested in. Products of the 1930s and 1940s are of interest. Hall's Autumn Leaf is widely collected. Teapots from the 1920s and a bit earlier are also quite collectible.

There is not a great amount of Hall whiteware that dates before 1920. The earlier marks are given below. I have not included any of the later marks for two reasons. First, these marks are generally known. A visit to almost any flea market will give you an opportunity to see numerous marked examples of Hall's ware from the 1930s and 1940s. It is as ubiquitous as Depression Glass. Second, some marks used in the 1930s were still in use as recently as the 1970s. One circular Hall mark (see next page) was used from 1912 to the 1970s.

101. Hall China Co. (continued)

(c.1905)

(c.1903 – c.1910)

(c.1912 – 1970s)

(1930s – 1970s)

This Hall mark dates from c.1912 to the 1970s. MADE IN U.S.A. was added about 1930. The numbers may indicate a dating system. See p. 211.

This Hall mark was used in the 1920s and early 1930s. MADE IN U.S.A. may be in the center of the circle after c.1930. A number may also be in the center, perhaps indicating a date. See p. 211.

HALL

6 CUP
MADE IN
U. S. A.

This mark was used for more than fifty years beginning just before 1920. There is usually a number under HALL. This might indicate a dating system. See p. 211.

This is probably a Hall China Co. mark from the late 1920s or early 1930s. I found it on a vitrified platter decorated in a style common to Hall's 1920s teapots; however, there is a fair chance it is a 1930s mark for the Hardesty China Co. of New Brighton, Pennsylvania. See Lois Lehner's *Complete Book of American Kitchen and Dinner Wares*, p. 74 for a brief history of this company.

102. Hampshire Pottery
Keene, NH
1871 – 1923

These first two marks were used mostly on whiteware souvenir pieces for sale at summer resorts of the 1890s and early 1900s. The marks would date from the late 1880s to c.1915.

The marks at left are printed in red. The signature in the center is J.S. Taft.

Hampshire Pottery

J.S.T. & Co.
KEENE, N.H.

In addition to the souvenir ware, they made ordinary whiteware as well as considerable art pottery. See Paul Evans's *Art Pottery of the United States.* Ordinary whiteware may not have been marked; some art pottery was marked as shown at left.

---

103. Hardesty China Co.
New Brighton, PA
1930s

See p. 60 for a possible mark.

---

104. Harker Pottery Co.
East Liverpool, OH
1840s – c.1970

This mark was impressed on yellow and Rockingham wares from 1847 to 1850.

(1892)

(1879 – 1890)

Barber said that they mark above was used on a portrait plate decorated by Harker for the Burroughs & Mountford Co. whose impressed mark was also on the plate. Barber gave the 1892 date. The mark may have been used by Harker to indicate decorating for other companies.

(1890 – c.1910)

(c.1895)

Note the H.P. Co. monogram on the above mark.

104. Harker Pottery Co. (continued)

(1890 – c.1920)

See p. 179 for a discussion of the infamous "inverted arrow mark." It is an upside down version of this mark at left. Unfortunately, controversy about the mark's existence has estranged two important camps doing American pottery marks research. The mark at the left is a valid mark.

(c.1920 – c.1940)

(c.1915 – 1930s)

COLUMBIA CHINAWARE was a mark used by Harker from c.1915 until the 1930s. See similar mark below at left.

(1930s)

This COLUMBIA CHINAWARE mark was used in the 1930s. Note the addition of ESTABLISHED 1873. This mark is polychrome.

(1930s & 1940s)

BAKERITE
OVEN-TESTED
MADE IN U.S.A.

(1930s & 1940s)

OVEN-TESTED

(1930s & 1940s)

The HOTOVEN mark is a distinctive American mark. One version is polychrome; one is not. CHINAWARE or COOKING WARE is under the mark.

*Early American
By Harker
Est. 1840*

(1930s)

Cameo Ware
BY
HARKER POTTERY CO.
PATENTED
U.S.A.

Cameo Ware was made in the 1940s. It is of interest to collectors. There are several versions of the mark. They all include CAMEO WARE.

The mark above with ROYAL DRESDEN would date about the same time.

Virtually all Harker marks not given on this or the previous page are from the 1950s and later.

105. Herold Pottery
Golden, CO
c.1908 – c.1914

This company became Coors Porcelain. See p. 178 for a possible Herold Pottery mark.

106. Hopewell China Co.
Hopewell, VA
1920s

Sol Ostrow was the founder of the company.

22 KARAT GOLD

The above is but part of a complex mark. See p. 197.

(1924)

The ship HOPEWELL is the most common mark.

(1925)

The mark at left is one that seems to go in any direction. The monogram in the center is certainly an *H* for Hopewell, however, it looks like a *Z*, if turned on its side. Note the *25* indicating the date.

107. Hull Pottery
Crooksville, OH
1905 – present

They are best know for their art pottery made after WWI. This ware is usually marked HULL. I have not made any attempt to date this art pottery. Their earlier ware was mostly kitchenware. These impressed marks were used on this earlier ware, I believe. See p. 178 for a discussion about the first mark given below.

These impressed marks were used from c.1908 to c.1930.

108. Huntington China Co.
Huntington, WV
1904 – 1911

I have not yet found any marks for this company.

109. Illinois China Co.
Lincoln, IL
C.1920 – 1946

This is the only Illinois China Co. mark I've seen. This seems strange for a company with a 20 year or so history. Based on ware seen, I would date the mark in the 1920s; however, it might have been used over the entire history. See Jo Cunningham's *The Collector's Encyclopedia of American Dinnerware* for a brief history.

110. International Pottery Co.
Trenton, NJ
1860 – c.1930

This company was a major player on the Trenton stage. It had a long and productive history. However, like most Trenton potteries, its fortunes waned in the early 1900s. It did continue to produce a nice semi-porcelain until the Great Depression. I have one example of c.1930 ware. It is a thin piece of semi-porcelain of good color with no crazing. Other wares from the 1920s or a bit earlier are better than most comparable East Liverpool, Ohio, wares.

Of particular interest to collectors today is their flow blue ware usually marked ROYAL BLUE. All of their Royal Blue was decorated with a rich cobalt blue, much of it flown (flow blue). In my opinion their flow blue designs are superior to any made in this country. Barber was equally impressed. Quoting from page 230 of his 1893 book:

> *Their flown blue services, produced within the past two years, are of exceptional merit and have been pronounced equal in all respects to the best of the kind produced in England. While no special effort has been made in the direction of decorative designs, many of their pieces are characterized by elegance of form and a richness and depth of blue ground seldom surpassed in this country or abroad. Their royal blue "Wilton" dinner service is especially praiseworthy.*

See p. 180 for more about their flow blue.

IRONSTONE CHINA
CARR & CLARKE

(1878 or 1879)

IRONSTONE CHINA
BURGESS & CAMPBELL

(1879 – c.1885)

The mark at far left with Carr & Clarke was used less than a year. Barber gave 1878 in an earlier book but 1879 in his marks book. Burgess & Campbell took over the company in 1879 using the same mark. See pp. 200 and 201 for more about this mark.

(c.1885 – c.1891)

impressed mark

RUGBY

FLINT CHINA
B. & C.
or
B. & C.

(1880s)

The impressed mark at far left is an early mark but, since it is found with flow blue decoration, it was undoubtedly still in use until 1891. The FLINT CHINA mark is probably a bit earlier. It marked a ware between white granite (ironstone) and semi-porcelain.

110. International Pottery Co. (continued)

The following marks were used from c.1890 to 1903. The first mark may have been used a bit earlier. The various ROYAL BLUE marks are usually, but not always, in flow blue. These flow blue marks may be very difficult to read. Because of this, I suspect much of this country's best flow blue is being attributed to English makers. English marks are usually in flow blue.

(1890s)

(c.1891 – c.1898)

(c.1891 – c.1898)

(c.1891 – c.1898)

(c.1895 – c.1902)

The above mark comes as a flow blue and an ordinary black mark.

(c.1895 – c.1902)

B - C
WILTON.

(1890s)

(c.1890 – c.1902)

The mark at left comes also with LOTUS and DIA-MOND.

WILTON has a cobalt blue design or border. It was a "still" not flow blue. The plate pictured on p. 230 of Barber's 1893 book is probably WILTON.

(c.1890 – c.1902)

The first mark below was used after 1903. Campbell (or C) is no longer on the mark. The next two marks were used c.1897. INTERNATIONAL was used after c.1910. See p. 66.

The I.P.Co. monogram on the Maltese cross marks at left is for International Pottery Co.

65

110. International Pottery Co. (continued)

(c.1910)

Note the similarity of this mark to one on p. 65.

(c.1915 – c.1930)

This rather common International Pottery Co. mark is the only later mark I've seen. Thus far, I've seen it only with AVON above the crown.

---

111. Iroquois China Co.
Syracuse, NY
1905 – 1930s; revived in 1940s and 50s

I have been unable to find any early marks for this company. The marks found are from the 1940s or 1950s. RUSSEL WRIGHT is on many later marks.

---

112. Jersey City Pottery
Jersey City, NJ
1820s – 1892

The earliest marks all had Jersey City and/or American Pottery (Co.) on them. They would be quite rare. I doubt if any collector today would find any ware so marked. About 1850 they became the first American potters to make whiteware exclusively. They began to make whiteware in 1840 and were the first to make it a commercial success.

(1850s)

R. & T.
(Rouse & Turner)

(1880s)

The I.V.W. is for Ivory White Ware. Barber said the V. was mistakenly used instead of W.

---

113. Johnson China Company
East Liverpool, OH
1930s

Their mark included JOHNSON'S and E. LIVERPOOL.

---

114. Kass China Co.
East Liverpool, OH
1930s – 1970s

The following mark is the only one I've seen. Gates and Ormerod show another mark with the company name in a wreath.

KASS
U.S.A.

115. Keswick China Co.
Fallston, PA
c.1900

Lois Lehner mentioned this company in her 1980 book on kitchen and dinner wares. I have not yet seen a mark for this company.

116. Keystone China Co.
East Liverpool, OH
c.1950

117. Keystone Pottery Co.
Trenton, NJ
1892 – 1930s

They made mostly sanitary ware. This is a Barber mark dating c.1904 or earlier.

118. Edwin M. Knowles China Co.
East Liverpool, OH
1901 – 1963
The Edwin M. Knowles name is again in use on limited edition ware.

Interestingly, there were only two marks used by this company during its first 25 years. The company initials were used for only a few years as a mark.

E.M.K
C. Co.   (before 1904)

The Knowles vase (looks like a balloon) mark was used from 1901 to 1948. For most of the time from c.1901 to c.1925 it was the only mark of the company. However, it is possible to date the mark by using several means. The most important is the Knowles dating system. It is a very simple system, one that anybody doing a careful and thoughtful study of marks would readily discover. Also, it is one that the casual student of marks can study, verify, and thus realize the importance of dating systems. See p. 208 for a section called "American Dating Systems."

118. Edwin M. Knowles (continued)

EDWIN M. KNOWLES DATING SYSTEM
From 1901 to 1909 the vase (or urn) mark will have no numbers or two digits under the mark. The numbers on these early marks are usually blurred. The earliest one that I could read was 83. The 8 was clear, the 3 was not; thus, the second digit may be a letter not a number. From 1910 to 1914 there are three digits under the mark. From 1915 to c.1930 there are three separate numbers under the mark. The first two digits (one before 1910) always indicate the year on an Edwin M. Knowles mark during this period. The following numbers are from actual marks. The third digit probably indicates the factory number.

83	1908
101	1910
112	1911
133	1913
15 1 11	1915
16–2–4	1916
23–3 6	1923
24–1–11	1924
30 2-3	1930

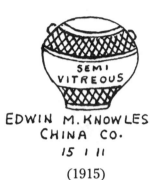

EDWIN M. KNOWLES
CHINA CO.
15 1 11
(1915)

The vase may say VITREOUS or SEMI-VITREOUS. VITREOUS was first used c.1915 or a bit earlier. SEMI-VITREOUS was used from 1901 onward.

About 1925 Knowles began to use other marks. Their IVORY mark dates c.1925 to 1929. All examples I've seen continued to use the dating system given above. Samples are given below.

THE
EDWIN M. KNOWLES
IVORY   (1926)
26-1-12

THE
EDWIN M. KNOWLES
IVORY   (1929)
29-2-11

During the 1930s, except 1930 itself, the vase mark was seldom (I believe never) used. The mark used was the ship mark given below. There are now two separate numbers under the mark. The first indicates the year, the second indicates the month. The ship mark is said to have been used before the 1930s; so far, I have not seen one.

32–2	1932 (Feb.)
34–12	1934 (Dec.)
35–3	1935 (Mar.)
38–10	1938 (Oct.)

MADE IN U.S.A.
36·4 (1936)

MADE IN U.S.A. was used after 1930.

68

118. Edwin M. Knowles (continued)

EDWIN M. KNOWLES DATING SYSTEM (continued)
During the 1930s Knowles introduced a few marks that seldom, if ever, used the dating system. In most cases (perhaps all cases) the ship mark did use the dating system. During the 1940s the vase mark was again use; however, it is a bit different from the earlier mark. The crosshatching is wider on the later mark. See comparison below:

EARLY MARK
(bottom of vase)
6 central diamonds

LATER MARK
(bottom of vase)
5 central diamonds

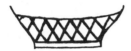

The dating system for the 1940s is the same as the 1930s system.

43-1	1943 (Jan.)
45-8	1945 (Aug.)
46-2	1946 (Feb.)
48-8	1948 (Aug.)

SEMI
VITREOUS

EDWIN M. KNOWLES
CHINA CO.
MADE IN U. S A.
46-2   (1946)

MADE IN U.S.A.
was used after 1930.

On some 1948 marks the word KNOWLES is printed across the vase. The numbers under the mark have no relation to the dating system described above. It seems that in 1948 this company abandoned their dating of marks in any consistent way. Some later marks seem to follow the system, many do not. The mark given below was used in the 1940s. It does seem to use the old system, at least in most cases.

KNOWLES
UTILITY
WARE
MADE IN U.S.A.
43-4

(1943)

118. Edwin M. Knowles (continued)

This is a typical 1950s Edwin M. Knowles mark. The distinctive K was used on many marks from c.1950 to 1963. This mark is dated 1953. The old Knowles dating system was infrequently used in the 1950s.

See Gates and Ormerod for more late Edwin M. Knowles Co. marks.

---

119. Knowles, Taylor and Knowles Co.
East Liverpool, OH
1854 – 1929

This company is the epitome of the early American whiteware industry. Companies like Knowles, Taylor and Knowles helped to make East Liverpool, Ohio, the center of the American whiteware industry. Their first whiteware dates back to 1872.

I've recently deciphered their dating system. See p. 73. See also p. 208 for a section called "American Dating Systems."

This earliest mark is from *The East Liverpool, Ohio, Pottery District* by William C. Gates, Jr. and Dana E. Ormerod. This is one of 27 marks reprinted from *Historical Archaeology*, Volume 16, Numbers 1 & 2, p. 116.

This mark was used from 1872 to c.1878.

Buffalo marks:
    These marks were used between 1878 and 1885.

There are a number of variations of the buffalo mark.

119. Knowles, Taylor & Knowles (continued)

Eagle trademark of the company:
These marks date from c.1880 to c.1890.

These marks and variations of these marks were used from c.1880 to c.1890.

(c.1880 – c.1890)   (c.1880 – c.1885)   (c.1880 – c.1885)

Barber showed a mark like the first mark above with a buffalo (bison) inside the circle instead of the eagle. Gates and Ormerod date this mark c.1900. I would date it c.1880. Jervis pictured this buffalo mark in his 1897 marks book. See p. 253. I have not yet seen the mark. Gates and Ormerod had not seen it when they published their book.

The BELLEEK mark below was used in 1889. The other marks were used between c.1890 to c.1900 or a bit later.

BELLEEK   K. T & K.   K. T. & K.
(1889)   GRANITE
                  (c.1890 – c.1900)   (c.1890 – c.1900)

71

119. Knowles, Taylor & Knowles (continued)

Eagle under monogram mark:

These marks date from c.1890 to c.1907. Above the mark is a K.T.K. (second K is backward) monogram. The third mark below is almost identical to a mark that was to be the first Knowles, Taylor & Knowles mark to use a dating system. See p. 74 for that mark.

(c.1890 – c.1907)   (c.1897)   (c.1900)

State, college or city marks:

These marks indicate shapes, decorations or patterns. They date from c.1885 to c.1905. They were used on table and toilet wares. Certain of these marks are used most often on toilet ware, but are also found on tableware. The reverse is undoubtedly true. For much more about these and other K.T.& K. marks see *The East Liverpool, Ohio, Pottery District* by William Gates and Dana Ormerod.

States:

See p. 73 for more state marks.

Colleges:

119. Knowles, Taylor & Knowles (continued)

Cities:

This is OBERLIN, not BERLIN. It is a college mark in fact.

This toilet ware mark is also found on tableware.

Other state marks; other shape marks

The mark at left was used from c.1905 to World War I. Gates and Ormerod showed a CALIFORNIA mark dating it c.1890. See p. 195 for this CALIFORNIA mark. They listed the following shape marks used from 1905: FANCY, QUINCY, ROCHESTER, and LUNA.

Other Knowles, Taylor and Knowles marks:

(1890s)

The mark at left and a similar mark were used on the famous Lotus Ware. The simple mark at above right was also used briefly to mark Lotus Ware.

K. T. & K
CHINA
(1890 – c.1905)

SEMI
VITREOUS
K. T. & K CO.
(after 1905)

K. T. & K
IVORY
(late 1920s)

The mark at right was found on a portrait plate decorated with a "modern" decal. K.T. & T. may have been one of the earliest to do so. See p. 227.

THE
KNOWLES, TAYLOR KNOWLES Co
MANUFACTURERS
EAST LIVERPOOL, OHIO
(c.1900)

K. T. & K.
S — V
CHINA.
3410 (1910)

K. T. & K.
S — V
IVORY.
49A (1929)

See dating system below.

KNOWLES, TAYLOR AND KNOWLES DATING SYSTEM

The Knowles, Taylor and Knowles Co. dating system is still tentative. I believe it to be correct; however, I've not yet acquired enough confirming dating information to declare the system absolute. The system is included here because I've not discovered a single mark, with one possible exception, that would invalidate the system. The K.T.& K. dating system is probably the oldest used in East Liverpool, Ohio. One K.T. & K. mark I've seen was dated 1904; one may have been dated 1900. Gates and Ormerod showed one Smith-Phillips mark dated 1904 in code. See p. 208 for a section called "American Dating Systems."

119. Knowles, Taylor & Knowles (continued)

DATING SYSTEM (continued)

The following details may need some refinement, particularly before 1905. From 1905 to 1926 the system is probably accurate. Again after 1926 there are some unanswered questions. I hope these questions will have been answered by the time another edition is released.

These two marks were used in the Knowles, Taylor and Knowles dating system.

K.T.&K Co.
326
(1906)

This Eagle mark was used from c.1900(?) to c.1915. This one dates 1906.

K. T. & K.
S ———— V
CHINA
145

(1905)

This S.V. mark was used from 1905 (possibly earlier) to 1926. Letters replaced numbers after 1914. See below (p. 75).

The following three-digit numbers were found under the Eagle (left) mark.

334   1904
315   1905
326   1906

The number 220 was found under one of two marks shown above. I failed to record which one it was. If it was under the Eagle mark it would most likely indicate 1900; however, the S.V. mark was probably not used until 1905.

From 1905 to 1915 the system dated both the Eagle mark and the S.V. mark the same way. From 1905 to 1909 the last of the three digits indicates the year. From 1910 to 1915 the last two of now four digits indicate the year.

145   1905   248   1908
315   1905   3410   1910
236   1906   3012   1912

119. Knowles, Taylor & Knowles (continued)

DATING SYSTEM (continued)

The Eagle mark was probably discontinued in 1914. It was used until then with dates. In 1915 the numbers under the mark were replaced with letters. The system now has three letters under the S.V. mark. I've seen no Eagle marks with letters under the mark. If there are, they would be using the same system. The third letter under the mark now indicates the year.

K.T. & K.	K.T. & K.
S———V	S———V
CHINA.	CHINA.
S D F	V H L
(1920)	(1926)

S H A	1915	R H G	1921
R G B	1916	P G H	1922
- - C	1917	S H I	1923
- - D	1918	R D J	1924
- - E	1919	- - K	1925
S D F	1920	V H L	1926

In 1927 the mark became a 27 between two other numbers. For example: 3 27 4

After 1927 the system seems to work as follows: under the mark is a number, a second number indicating the year, and an A or B.

48A	1928
39B	1929
41B	1931(?)

K.T. & K
S——— V
IVORY.
49B   (1929)

Although Knowles, Taylor and Knowles failed in 1929, becoming a part of the American Chinaware Corporation, it is not unlikely they continued to use their old mark until 1931. See above. In her 1982 book Jo Cunningham shows the Pope-Gosser name on a 1931 American Chinaware Corporation mark. Although Pope-Gosser was a member of the corporation, Knowles, Taylor and Knowles was the leading member and, thus, most likely to continue to use their old mark. All activities ceased in 1931.

As stated, the K.T. & K. dating system is still tentative.

120. Kurlbaum & Swartz
Philadelphia, PA
1851 – 1855

They made early hard-paste porcelain. It would be very rare.

K & S (very rare mark)

---

121. Homer Laughlin China Co.
East Liverpool, OH
1877 to the present

    As Knowles, Taylor & Knowles epitomizes the early American whiteware industry, Homer Laughlin epitomizes the industry as it moved into the modern period. This company's development of the continuous tunnel kiln in 1923 could well be considered the watershed of the American early and modern periods. Laughlin's use of the American Eagle atop a vanquished British Lion to mark much early whiteware is also noteworthy. And this was at a time when many companies were hiding their ware behind marks replicating the British Coat of Arms.

    Gates and Ormerod show a mark with LAUGHLIN BROS. under a shield that was used before 1877. I have not yet seen this mark.

PREMIUM STONE CHINA
HOMER LAUGHLIN

(c.1877 – c.1890)

PREMIUM STONE CHINA
HOMER LAUGHLIN

(c.1877 – c.1890)

Although the marks above are quite similar, based on ware I've seen, I would date the first mark a bit earlier than the second.

(c.1890 – c.1900)

Various versions of this mark were used to mark ironstone and semi-vitreous ware.

"AN AMERICAN BEAUTY"

(c.1897)

About 1897 this mark began to be used on semi-porcelain with pattern or shape names above.

121. Homer Laughlin China Co. (continued)

(1886 – 1889)

(c.1890 – c.1900)

(c.1900)

This is another version of a mark given on p. 76. The COLONIAL mark was used on some very good flow blue ware.

The above stamped or impressed mark was used only in 1886 according to Gates and Ormerod. See p. 181 for more about this mark.

The above mark is a fancy H.L. monogram for Homer Laughlin.

(c.1897 – c.1905)

Instead of GOLDEN GATE, the mark at left may say:
1. COLONIAL
2. AN AMERICAN BEAUTY, etc.

(c.1905)

Some interesting and "artistic" decals were used on this ART CHINA ware; however, it would not be considered art pottery in the traditional sense. GOLDEN FLEECE may be under the ART CHINA mark above.

The mark at the right was used to about World War I.

(c.1897 – c.WW I)

Homer Laughlin marks used in the early 1900s are included with the dating system given here.

HOMER LAUGHLIN CHINA CO. DATING SYSTEM

The Homer Laughlin dating system has been widely publicized. The information is usually given as provided by that company. After several years of research, I can say that the company supplied information is generally reliable with the exception of the first ten years; consequently, contrary to the common belief, Homer Laughlin was not the first to use a dating system. They were not even the earliest East Liverpool, Ohio, company to date their wares. Knowles, Taylor and Knowles, Edwin M. Knowles, Smith-Phillips and possibly others were ahead of them. The Knowles, Taylor and Knowles

121. Homer Laughlin China Co. (continued)

HOMER LAUGHLIN DATING SYSTEM (continued)

Co. was probably first. The J.& E. Mayer Co. of Beaver Falls, Pennsylvania, had all of the East Liverpool, Ohio, companies beat. See p. 208 for a section called "American Dating Systems."

Below are the two versions of the Homer Laughlin monogram and signature mark used from c.1900 to c.1930. Monograms used on other marks are included on following pages.

HOMER LAUGHLIN

(c.1900 to 1919)

HOMER LAUGHLIN

(1920 to c.1930)

The following information will help the collector to quickly distinguish between pre-1920 and post-1920 Homer Laughlin marks without dealing with the dating system. Every pre-1920 mark I have seen conforms to the first sample mark shown above. Every post-1920 mark conforms to the second sample mark shown above. I have studied so many marks that I can say the distinction is absolute. In seven years I've not seen a single exception!

Concerning the two marks, note the difference between the first *L*s of the two Laughlins. Also, note the horizontal line connecting the *H* and *C* of the monogram. On the earlier mark the line goes through the left vertical line of the *H* and through the *C* on the right. It does not on the later mark. Below is given a Homer Laughlin mark used in the 1960s and later. It has the open loop on the first *L* of Laughlin; however, note the different monogram style. Also, MADE IN U.S.A. was never used on pre-1920 Homer Laughlin marks.

HOMER LAUGHLIN

MADE IN U.S.A.

(1960s and later)

MADE IN U.S.A. was not used on Homer Laughlin marks before 1922. The study of hundreds of this company's marks has uncovered only one possible exception to the rule. This mark possibly indicated a 1921 use of MADE IN U.S.A. This will be discussed later on in the dating system.

121. Homer Laughlin China Co. (continued)

HOMER LAUGHLIN DATING SYSTEM (continued)

Below are given the details of the Homer Laughlin dating system in reality, not in theory. On p. 225 is given the information as presented in my earlier book.

1900 – 1910:

According to the theory, Homer Laughlin marks during this period had three numbers under the mark. The first indicated the month (1 to 12); the second indicated the year (0 to 9); the third number indicated the factory (1 to 3). Lois Lehner in her 1980 book and her new book incorrectly dated a 1914 mark as a 1904 mark.

I have not seen even one verifiably dated mark from this period. I have seen some blurred marks that might be from the period. If Homer Laughlin did date these early marks, it was quite infrequently. Personally, I don't believe they dated their 1900 to 1910 marks. I'll have to see a verifiable mark to believe it.

What one does find from this period are monogram with signature marks accompanied by an identifying shape or pattern word. These marks are given below. HUDSON seems to be the most common. It was used from 1903 (from calendar plate) to c.1920 (possibly later). The other marks are less frequently found. If there are no numbers under the mark, it was used before c.1910. If the mark has letters and a number under the mark, see the 1910 to 1919 part of the dating system given later on.

HOMER LAUGHLIN
Hudson

(1903 – c.1920)

HOMER LAUGHLIN
The Angelus

(c.1908 – c.1915)

HOMER LAUGHLIN
Colonial

(before 1910)

HOMER LAUGHLIN
Niagara

(c.1909)

Before 1910 these marks will not use the dating system. GENESEE was probably not used in this early period; however, if found without numbers, it would indicate a pre-1910 usage. See next page. Gates and Ormerod also mentioned a KING CHARLES and a REPUBLIC mark. I've not yet seen these marks.

121. Homer Laughlin China Co. (continued)

HOMER LAUGHLIN DATING SYSTEM (continued)

1910 – 1919:

During 1910 to 1919 the dating system began to be used in fact, not just in theory. The first number under the mark is the month (1-12) of manufacture. The second single digit number is for the year. The third part is a letter (or letter with number) indicating the factory. They include N, L, and N5.

4 1 L	April 1911	factory L	Sample mark:
8 2 N	August 1912	factory N	
10 3 N	Oct. 1913	factory N	
1 4 L	Jan. 1914	factory L	
5 5 N	May 1915	factory N	
5 6 L	May 1916	factory L	
12 7 N5	Dec. 1917	factory N5	
3 8 N	March 1918	factory N	
7 9 L	July 1919	factory L	

HOMER LAUGHLIN
Jerasee (1916)
5 6 L

The 1911 and 1912 dates given above are simulated. The earliest Homer Laughlin mark with a date that I've seen is 1913.

NOTE: During this period, the year is given only as a single digit.

1920 and 1921:

During 1920 and 1921 the number for the year is almost always a 20 or 21. The monogram and the signature have changed slightly. See p. 78.

2 20 N5	Feb. 1920	factory N5
3 20 L	March 1920	factory L
8 21 N	Aug. 1921	factory N
12 21 N	Dec. 1921	factory N

HOMER LAUGHLIN
2 20 N5 ·

(1920)

This mark is possibly an exception to the rule above. It is the only Homer Laughlin mark I've found that does not fit the rules as given in this book. This is possibly for January 1921, factory N. If so, it is a very rare exception to the rule. Possibly it is just an incorrect or incomplete mark.

HOMER LAUGHLIN
MADE IN U.S.A.
I I N

(1921?)

121. Homer Laughlin China Co. (continued)

HOMER LAUGHLIN DATING SYSTEM (continued)

1922 – 1929:

From 1922 to 1929 the system works as follows: a letter (A to L) has replaced the month number; the single digit number in the middle is the year (1922 to 1929); the factory letter (or, letter with number) is last. MADE IN U.S.A. was first used on Homer Laughlin marks in 1922. (See previous page for a possible 1921 use of MADE IN U.S.A.)

L 2 N	Dec. 1922	factory N	Sample mark:
B 3 N	Feb. 1923	factory N	
K 4 L	Nov. 1924	factory L	
D 5 N5	April 1925	factory N5	
F 6 L	June 1926	factory L	
J 7 N5	Oct. 1927	factory N5	
A 8 N	Jan. 1928	factory N	
C 9 N	March 1929	factory N	

HOMER LAUGHLIN
MADE IN U.S.A.
K 3 N

(1923)

1930 and later:

From 1930 onward the dating system is quite simple. The middle two-digit number is the year: B 33 N4 is for 1933; D 42 N5 is for 1942; K 55 N5 is for 1955.

From the 1930s onward many Homer Laughlin marks were not dated. Below is a sampling of later marks that I often find at flea markets. Some later Homer Laughlin ware is quite collectible. For a much larger selection of later marks and the approximate date when used, see "The East Liverpool, Ohio, Pottery District" by William Gates and Dana Ormerod as published in *Historical Archaeology* Volume 16, Numbers 1 & 2.

(all c.1930 marks below)

Trellis
L
L9N
(1929)

Ivory Tone
T

Trellis
C

Ivory Color
L.C.

Ivory Color
C

Ivory Color
L

The first mark above is a Homer Laughlin mark dated 1929. IVORY TONE with T (Trellis) marked ware was found with the TRELLIS marked ware. The ware was identical and undoubtedly Homer Laughlin. The word TRELLIS on the TRELLIS with *C* mark is identical to the TRELLIS on the first mark, thus indicating a probable Homer Laughlin mark; however, since the Crooksville China Co. made a "trellis" ware, I'm not yet ready to rule out the mark being a Crooksville mark. See p. 39. IVORY COLOR is also found with the Homer Laughlin trellis shape and decoration. I had thought the L.C. was for the Limoges China Co. Apparently it is for Laughlin China or Company. Putting all the information together seems to make all these Homer Laughlin marks. I can't explain the solitary *C* under two of the marks.

81

121. Homer Laughlin China Co. (continued)

Other later Marks:

OVEN SERVE MADE IN U.S.A.

Various versions of OVEN SERVE were used from the 1930s to the 1950s. Later OVEN SERVE marks use a different monogram. See p. 83.

Eggshell NAUTILUS U.S.A.

B 36 N5

Eggshell NAUTILUS U.S.A

J 47 N5

(c.1935 to c.1955)

Marks with EGGSHELL and/or NAUTILUS were used from c.1935 to c.1955. These marks were almost always dated. Wares with these marks are fairly common at flea markets.

ART WELLS GLAZES

(1930s)

WELLS MADE IN USA.

(1930s)

HomerLaughlin VIRGINIA ROSE MADE IN U.S.A.

D 48 N8

(1930s – c.1960)

The VIRGINIA ROSE shape and/or decoration was used from the 1930s to c.1960. The VIRGINIA ROSE decoration is very popular. These marks are usually dated.

Fiesta HLC USA

See the Gates and Ormerod book for details of the various FIESTA marks used from the 1930s onward. There are numerous books and articles dealing with the ever-popular Fiesta Ware.

KRAFT-BLUE HomerLaughlin MADE IN U.S.A.

(c.1950)

This 1950s ware is quite collectible. It can be found at flea markets but is not common. There is a KRAFT-PINK also.

Wild Rose U.S.A.

C 62 N6

(c.1945 to at least 1962)

121. Homer Laughlin China Co. (continued)

TUDOR
ROSE

(c.1945 – c.1955)

This mark also has one
or two lines under the OSE
of ROSE.

The monogram at left was in use from 1920 to c.1960 on various Homer Laughlin marks. In the 1920s it was used only with the Homer Laughlin signature. See p. 81. From the 1930s onward it was used as a part of many marks.

H L co

)|(e

H · L · Co

The six Homer Laughlin monograms above were used on/in various marks in the 1930s, 1940s and possibly the 1950s.

The monogram at left is for Household Institute. It is a Homer Laughlin mark of the 1940s.

)|(c   )|(c

A mark with one of the monograms above indicates a very late Homer Laughlin mark dating from the 1960s to the present.

122. Lenox, Inc. (Ceramic Art Co.)
Trenton, NJ
1889 to the present

This remarkable company has now been making quality porcelain for more than 100 years. No other American company has been able to commercially produce porcelain for general home use for more than a decade or two. I believe Lenox is currently the only American maker of fine porcelain dinnerware. (See Pfaltzgraff on p. 113.) The Gorham Co. attempted to enter the market in the 1970s but is no longer making porcelain dinnerware in this country. The ivory-like porcelain of Lenox is as distinctive as Irish Belleek.

The marks used by Lenox to about 1930 are given on the following page. For some detailed information about Lenox and its marks, see the *Official Price Guide to Pottery & Porcelain* by House of Collectibles.

122. Lenox, Inc. (continued)

CERAMIC ART CO. in a wreath was used on special decorative work in the 1890s.

BELLEEK

(before 1895)

LENOX

(1896 – 1906)
decorated ware

The mark above was used on both decorated and undecorated (mostly for "home" decorating) wares between 1889 and 1896. Undecorated ware continued to have this mark until 1906. Note the complex C.A.C. monogram on the first three marks.

After 1924 the *L* in a wreath was used on all wares. MADE IN U.S.A. was first used in 1930.

LENOX

(1906 – 1924)
decorated ware

BELLEEK

(1906 – 1924)
undecorated ware

---

123. Limoges China Co.
Sebring, OH
1900 – 1955

For a short time this company was called the Sterling China Co. The first two marks given below may be for this period. For more about Sterling China marks see p. 188.

Sterling China

(possibly c.1900; however, see p. 188 for Sterling China)

SEBRING.OHIO

(c.1900 – c.1910)

LIMOGES
CHINA

(c.1900 – c.1910)

LIMOGES
CHINA

(c.1910 – c.1915)

123. Limoges China Co. (continued)

Based on marks seen, I would say the Limoges China Co. was in retreat in the 1930s. Marks before c.1930 and after c.1940 are rather common. This isn't true of the 1930s. JIFFY WARE dates from the 1930s but isn't common. (See p. 181 for a JIFFY WARE mark.) Most PEASANT WARE seems to be from the 1940s. Only PEACH-BLO seems to be a common 1930s mark.

There are several other PEACH-BLO marks.

Limoges China Co. marks from the 1940s are fairly common. These are two representative examples. Note the use of AMERICAN LIMOGES during this period.

LINCOLN CHINA CO. was used as a mark by the Limoges Co. c.1950 because of legal problems.

124. Maddock Companies, various
1882 – c.1929

The Maddock companies are most remarkable. Most Trenton potteries were on the decline by the early 1900s; consequently, Barber's 1904 marks book is still relatively valid today for most of the Trenton companies. This certainly isn't true for the Maddocks. Thomas Maddock & Sons became Thomas Maddock's Sons Co. in 1902. They continued to make mortars and pestles as had the company before 1902. These are frequently found at flea markets. They were also a major decorating company in the early 1900s. They decorated their own or other Trenton whiteware until 1912 (see also pp. 182 and 183). They were associated with a New Jersey China Pottery Co. c.1910 (see next page). This name is sometimes found on pieces decorated by Thomas Maddock's Sons. In 1912 they began to import and decorate German porcelain blanks. This continued to c.1915. Their name is also found on specially decorated flow blue ware from the early 1900s.

The Maddock Pottery (Lamberton Works) is also quite remarkable. Their ROYAL PORCE-LAIN (see next page) was some of the best semi-porcelain made in this country. Thinner pieces are so translucent as to be possibly considered porcelain. Thicker pieces are not overtly translucent. The ROYAL PORCELAIN mark is a copy of an English Maddock's mark. See discussion below with mark.

The Maddock name is very common on hotel and railroad wares found at flea markets. This ware is marked LAMBERTON CHINA, MADDOCK'S TRENTON CHINA, TRENTON CHINA, MADDOCK'S AMERICAN CHINA, etc. In the mid-1920s the Scammell China Co. took over the Maddock Pottery Co. They continued to make a TRENTON CHINA and a LAMBERTON CHINA. See their marks under Scammell China Co. on pp. 128 and 129.

Thomas Maddock & Sons
Trenton, NJ
1882 – 1902

dinnerware	sanitary ware	This c.1900 mark is impressed on mortars with pestles.

Thomas Maddock's Sons Co.
Trenton, NJ
1902 – c.1915+

The mark at left is found impressed on mortars with pestles.

This after 1902 mark is impressed or stamped.

(after 1902)

124. Maddock Potteries (continued)

Thomas Maddock's Sons Co. (continued)

These Thomas Maddock's Sons marks are decorator marks used from c.1905 to c.1915. See p. 183 for a Thomas Maddock's Sons mark used on flow blue ware. They are usually found on pieces that are dated, such as Masonic, commemorative, etc. Until 1911 ordinary American whiteware was usually used for decorating. They were probably using their own whiteware until 1912. In 1912 they began importing German porcelain blanks. The NEW JERSEY CHINA POTTERY mark shown below is sometimes found with the decorator mark. Since other Maddock companies made LAMBERTON CHINA, TRENTON CHINA, and AMERICAN CHINA, they probably named their whiteware NEW JERSEY CHINA and their company New Jersey China Pottery Co. This company didn't last long. I've found no evidence of NEW JERSEY CHINA being made after 1912.

Tho's. Maddock's
Son's Co.
Trenton, N. J.

(c.1905 – c.1915)

Tho's. Maddock's Sons Co,
Trenton, N. J.

(c.1905 – c.1915)

The above marks are fairly common; after 1912 they marked imported porcelain ware.

NEW JERSEY

CHINA
POTTERY COMPANY

This c.1910 mark is found with the Thomas Maddock's Sons Co. mark shown above. It was probably not used after 1912.

Maddock Pottery Co. (Lamberton Works)
Trenton, NJ
1893 – c.1923

(c.1893 – c.1900)

This Maddock's ROYAL PORCELAIN mark is found on a very good semi-porcelain. Thin pieces are so translucent as to be virtually true porcelain. I've yet to see one piece that showed even a hint of crazing. Some pieces are ordinary in shape and decoration; others are comparable to fine English porcelain. The mark itself is a virtual copy of an English Maddock's mark. See p. 204. The American whiteware is superior to that with the English mark!

124. Maddock Potteries (continued)

Maddock Pottery Co. (Lamberton Works)(continued)

(c.1900 – c.1905)

See p. 181 for more about this
and later LAMBERTON CHINA
marks.

M
CHINA
L

(c.1900 – c.1915)

M
LAMBERTON
CHINA

(c.1910 – c.1920)

The next two marks were used on hotel and railroad china from c.1910 to c.1920+. The LAMBERTON CHINA mark was stamped on hotel ware. MADDOCK'S TRENTON CHINA was impressed on railroad ware.

Lamberton China

TRENTON CHINA
MADE IN AMERICA

(c.1920+)

MADDOCK'S
TRENTON CHINA

(impressed)

The TRENTON CHINA mark above could be a c.1920 mark for the Maddock Pottery Co. or it could date a bit later, after the company became the Scammell China Co. It is undoubtedly a transition mark. See p. 128 for similar Scammell marks.

John Maddock & Sons
Trenton, NJ
1894 – c.1929

John Maddock was a son of Thomas Maddock. Although they made mostly sanitary and specialty wares, Barber said the first mark given below was used on "Coalport" china. From c.1910 to the 1920s they made hotel and railroad china marked MADDOCK'S AMERICAN CHINA. The mark below at far right is a very common mark found impressed on hotel ware.

(c.1900 – c.1915)

VITREOUS GLAZE may be
above the mark at left.

MADDOCK'S
AMERICAN CHINA

(c.1910 to 1920s)
(impressed)

The c.1915 mark at left was used on
railroad ware.

125. Maryland Pottery Co.
Baltimore, MD
1879 – c.1910

The D.F. Haynes, connected with this company for about two years, acquired the Chesapeake Pottery in 1882. This company, like the other two big Baltimore potteries, produced some fine whiteware with excellent decoration. Although small compared to the Trenton, New Jersey, or East Liverpool, Ohio, pottery industries, the Baltimore pottery industry was a credit to the city as well as the nation. The Maryland Pottery Co. made only sanitary ware after c.1895.

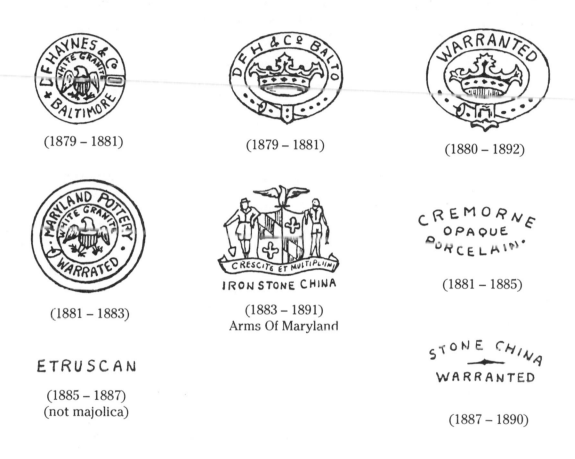

(1879 – 1881)

(1879 – 1881)

(1880 – 1892)

(1881 – 1883)

(1883 – 1891)
Arms Of Maryland

CREMORNE
OPAQUE
PORCELAIN

(1881 – 1885)

ETRUSCAN

(1885 – 1887)
(not majolica)

STONE CHINA
WARRANTED

(1887 – 1890)

126. Mayer Pottery Co.
Beaver Falls, PA
1881 – c.World War I

The Mayer Pottery Co. is quite important. They were America's most prolific maker of tea leaf luster ware. They also made some good flow blue ware. They developed the earliest true dating system for whiteware in this country. A few American companies such as the Dresden Pottery (Potters' Cooperative Co.) put actual dates of manufacture on their marks from time to time in the 1890s and earlier (Note: a date on a mark may mean any number of things); however, it was J. & E. Mayer that first developed an actual dating system.

About 1916 this company began to make hotel china. The mark became MAYER CHINA. (See p. 197 for samples of these later marks.) This company continues to operate; however, it is the early ware that is of real interest to collectors.

126. Mayer Pottery co. (continued)

Their dating system is explained along with the following marks. See pp. 218 and 219 for more about the Mayer dating system.

(1881 – c.1890)

This mark is by far the most commonly found J. & E. Mayer mark. In the 1880s it was the company's only mark. Earlier marks were in black; later marks were in brown. Nearly all tea leaf luster ware has this mark or the dated stone china mark below.

(probably Aug. 1899)

(April 1900?)

In the 1890s J. & E. Mayer introduced semi-porcelain. The marks used are given; however, the company continued to use the stone china mark on that type of ware. At some point in the 1890s, perhaps as early as 1890, they began to use a dating system on these marks. See examples at left. The H and 9 mark is probably for August, 1899. The D and O mark could be for April, 1890 or 1900. I've not yet seen enough of these dated marks to be sure. See pp. 218 and 219.

These marks were used on semi-porcelain in the 1890s.

Pennsylvania Coat Of Arms

After 1900 the stone china mark was dropped. The Pennsylvania Coat of Arms mark continued to be used with either SEMI-VITREOUS CHINA or IRON STONE CHINA above the mark. Also, there are numbers on both sides of the mark. The number on the left is probably the month and the number on the right is probably the year. Again, I have not seen enough of these marks to be positive. Also, I'm not sure how far into the 1900s these marks continued to be used.

126. Mayer Pottery Co. (continued)

(c.1900 – c.1910)
(August, 1901?)

(c.1900 – c.1910)
(January, 1902?)

(c.1900 – c.1910)
(March, 1901?)

Barber said there were three other special marks used before 1896. They were DIANA, POTOMAC and WINDSOR; however, they were not pictured. In a 1940s marks book, C. Jordan Thorn showed a suspicious-looking POTOMAC mark. He used the exact outline of the Knowles, Taylor and Knowles DAKOTA mark (see p. 186), but with POTOMAC in the center. Thorn got the mark from Jervis' 1897 book. See p. 255. The following marks date c.1900.

In addition to LINCOLN, the mark at left comes with:
1. GENOA
2. JUNO
3. DAYBREAK
4. DUQUESNE

126. Mayer Pottery Co. (continued)

The MARINE mark below would date c.1905 to c.1915. Petra Williams says a MARINE mark was used on Mayer Pottery Co. flow blue ware. The MARINE marked pieces I've seen are in blue but not the cobalt blue associated with flow blue. The "flown" appearance is caused by the blue paint being sprayed over the whiteware's surface.

The Mayer Pottery Co. did make a flow blue, however. Like most British flow blue marks, the marks are in flow blue. These marks are often difficult to read. One is lucky to make out "J. & E. Mayer" or "Beaver Falls, Pa." on the mark. I have one of these marks on p. 183. The Mayer flow blue marks appear to be unique to that type of ware. I believe they were used at least as early as the 1890s. Barber was unaware of these marks.

(c.1905 – c.1915)

---

127. J.W. McCoy Pottery
Roseville, OH
1900 – 1911

They made and marked some art pottery. See Paul Evans's *Art Pottery of the United States*. They also made utilitarian yellow ware and possibly whiteware.

---

128. Nelson McCoy
Roseville, OH
1910 to the present

This company made no early whiteware. McCoy did not mark ware until the 1930s. The word *McCoy* on a mark dates from the 1940s and later.

---

129. McNicol Burton & Co.
East Liverpool, OH
c.1870 – 1892

McN.B. & Co. was used on various marks from the late 1880s to 1892.

(c.1890)

---

130. D. E. McNicol Pottery Co.
East Liverpool, OH
1892 – 1950s

The D.E. McNicol Co. is fairly typical of East Liverpool, Ohio, companies. The whiteware itself is typical of the general East Liverpool ware. The company produced enough ware that many of their marks will be encountered by the collector. Also, since they made much specialty ware, such as calendar plates, commemorative items and the like, much has survived for us to find today.

130. D. E. McNicol Pottery Co. (continued)

(c.1892 – c.1900)

(c.1895 – c.1900)

(c.1900)

(c.1900 – c.1920)

(c.1905 – c.1915)

(c.1895 – c.1905)

(c.1900 – c.1910)

(c.1900)

The mark at left is from Gates and Ormerod. It is one of 27 marks reprinted from *Historical Archaeology,* Vol. 16, Numbers 1 & 2, p. 187.

(c.1905 – c.1915)

(c.1910 – c.1920)

D. E McNicol
East Liverpool, O.

(c.1915 – c.1929)

This mark has 2 numbers or 3 letters under it. See below.

The third mark above was the first D. E. McNicol mark to use a dating system. I've uncovered the general outline for this system. I've yet to fill in all the details. See the next page for the general outline to the system.

130. D.E. McNicol Pottery (continued)

D. E. McNicol
EAST LIVERPOOL, O.
8 9

(c.1915 – c.1920)

D. E. McNicol
EAST LIVERPOOL, O.
X F S

(c.1920 – c.1929)

From c.1915 to c.1920 all the D.E. McNicol factories in East Liverpool, Ohio, and the one in Clarksburg, West Virginia, used the above mark with no numbers or two numbers under the mark. By 1920 a new factory had opened in East Liverpool. From then to c.1929 East Liverpool marks included three *letters* under the mark. The first letter indiates one of the four East Liverpool factories (V, W, X or Z). The other two letters are probably a dating system. I've not yet decoded it.

In the 1920s the Clarksburg factory used the mark below. Between c.1915 and 1920 the mark was infrequently used. In the 1920s the mark was dated.

D. E. McNicol
CLARKSBURG, W.VA.
10 25

(1925)

HOLD FAST BABY PLATE
MADE BY
THE D.E. MC NICOL POTTERY
EAST LIVERPOOL, O.
PATENT APPLIED FOR

(before 1920)

(c.1920)

As did many others, D.E. McNicol had troubles in the 1920s. They left East Liverpool to concentrate on their West Virginia operations. They survived there from the 1930s to the 1950s making hotel or institutional ware marked McNICOL CHINA or (LIBERTY) VITRIFIED CHINA. D. E. McNICOL and/or CLARKSBURG, W. VA., will accompany all marks with VITRIFIED CHINA or LIBERTY VITRIFIED CHINA. See also Albert Pick on p. 115.

Various McNICOL CHINA marks like the one at left and other D. E. McNicol marks with VITRIFIED CHINA or LIBERTY VITRIFIED CHINA date from c.1930 through the 1950s.

131. T. A. McNicol Pottery Co.
East Liverpool, Ohio
1913 – 1929

(1923)

T. A. McNicol was a brother of D. E. McNicol. Note how similar this mark is to one of the D. E. McNicol marks. Also, note the dating system. The last two numbers indicate the year, in this case 1923.

---

132. Other McNicol potteries

McNicol-Smith Company
Wellsville, OH
1899 – 1907

(1899 – c.1901)   (1899 – c.1907)   (c.1903)

The first mark above is from Gates and Ormerod. It is one of 27 marks reprinted from *Historical Archaeology,* Volume 16, Nos. 1 & 2, p. 196. The second one is the most common McNicol & Smith mark.

The center of the above mark is an M. & S. monogram.

McNicol-Corns Company
Wellsville, OH
1907 – 1928

This mark at left is the only one I've seen for this company. This seems remarkable for a company that operated for twenty years. I can only conclude this company was not very productive. For a few years after 1928 the company was called the Corns China Co. See p. 183 for a recently seen McNicol-Corns mark.

Corns China Company
Wellsville, OH
1928 – 1932

I've not yet seen any marks for this short-lived company.

133. Mercer Pottery Co.
Trenton, NJ
1868 – c.1930

The Mercer Pottery Co. would have to rank as one of Trenton's leading potteries of the 1880s and 1890s. I find more Mercer marked ware from before 1900 than ware from any other Trenton pottery with the possible exception of the Willets Manufacturing Co. I've seen every Barber mark, some many times, except the TACOMA mark; however, I've seen but one Mercer mark not given by Barber. See p. 184 for that mark.

Mercer is typical of the Trenton potteries. While many of these companies continued to about the time of the Great Depression, very little of what can be found of their ware dates from beyond the very early 1900s. Most of the Trenton companies that continued into the 20th century converted to making sanitary porcelain. Therefore, the collector is more likely to find early Trenton whiteware than later ware. Barber's 1904 marks book is still reasonably valid with regard to most Trenton potteries.

The Mercer Pottery Co. is also important as one of America's outstanding makers of flow blue ware. I would rank them with Burgess and Campbell of the International Pottery Co. as making this country's best flow blue. Their flow blue is of a rich cobalt blue with a considerable flowing effect. The whiteware itself, both ironstone and semi-porcelain, is superior to the whiteware of Burgess and Campbell. They did not, however, attempt as many designs or patterns as Burgess and Campbell.

(1879 – c.1885)

(c.1880 – c.1885)

(1880s)
(impressed mark)

MERCER POTTERY
TRENTON, N.J.

(1880s)
(impressed mark)

(1890s)

(1890s)

These two 1890s marks include complex M.P. Co. monograms. Both were used on flow blue ware.

133. Mercer Pottery Co. (continued)

As were the last two marks on p. 96, several of these marks were used on flow blue ware.

(1890s)

(1890s)

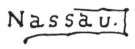

(1890s)

(c.1897)

Bordeaux
Mercer

(c.1900) See p. 168 for a varia-tion of the BORDEAUX mark.

(1890s)

(1890s)

(c.1900)

The mark to the left also comes with:
1. TRINIDAD
2. SMYRNA
3. ARDMORE

---

134. Millington, Astbury & Poulson
Trenton, NJ
1859 – 1862

(impressed mark)

---

135. Monarch Dinnerware Co.
Chester, W V
1940s

Their mark is MONARCH DINNERWARE CO.

136. Morgan Belleek China Co.
Canton, OH
1924 – 1931

Wares are marked MORGAN BELLEEK.

137. Morley & Co.
Wellsville, OH
1879 – c.1884

Another version of this mark
says MAJOLICA.

138. George Morley & Son(s)
East Liverpool, OH
1885 – c.1890

This is the same Morley that had operated earlier in Wellsville,
Ohio. See above.

The version of the above mark without company initials might well be mistaken for an English mark because of its complexity and artistic accuracy. My drawing doesn't really do justice to the original.

The two marks below are from *The East Liverpool, Ohio Pottery District* by William Gates and Dana Ormerod. They are two of 27 marks reprinted from *Historical Archaeology,* Volume 16, Numbers 1 & 2, p. 200.

139. Mount Clemens Pottery
Mount Clemens, MI
1915 – 1960s and later

Although this company continued to produce into the 1960s and later, all of the marks I've seen with the monogram given below date from the 1920s to the 1940s. Most date c.1930 to c.1935. In her 1988 book, Lois Lehner shows many very late marks for the company.

(1935)

140. Mountford & Co.
East Liverpool, OH
1891 – 1897

Gates and Ormerod credit the first mark given below to this company. The second mark is probably for the same company; however, it could be for Murphy & Co., the company that was a continuation of Mountford & Co.

   The mark at left could be for this company or for Murphy & Co. See below.

141. George C. Murphy & Co.
East Liverpool, OH
c.1898 – 1904

This company took over Mountford & Co. See above.

Note the G.C.M. & Co. monogram on the mark above.

See Mountford & Co. for another possible George C. Murphy & Co. mark.

142. Mutual China Co.
Indianapolis, IN
1915 – 1970s

Mutual China was a retailing concern that marked both foreign and American wares.

143. National China Co.
East Liverpool and Salineville, OH
1900 – 1929

The National China Co. is the most important early American pottery not mentioned in Barber's 1904 marks book. The National China Co. produced a great deal of ordinary whiteware; however, they also produced some excellent ware thin enough and translucent enough to rival true porcelain. Some of their decal decorations are also noteworthy.

In 1911 the National China Co. moved to Salineville, Ohio. Their Salineville produced ware is generally inferior to their ware produced earlier in East Liverpool. Much of their later ware, particularly from the 1920s, is an inferior whiteware subject to serious crazing. Apparently the company did not prosper after the move. I find much more of the earlier ware.

N. C. Co.
E.L.O.

(1900 – 1911)

The plain mark above is probably the most common National China Co. mark. It is common on calendar plates.

N. C. Co.
HOTEL
E.L.O.

(1900 – 1911)

The NATIONAL China Co.
E.L.O.

(1900 – 1911)

(1900 – 1911)

The WESTERN GEM mark was used on some excellent ware; however, once in a while, some very ordinary pieces have the mark.

(1900 – c.1915)

The above mark was used on some excellent ware. Although used in the early years, I believe it was also used after 1911, to about 1915.

(c.1900)

I have seen the above mark only twice. In both cases it marked ware I would classify as majolica, similar to the Chesapeake Pottery's CLIFTON ware.

NATIONAL
CHINA
COMPANY

(c.1911 – c.1925)

In the 1920s the mark at the left was usually dated.

143. National China Co. (continued)

(c.1916 – c.1929)

WHITE GRANITE

(c.1911 – c.1929)

(1911 – c.1920)

(1911 – c.1920)

This mark was used on some good whiteware; however, by the late 1920s, it marked some very poor whiteware. The later marked ware has MADE IN U.S.A. under the mark.

KERMIT was used primarily on toiletware.

PERFECTION was used on toiletware. It was probably the latest use of the British Coat of Arms on American whiteware. See p. 232.

Variations of the monogram at left were used on National China Co. marks after 1911. NATIONAL DINNERWARE was used at this time. See example on p. 231.

Gates and Ormerod, using company catalogs, etc., show a few other possible National China Co. marks. I have included only marks actually seen on ware.

---

144. National Silver Co.
New York, NY
1930s – 1950s

This company distributed wares made by other American companies. Although the company may have continued beyond the 1940s, virtually all of the NASCO marks date from the 1930s and 1940s. The NASCO mark below with *Japan* would be an exception. It would date in the 1950s or later. Of course, it would not be an American whiteware mark.

NASCO
PLATINUM
&
22 KT. GOLD
DECORATION

(1930s, 1940s)

NASCO
JAPAN

(1950s or later)

145. New Castle Pottery Co.
New Castle, PA
1901 – 1905

NEW CASTLE CHINA
NEW CASTLE, PA.

---

146. New England Pottery Co.
East Boston, MA
1875 – c.1914

A pottery was established in East Boston as early as 1854 for the manufacture of whiteware. In 1875 Thomas Gray and L. W. Clark took over the pottery, now called the New England Pottery Co. In his 1893 book, Barber pictured some very nice whiteware made by this company. I've seen only a few New England Pottery Co. marks. Although most of the ware was quite ordinary, I have recently seen some exquisite New England Pottery Co. ware. I suspect ware made by this company is more common in Massachusetts and the rest of New England. Note the N.E.P. monogram on several of the marks. The *G* and *C* on two of the marks are for Gray and Clark.

(1878 – 1883)

(1883 – 1886)

(1886 – 1888)

(1886 – 1892)

(1888 – 1889)

The above mark was used on a special order. It was not a regular mark. It is pre-1904.

(1889 – 1895)

(1887 – c.1904)

(1897 – 1904 or later)

147. New Jersey Pottery Co.
Trenton, NJ
1869 – 1883

This company joined the Union Pottery Co. of Trenton in 1883. Elias Cook had been involved with the forming of both these companies in 1869. See p. 152.

148. New Milford Pottery Co. and Wannopee Pottery
New Milford, CT
1886 – 1903

This company began making ordinary whiteware. Between 1890 and 1892 the company changed hands and became known as the Wannopee Pottery. Art pottery became important after the change. The names Lang & Schafer and Lang & Osgood were associated with these companies. See Paul Evans's *Art Pottery of the United States* for more about their history.

New Milford Pottery Co. marks 1886 – c.1891

Wannopee Pottery marks c.1891 – 1903

149. New Orleans Porcelain Mnfg. Co.
New Orleans, LA
1880s

No marks are known for this company.

150. New York City Pottery
New York, NY
1853 – 1888

Morrison & Carr were the first owners; from 1871 to 1888 James Carr operated the company alone.

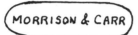

(1860)
(Impressed mark)

(1871)
Note the J.C. monogram.

(1871)
The above mark was a special mark for the James L. Howard Co.

(1879)

The next five marks date from c.1872 to 1888.

  This mark was used on hotel china.

NOTE: The squares and circle enclosing three of the above marks are probably not actually part of the marks. Barber often used this device to highlight selected marks.

---

151. Oakwood China Co.
Chester, WV
Ravenna, OH
Sebring, OH
1915 – 1950s and later

This decorating company marked both American and foreign blanks. Marks that include Chester, West Virginia or Ravenna, Ohio, would date 1915 to the 1920s. Marks with Sebring, Ohio would date from the 1930s and later. See *The East Liverpool, Ohio, Pottery District* by Gates and Ormerod for examples of the early marks.

152. Ohio China Co.
East Palestine, OH
1896 – 1912

(1896 – c.1902)

(c.1902 – c.1912)

(c.1902 – c.1912)

See p. 180 for more about IMPERIAL CHINA marks.

The above mark is an O.C. Co. monogram.

153. Ohio Pottery Co.
Zanesville, OH
c.1900 – 1923

After c.1915 this company began to make kitchen and dinner wares. Lois Lehner said they developed a true hard-paste porcelain marked PETROSCAN. See her 1988 book for some marks. This company became the Fraunfelter China Co. in 1923.

154. Ohio Valley China Co.
Wheeling, WV
1887 – c.1894

Barber was quite interested in this company, mentioning it several times in his various books. He was most interested in the artistic ware made of true hard porcelain. I've come across only one piece of the company's ware. It was a quite remarkable piece of true porcelain made in the form of a circular plaque pierced for hanging. It was covered with beautifully modeled, applied roses with leaves and branches. It had no coloring — just the white porcelain. At a distance it looked like a fine example of Irish belleek. Upon closer examination, it had a different white coloring and the ware was much thicker than true belleek. Nevertheless, it was an outstanding example of American artistry. It had the shield mark below. Ohio Valley China Co. ware is probably rather rare.

Before 1891 this company was called the West Virginia China Co. These marks date from 1891 to c.1894.

O.V.

155. Oliver China Co.
Sebring, OH
1899 – c.1908

VERUS
PORCELAIN

VERUS is probably the earliest Oliver China Co. mark.

THE OLIVER
CHINA CO
SEBRING, OHIO

This ROCOCO mark is from Gates and Ormerod. It is one of 27 marks reprinted from *Historical Archaeology,* Vol. 16, Nos. 1 & 2, p.209.

---

156. Onondaga Pottery Co.
Syracuse, NY
1871 – 1960s

This company has continued to operate from the 1960s to the present. After 1966 it was called the Syracuse China Co.

IRONSTONE CHINA
O. P. Cº

(1874 – 1893)
Arms of New York

IMPERIAL
GEDDO

(1890 – 1893)

O. P. CO.
CHINA
SEMI-VITREOUS

(1886 – 1898)

(1893 – 1895)

O. P. CO.
SYRACUSE
CHINA

(1897 – c.1935)

See below.

(1895 – 1897)

This company began using a dating system in the 1920s. I have not yet found any evidence of a dating system used before 1920; however, I have not seen enough early marks to totally rule out company claims of an early dating system. See p. 220. The middle SYRACUSE CHINA mark above with a letter and a number under it was used from the 1920s to the mid-1930s and possibly later.

156. Onondaga Pottery Co. (continued)

ONONDAGA DATING SYSTEM: 1920 to 1959

There is a number and a letter under the mark. Sometimes the letter is first; sometimes the number is first. The letter is for the year of manufacture. The number is probably for the month. After 1945, two letters give the year.

A for 1920	K for 1930	U for 1940	EE for 1950
B for 1921	L for 1931	V for 1941	FF for 1951
C for 1922	M for 1932	W for 1942	GG for 1952
D for 1923	N for 1933	X for 1943	HH for 1953
E for 1924	O for 1934	Y for 1944	II for 1954
F for 1925	P for 1935	Z for 1945	JJ for 1955
G for 1926	Q for 1936	AA for 1946	KK for 1956
H for 1927	R for 1937	BB for 1947	LL for 1957
I for 1928	S for 1938	CC for 1948	MM for 1958
J for 1929	T for 1940	DD for 1949	NN for 1959

Sample Marks

O.P.CO.
SYRACUSE
-CHINA-
F-10

(1925)

O.P.CO.
SYRACUSE
CHINA
N-1

(1933)

O.P.CO.
SYRACUSE
CHINA
5-F
GLENDALE
COPYRIGHTED 1923

(1925)

GLENDALE was found with the 1925 mark above. COPYRIGHTED 1923 does not determine the date, just the earliest possible date for the mark.

9-KK
SYRACUSE
China

(1956)

8-NN
SYRACUSE
China
U.S.A.

(1959)

I have not attempted to date any marks beyond the 1950s. See Lois Lehner's *Complete Book of American Kitchen and Dinner Wares* for company provided dating information.

By the early 1900s the Onondaga Pottery Co. had become an important maker of hotel porcelain. Most of what one finds today is hotel ware. Much of this hotel ware is more interesting and collectible than most hotel ware.

OLD IVORY is a very common Syracuse China mark. This mark was accompanied by a separately printed 1929, probably the earliest use of the mark; however, the mark was used for many years, possibly to c.1950.

157. Ott & Brewer
Etruria Pottery
Trenton, NJ
1863 – 1893

This company began in 1863 as the Etruria Pottery of Bloor, Ott & Booth. In 1865 John Hart Brewer joined the company. Booth had already left the company. William Bloor, who had come from East Liverpool, Ohio, in 1863, returned there in 1870 where, about five years later, he helped start the Dresden Pottery of Brunt, Bloor, Martin & Co.

From 1870 to 1893 the company was called the Etruria Pottery of Ott & Brewer or simply Ott & Brewer.

IRON STONE CHINA
ETRURIA POTTERY Co

(c.1863 – c.1869)

This early Etruria Pottery Co. mark is undoubtedly rare. I found it on a tea set with a moss rose decoration. They are among the earliest marked pieces of American whiteware I've found thus far. Note the E.P. Co. monogram in the center of the shield. This is for Etruria Pottery Co. After 1870 the monogram became O. & B. for Ott & Brewer. See the first mark given below.

The two marks given below were used in the 1870s. Note the O. & B. monogram on the central shield.

IRONSTONE CHINA

(1870s)

(1870s)

The following several marks were used from the late 1870s through the 1880s on various grades of whiteware excluding true porcelain.

(c.1880 & probably earlier)

(1880s)

O.-B.
CHINA

(after 1880)

157. Ott & Brewer (continued)

The following three marks were used in the 1880s on various grades of whiteware excluding true porcelain.

(c.1885)

This 1880s marks is often impressed

(after 1880)

Ott & Brewer began experimenting with the making of true porcelain in the middle and late 1870s. Between 1882 and 1883 they developed a true belleek. Barber believed it to be superior to the Irish belleek it was imitating.

Quoting from p. 216 of Barber's 1893 book:

The ware now manufactured by the Ott & Brewer Company at the Etruria Pottery is made entirely from American materials, and is a vast improvement over the body and glaze first introduced by the Bromleys ten years ago. The rich iridescence of the nacreous glaze is fully equal to that of the Irish Belleek which is produced from salts of bismuth colored with metallic oxides; in delicacy of coloring and lightness of weight the Trenton ware is even superior.

The following marks date from 1882 (possibly a bit earlier for some) to 1893 when the company ceased production.

(c.1880 – c.1882)

(c.1882 – c.1884)

(c.1884 and later)

The above mark is the most common Ott & Brewer belleek mark. It probably was not used until 1884.

O.& B.

Barber said the O. & B. initials were used to mark fine belleek c.1885.

(c.1884 – c.1893)

This common mark is often found on belleek made for Tiffany & Co. and others.

157. Ott & Brewer (continued)

These two uncommon marks were also used to mark porcelain and belleek in the 1880s. The first mark was likely used to mark ware to be exhibited in or exported to a foreign country.

MANUFACTURED BY
OTT & BREWER
TRENTON, N.J. U.SA.

---

158. Edward J. Owen China Co.
Minerva, OH
1902 – c.1930

(1902 – c.1905)

The rather uncommon mark above was the first Edward J. Owen mark. Shortly after 1904 it was replaced by the mark at right.

(c.1905 – c.1915)

(1920s)

Shortly after winning a prize at the St. Louis Exposition in 1904, the company adopted the mark above. RANSOM and ROYAL IVORY were also used with OWEN CHINA in the mid to late 1920s.

See p. 180 for an IMPERIAL CHINA mark I incorrectly ascribed to this company previously.

---

159. J.B. Owens Pottery
Zanesville, OH
1885 – 1907

They made mostly art pottery. See Barber's 1904 marks book or Paul Evans's *Art Pottery of the United States.*

---

160. Oxford Pottery
Cambridge, OH
1914 – 1925

They made mostly utilitarian kitchen ware; I am not sure if it was marked. Items marked OXFORD WARE or OXFORD STONEWARE were made by Universal Potteries in the 1930s or later.

161. Paden City Pottery Co.
Paden City, WV
c.1910 – 1963

They made their first whiteware in the 1920s; most Paden City ware dates from the 1930s and later. Most Paden City marks are dated as samples below show. See other Paden City marks on pp. 185 and 186.

Regina
P. C. P. Co.
E 33

(1933)

This common Paden City mark was used in the 1940s and 1950s.

(1951)

---

162. Pearl China Co.
East Liverpool, OH
1930s to present

Their mark was used on ware made at other factories. They apparently marked only American ware. See *The East Liverpool, Ohio, Pottery District* by Gates and Ormerod for more about this selling company.

This is a 1930s and 1940s mark. Pearl China Co. marks were not used after the 1950s.

---

163. Pennsylvania China (Pottery) Co.
Kittanning & Ford City, PA
c.1905 – 1913

This company was a continuation of the Wick China Co. They also operated the Ford China Co. from c.1911 to 1913 or later. I believe they primarily made hotel ware at Ford City. See VICTOR mark below.

The mark at left is from John Ramsay. His marks are often quite inaccurate. The actual mark may be identical to the AURORA CHINA mark of the Wick China Co. on p. 163, except for monogram. The monogram itself might really be P. C. Co. Ramsay made such mistakes.

VICTOR

VICTOR is a possible Pennsylvania China Co. mark. It is always impressed on plain hotel ware. See p. 193 for a discussion about the mark.

164. Peoria Pottery Co.
Peoria, IL
1873 – 1904

The American Pottery Co. made whiteware in Peoria from 1859 to c.1863. The company was taken over by others who did not make whiteware again until the 1880s.

This impressed mark was used on whiteware between 1860 and c.1863.

The two marks below were used from 1888 to 1890 while the company was converting from stoneware to whiteware.

(1890 – 1899)

The company monogram was used on cream-colored ware from 1890 to 1899.

(1890 – 1899)

(1890 – 1904)

(1890 – 1904)

(1889, 1890)

The ironstone china mark above is probably the most common Peoria Pottery Co. mark. It was used from 1890 to 1904.

165. Pfaltzgraff Pottery
York, PA
early 1800s to the present

The early products of this company do not fit the scope of this book. They made no early whiteware; however, since World War II, they have become a major producer of kitchen and dinner wares. Even this ware would not be considered whiteware. In 1989 Pfaltzgraff was making some ware that appears to be whiteware. I believe I've read that Pfaltzgraff was making porcelain in 1990. See Lehner's 1988 book for more about this company and its marks.

166. Philadelphia City Pottery
Philadelphia, PA
1868 – c.1910

This company was also called J.E. Jeffords & Co. Note the J.E.J. Co. monogram on the mark at left.

(c.1897)

167. Phoenix Pottery
Phoenixville, PA
1867 – 1894

In the period 1872 to 1876 some Parian ware and lithophanes were made in addition to yellow and Rockingham wares and terra-cotta animal heads. Some ware was marked "Phoenix Pottery." From 1877 to 1879 Phoenix Pottery was under Beerbower & Griffen. See p. 21.

In 1879 the company became Griffen, Smith & Hill. The Phoenix Pottery is best known for Etruscan Majolica, made from 1880 to 1890. The following marks and information are for this majolica.

(1880 – 1890)

(1880 – 1890)

Note the G.S.H. monogram.

(1880 – 1890)

The above marks are impressed. The IVORY mark was used on uncolored ware. More information and marks are on the next page.

167. Phoenix Pottery (continued)

These impressed marks were also used on majolica made between 1880 and 1890.

ETRUSCAN   ETRUSCAN MAJOLICA

In addition to the factory marks, there were usually other marks impressed in the ware, and as these are occasionally found alone, they are given here to facilitate identification of Phoenix Pottery majolica. These supplementary marks consist of letters and figures, the former indicating the shape of the piece, the latter the style of decoration. The letters run from *A* to *O*, as follows:

A1, A2, etc., occur on individual butter plates, round, leaf or flower shape.
B1, B2, etc., on pickle dishes, usually of irregular leaf shape.
C1, C2, etc., on cake trays or dishes, of leaf or flower shape, irregular or round.
D1, D2, etc., on plates of various patterns, round, conventionalized leaf or shell shape.
E1, E2, etc., on hollow vessels, such as pitchers, coffee and tea pots, syrup jugs, sugar and slopbowls.
F1, F2, etc., on cuspidors and jardiniers.
G1, G2, etc., on cake baskets.
H1, H2, etc., on bonbon dishes, deep and oval.
I1, I2, etc., on covered boxes.
J1, J2, etc., on compotes (Barber used *comports*)
K1, K2, etc., on paper weights, pin trays or small flower jars, and occasionally cheese dishes and other trays.
L1, L2, etc., on celery vases, mugs, pepper and salt shakers, jewel trays and compotes with dolphin-shaped feet.
M1, M2, etc., on bowls, covered jars, bonbon dishes and occasionally on plates.
N1, N2, etc., on covered cheese and sardine boxes.
O1, O2, etc., on cups and saucers.

SAMPLE MARKS

A 8   B 5   C 11   G 2   M 15   K 3   D 1   H 6

E 4   I 15   J 7   F 12   N 3   O 10   L 9   C 13

The information above is from Barber's 1904 marks book. I changed his *comport* to *compote* in two cases. Victorians sometimes called low compotes *comports*. They did not use the term *compote*. We would call both compotes.

168. Albert Pick & Co.
Chicago, IL
c.1900 – c.1950

Pick was a distributor, not a manufacturer. His mark will be on wares made by other companies. The first mark below was used from c.1900 to c.1910 and possibly later; however, I've not yet seen their mark on wares made between c.1910 and c.1920. The second mark was used in the 1930s and 1940s when Pick was fairly active. Pick marks are usually found in conjunction with the manufacturer's mark. See also p. 168.

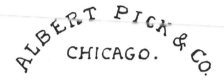

(c.1900 – c.1910)

(1930s and 1940s)

Albert Pick was associated with a number of manufacturers, but D. E. McNicol marks are the most common. L. Barth & Co. was a New York distributor.

---

169. Pickard China
Chicago, IL & Antioch, IL
1894 to the present

The early ware of Pickard was hand-painted European (mostly French) porcelain. Most was artist-signed. The earliest artists were American. The marks below or similar marks were used from 1895 to c. 1912 or 1919. Current price guides often give very specific dates for the early pieces. Apparently the early marks can be dated 1895–1898, 1898–1904, 1905–1910, 1910–1912 and 1912–1919. I am not familiar with all these marks; however I believe the first mark below is the oldest.

In the 1920s and 1930s EDGERTON, RAVENSWOOD* and PICKARD without the word CHINA were used to mark hand-decorated imported blanks. From c.1940 the term PICKARD CHINA and/or MADE IN U.S.A. was part of the mark. The ware so marked was now an American porcelain developed by Pickard in the 1930s.

(probably 1895-1898)

(after 1898)

*See p. 187 for a RAVENWOOD (not RAVENSWOOD) mark also used on hand-painted porcelain.

170. Pioneer Pottery Co. 1885 – c.1902
Wellsville China Co. c.1902 – c.1960
Wellsville, OH

Financial problems led the Pioneer Pottery Co. to be reorganized as the Wellsville Pioneer Pottery in 1896. About 1902 it became the Wellsville China Co. which continued until c.1960. See p. 118 for another Pioneer Pottery Co.

Pioneer Pottery Co. marks used between 1885 and 1896:

The ribbon at the bottom of the above mark may have the Latin LABOR OMNIA VINCIT instead of STONE CHINA.

PIONEER POTTERY WORKS.

Gates and Ormerod believed Pioneer was inactive between c.1891 and 1895. This mark's similarity to one below tends to refute that.

Wellsville Pioneer Pottery Co. marks used from 1896 to c.1902:

W. P. P. Co.
SEMI-PORCELAIN

Note the similar mark above.

Wellsville China Co. marks used between c.1902 and c.1950. See the book by Gates and Ormerod for many later marks.

(c.1902 – c.1910)

(c.1904)

Barber said this mark was used on special customer orders.

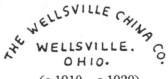

(c.1910 – c.1920)

The above mark was also used with dates in the 1920s. See next page.

116

170. Pioneer Pottery (continued)

Wellsville China Co. marks (continued)

THE WELLSVILLE CHINA CO.
WELLSVILLE.
OHIO.
1-27   (1927)
(1920s)

W.C.Co.
S.V.
CHINA

(c.1915 – c.1925)

THE Wellsville

(c.1915 – c.1920)

W.C.Co.

(1920s)

The above mark is a continuation of a mark used without dates from c.1910 to 1920. It is the most common early Wellsville mark.

Similar S.V. marks were used by many companies c.1910 to c.1930; however, it is not a common Wellsville mark.

WELLSVILLE DeSoto CHINA OHIO. U.S.A.

(1930s)

WELLSVILLE BAKE RITE CHINA OHIO. U.S.A.

(c.1935 – c.1945)

WELLSVILLE VITRIFIED CHINA OHIO. U.S.A.

(c.1933)

It is fairly easy to distinguish early Wellsville marks from later ones. Before 1930 all the marks used W.C. Co. initials or THE WELLSVILLE or THE WELLSVILLE CHINA CO. After 1933 the ware made is primarily a vitrified hotel ware. All the marks now say WELLSVILLE CHINA or WELLSVILLE CHINA CO. Note that the word THE does not precede the word WELLSVILLE.

The above mark was found on hotel ware. Gates and Ormerod give 1933 as the year Wellsville began making vitrified hotel ware.

A sampling of later marks are given below. They date to c.1955. For a larger sampling of marks dating from c.1933 to c.1960 see *The East Liverpool, Ohio, Pottery District* by William Gates and Dana Ormerod. These marks were used on hotel ware from c.1935 to c.1955.

WELLSVILLE CHINA

WELLSVILLE CHINA "BELMONT"

WELLSVILLE CHINA "MAJESTIC"

WELLSVILLE CHINA "WILLOW"

171. Pioneer Pottery Co.
East Liverpool, OH
1935 to 1980 or later

This company has no connection to the earlier Pioneer Pottery Co. The mark shown is the only one I have seen. Gates and Ormerod say it was used between 1935 and 1958. See their *The East Liverpool, Ohio, Pottery District* for more about this company.

(1935 – 1958)

---

172. Pope-Gosser China Co.
Coshocton, OH
1903 – 1929; 1935 – 1958

(c.1904, 1905)

Lehner quotes Jervis as saying this mark was used in 1913. I believe Jervis or Lehner meant 1903. I've seen the mark but once on a fine semi-vitreous piece. This mark is likely the first Pope-Gosser mark used after their early experimentation with true porcelain.

(c.1905 – c.1915)

The mark at left is the most common early mark. I've found it on several calendar plates as well as other pieces. The quality of the whiteware varies from excellent to terrible. One 1907 calendar plate was of particularly poor quality — much like their 1920s ware. Another plate from about the same period could almost pass as porcelain.

(1920s; 1940s)

This is the most common Pope-Gosser mark. It was used throughout the 1920s almost always with dates. See example at left. The 1920s ware is usually of poor quality. From 1929 to c.1931 Pope-Gosser was a member of the ill-fated American Chinaware Corporation. Pope-Gosser and other members continued to use their own marks, at least at times, during this period. See p. 186 for a discussion about this. Very little was made at Pope-Gosser in the 1930s when reorganization was taking palce. By 1940 they were again quite active.

172. Pope-Gosser China Co. (continued)

POPE-GOSSER
U.S.A.

(late 1920s; 1930s)

I dated this mark c.1920 previously. I now believe it was used no earlier than the late 1920s. Quite possibly it was used only in the 1930s. I don't believe it was used beyond c.1940.

POPE-GOSSER
— . —
· CHINA ·
MADE IN U.S.A.

STERLING
40

(1920s;1940s)

This mark was used in the 1920s and the 1940s. See previous page. In the 1920s the whiteware marked was usually of poor quality. The 1940s ware is of better quality, more like some of the good pre-1920 ware made by Pope-Gosser. The 1940s dating included just two digits under the mark. The 40 under the mark at left is for 1940. Some 1940s marks are not dated. This STERLING mark was also found without a number. I don't believe marks after 1944 were dated.

(c.1950)

(1950s)

I found this mark on a set of plates with dogwood decals so popular in the early 1950s. I suspect the mark was also used before 1950.

The wreath mark is the most common 1950s Pope-Gosser mark. Like the 1940s mark above, it may or may not include a date. This particular wreath mark also had BY STEUBENVILLE under the wreath. The Steubenville Pottery Co. absorbed Pope-Gosser c.1958. After that the story gets a bit complicated. See p. 74 of Lehner's 1988 pottery book for more about this example of U.S. pottery cannibalization during the import-flooded 1950s.

POPE GOSSER
CHINA
MADE IN USA

by
Steubenville

(c.1959 or later)

ROSE POINT shape or a pattern name may have been with the mark at left. When I saw the mark several years ago, I was so shocked to see the BY STEUBENVILLE that I may well have failed to notice a pattern or shape name under the wreath.

173. Porcelier Manufacturing Co.
Greensburg, PA
c.1930 – 1954

Lehner said this company was first in East Liverpool, Ohio, for about two years. They made vitrified whiteware. It is not early but is quite collectible. Although I live but 25 miles from where the factory was, I've found but one Porcelier marked piece at local flea markets. The pieces I've seen were in Maryland and Virginia! The word PORCELIER is on most marks. I do not yet know if it is possible to tell earlier marks from later marks.

All the marks I've seen had this design. There is various information under the mark that might help to date Porcelier marks.

174. Potters' Cooperative Co.

See Dresden Pottery.

175. Pottery Guild
New York, NY
1937 – 1946

This company was a selling organization started by J. Block who also started the Block China Co. Jo Cunningham said they marked much ware made at the Cronin China Co. of Minerva, Ohio. See pp. 34, 52, 235–237 of Cunningham's *The Collector's Encyclopedia of American Dinnerware* for more information about the Pottery Guild.

176. Prospect Hill Pottery
Trenton, NJ
1872 – 1894

This is one case where Barber was essentially incorrect; however, he carefully worded his information so as not to be technically incorrect. The Isaac Davis period (1872 to 1879) was actually a phase of the Trenton Pottery Co. and should be included there. See pp. 148 and 149 for the Trenton Pottery Co. Nevertheless, I've chosen to keep this material together for continuity. These are Ramsay's dates, not Barber's. From 1872 to 1879 the company was under Isaac Davis alone. From 1879 to 1894 it was under Dale & Davis. Under Dale & Davis it was called the Prospect Hill Pottery.

176. Prospect Hill Pottery (continued)

IRONSTONE CHINA
I. DAVIS

(1872 – 1879)

PATENTED AUG. 26th. 79.
I. DAVIS.

(1872 – 1879)

I. DAVIS

(1872 – 1879)

D-D

(c.1890 – 1894)

DALE & DAVIS.

(1880 – 1894)

D. & D.
CHINA

(c.1890 – 1894)

---

177. Purinton Pottery Co.
Shippenville, PA
1941 – c.1960

Their casually hand painted decorations are similar to Stangl Pottery, Watt Pottery, Southern Potteries, Inc. and particularly Blair Ceramics. For some history and beautiful pictures of ware made by all these potteries, except Watt, see Jo Cunningham's *The Collector's Encyclopedia of American Dinnerware*.

Purinton
SLIP WARE

painted

---

178. Red Cliff Co.
Chicago, IL
c.1950 – 1977

My research generally ends with the 1950s. As a general rule I don't find much later ware at flea markets. Red Cliff is a major exception. Because of their old English styles and decorations (tea leaf luster, for example), Red Cliff marked ware is frequently mistaken for the English ironstone it quite successfully duplicates. Annise Doring Heaivilin's *Grandma's Tea Leaf Ironstone* explains much about Red Cliff, particularly their tea leaf ware. This information is under Hall China in her book because they made the ware. This ware was made exclusively for Red Cliff, who distributed it. Apparently tea leaf ware was made only in the late 1950s and early 1960s. Gates and Ormerod say the ironstone mark given was used until 1977.

178. Red Cliff Co. (continued)

This mark was used from c.1957 to 1977. The R.C. monogram was used alone to mark wares during the same period.

---

179. Red Wing Potteries, Inc.
Red Wing, MN
1936 – 1967

This company was preceded by the Red Wing Stoneware Co. that dated back to the 1870s. As early as the 1920s they began to make ware that would be considered art pottery. I am not sure if this ware was true whiteware; however, it wasn't traditional stoneware either. In the 1930s they made Rum Rill kitchenware. This "craft-type" ware may not have been true whiteware either. Not until the 1940s was ware made that truly had the appearance of whiteware. Most dinnerware encountered comes from the late 1940s and particularly the 1950s.

These Rum Rill marks were used in the 1930s.

These marks were used on art or "craft" pottery between 1936 and 1967.

This mark was used on dinnerware from c.1947 to c.1960.

See *Red Wing Dinnerware* by David Newkirk and Stanley Bougie for more about this company.

**180. Paul Revere Pottery
Saturday Evening Girls**
Boston, MA
c.1909 – 1942

They made art pottery primarily. See Paul Evans's *Art Pottery of the United States* for more about this pottery and its marks. See also p. 202.

---

181. Robinson, Ransbottom Pottery Co.

I don't believe any of their ware would be considered whiteware. Prior to the 1920s they made stoneware. The initials R.R.P. Co. and the word Roseville are often used on their marks and confused with wares made by the Roseville Pottery Co. See Lois Lehner's *Complete Book of American Kitchen and Dinner Wares* for more about this company and its marks.

182. Rookwood Pottery Co.

Rookwood is probably the most famous maker of art pottery in the United States. Barber's 1904 marks book would be a good place to begin a study of Rookwood marks. Barber has more than 6 pages of Rookwood marks and information.

183. Roseville Pottery Co.

This company is famous for its art pottery made in the early years. I would call their later ware "craft" pottery. Evans calls it industrial art pottery. For a beginning study of Roseville, see Paul Evans's *Art Pottery of the United States.*

184. Royal China Co.
Sebring, OH
1933 – 1969 (as an independent company)

Royal China was taken over by the Jeannette Glass Corporation in 1969.

(1930s+)

Although Gates and Ormerod say this mark was possibly used to the late 1950s, based on ware seen, I doubt that it was used beyond the 1940s. I believe it to be the earliest mark for the Royal China Co.

(1930s; 1940s)

This version of the crown mark is not too common. It is also an early mark — possibly as early as the mark above. Note the similar placing of Sebring and Ohio to the above mark.

(1950s)

This rather common version of the crown mark was not used until the 1950s. It is often dated as on the sample 1954 mark shown here.

184. Royal China Co. (continued)

(1950s)

This is probably the most common Royal China Co. mark. Homer Laughlin in the 1950s used a mark seemingly in imitation of this Royal China mark. See p. 187 for a comparison of these two marks as well as a ROYAL-STETSON mark.

(1950s)

This BLUE WILLOW and other BLUE WILLOW and PINK WILLOW marks were used in the 1950s and perhaps a bit later. The BLUE WILLOW and PINK WILLOW marks of the 1950s are the most common Royal China Co. marks seen at antique flea markets. On p. 249 of Jo Cunningham's 1982 dinnerware book are shown many CAVALIER IRONSTONE patterns including a blue willow pattern. CAVALIER IRONSTONE marked ware is from the late 1960s. Willow ware was probably made and marked by the Royal China Co. from c.1950 to 1969.

Royal used various marks with UNION MADE and/or the seal of the National Brotherhood of Operative Potters. See p. 225 of *The East Liverpool, Ohio, Pottery District* by William Gates and Dana Ormerod. Although I've seen too few examples of these marks to date them directly, based on numerous similar marks used at various other companies, I would date them c.1935 to the early 1950s. See the Gates and Ormerod book for many more Royal China Co. marks used to 1970. This includes a number of 1930s and 1940s marks I have not yet seen.

---

185. Rum Rill
See Red Wing Potteries, Inc.

---

186. Sabin Industries
McKeesport, PA
late 1940s to early 1960s

This company was located not far from where I live. I frequently find variations of the mark given below on plates at ordinary flea markets, bazaars and yard sales. Much Sabin marked ware is 1950s ware at its worst. In my opinion it is generally tasteless and gaudy. I'd compare it to those paintings on black velvet. Nonetheless, it is worth collecting. It is representative of a segment of our culture.

(1950s)

There are a number of variations of this 1950s mark. CREST-O-GOLD is often on the mark. SABIN is infrequently found. See also SABINA LINE on p. 187.

187. Salem China Co.
Salem, OH
1898 – 1967

Jo Cunningham in *The Collector's Encyclopedia of American Dinnerware* says that this company was fairly inactive and financially troubled until 1918 when F.A. Sebring took over. Barber, in his 1904 marks book, fails to mention the company at all. This led me to believe in the past that little was produced or marked by Salem until after the 1918 Sebring takeover. Recently, I have found several early marks. The most important one is given first below.

(c.1898 – c.1905)

This is the earliest Salem China Co. mark. I found it on an excellent piece of semi-porcelain. I first suspected it to be English. I've seen the mark only once. See p. 175 for documentation of the EXCELSIOR PORCELAIN mark. Salem also made an early ironstone ware. I've not yet seen this mark, if in fact the ironstone was marked.

SACHCO.

(c.1905 – c.1910)

This mark was on a semi-porcelain bowl with a cherries decal typical of the fruit and flowers decorations of the early 1900s.

SALEM CHINA Co.
SALEM, OHIO

(c.1910 – c.1915)

This plain mark was used before the 1918 Sebring takeover at the Salem Co. Like the other early marks, I have seen it but once.

SALEM
S-V
CHINA

(c.1918 – c.1925)

The ubiquitous S-V (Semi-Vitreous) mark was used by many companies beginning with K.T. & K. c.1905. Salem probably didn't use it until 1918. They used it to c.1925. In the 1920s the marks are frequently dated.

Made in

America

(c.1925 – c.1930)

187. Salem China Co. (continued)

ANTIQUE
IVORY
FROM
SALEM
PAT AUG 3-27

(1927 – c.1935)

Briar Rose
Made in
America

(c.1930 – c.1935)

Briar Rose
by
Salem

(c.1935 – c.1940)

(c.1935 – c.1945)

TRICORNE
BY
Salem
U. S. PATENT
D. 94245

(c.1939 – c.1950)

TRICORNE is a 1940s mark for a shape with sharp angularity. Plates had three sides. The same angularity is seen on STREAMLINE except plates are round. STREAMLINE is also from the 1940s.

VICTORY
by
SALEM
CHINA CO.
SALEM-OHIO

(c.1944 – c.1950)

The various designs below are not marks but parts of many Salem China Co. marks.

Made in
America

MADE IN AMERICA (not MADE IN U.S.A.) was used c.1925 to c.1935.

BY SALEM

BY SALEM in various styles was used on many Salem marks from c.1935 to c.1965.

by
SALEM

BY SALEM in a box, as seen at left, was used in the late 1940s and the 1950s.

The design at left was an integral part of most 1960s marks. Salem ceased manufacturing in 1967; however they continued as a distributor of mostly foreign ware. This design can be found on this ware imported after 1967.

188. Saxon China Co. c.1900 – 1929
French-Saxon China Co. 1935 – 1964
Sebring, OH

Gates and Ormerod said Fred Sebring took charge of the Saxon China Co. of Sebring, Ohio 1911. Lehner in her 1980 book said Jervis mentioned a merger between the Saxon China Co. and the French China Co. in 1907, indicating Saxon existed before that year.

The Saxon China Co. had a close relationship with the French China Co. from 1907 onward. The more I study the whiteware and marks of these two companies, the more evident this closeness becomes. After the failure of the American Chinaware Corporation, the French China Co. and Saxon China were officially united as the French-Saxon China Co.

SAXON
CHINA

(c.1900 – c.1907)

The ware I've seen with this SAXON mark was quite old, possibly pre-dating 1900. If Jervis's 1907 date is correct, I would date the mark c.1900 to 1907.

Lebeau
Porcelain

(c.1907 – c.1920)

The LEBEAU PORCELAIN(E) mark is Saxon's version of the French China Co.'s LA FRANCAISE mark. Quite possibly LEBEAU PORCELAIN and LA FRANCAISE as displayed on the fleur-de-lis were both introduced in 1907. See French China Co. See p. 182 for a discussion and documentation of LEBEAU PORCELAIN(E).

S. C. Co.
——————
MARTHA
WASHINGTON
6 - 1

(probably 1926)

S.C.Co.
——————
5 B

(1925)

These plain marks are virtually the same as those used by the French China Co. in the 1920s. See French China Co. It is not uncommon to find both French and Saxon marked whiteware in the same set of dishes. This mixing probably came about by accident as consumers of the 1920s saw the ware was often identical in shape and decoration. See p. 221 for a discussion of the Saxon dating system.

(late 1920s)

This late 1920s Saxon mark parallels a French China Co. mark of the late 1920s. See p. 51. Neither used a full name until these marks, used just before their 1929 closings; however, the Saxon Co. did use SAXON CHINA for a short time in the early 1900s.

188. Saxon China Co./French-Saxon China Co. (continued)
c.1935 – c.1960

French-Saxon China Co. marks:

MADE IN
SEBRING
U. S. A.
WARRANTED
22 K GOLD

(c.1935 – c.1940)

UNION MADE
U. S. A.
Pine Cone
2837·5·54

(1950s)

This shield mark is by far the most common French-Saxon China Co. mark. It is a carry-over of the last Saxon China Co. mark used in the late 1920s. See p. 127. This mark was used from c.1935 to c.1960. Some 1950s marks were dated as on the mark at left. The 54 in this case is probably the year when the PINE CONE decoration was introduced, not the year of manufacture as is the usual case. Pine cones like dogwood blossoms were common 1950s decorations.

(c.1945 – c.1955)

(c.1940 – c.1955)

The mark at far left also says ALOHA DINNERWARE. UNION MADE as given on the above mark was used possibly as early as 1935. The OPERATIVE POTTERS mark at near left was used by many companies starting c.1940 or during World War II. See p. 200 for more discussion about various "union" marks.

---

189. Scammell China Co.
Trenton, NJ
c.1924 – 1954

The Scammell China Co. was a continuation of the Maddock Pottery Co. See pp. 86 – 88.

Like the Maddock Pottery Co., the Scammell Co. continued to make and mark LAMBERTON CHINA, as did the Sterling China Co. of East Liverpool, Ohio, that took over Scammell in 1954. See Sterling China Co. on p. 135. See also p. 181 for a discussion of the long history of LAMBERTON CHINA.

TRENTON CHINA
MADE IN AMERICA

(c.1920 – c.1925)

SCAMMELL'S
TRENTON CHINA

(c.1925 – c.1940s)

SCAMMELL'S
Lamberton China

(c.1925 – c.1940)

The mark above was used c.1920 to c.1925. It is probably a transition mark used primarily before Scammell took over the Maddock Pottery Co. See p. 88.

Versions of the mark above with MADE IN AMERICA under TRENTON CHINA would most likely date c.1925 to c.1935.

This mark is a continuation of a mark used by the Maddock Pottery Co. See p. 88.

189. Scammell China Co. (continued)

(1927)

This special 1927 mark was used to mark ware made for the centennial of the Baltimore and Ohio Railroad. The ware so marked was decorated with under the glaze blue transfer designs similar to 19th century Historical Staffordshire ware but depicting B. & O. Railroad scenes. The same mark was found with SHENANGO CHINA instead of SCAMMELL'S LAMBERTON CHINA. See p. 132.

(c.1924 – 1954)

This is the most common Scammell mark. Variations of this mark were probably used from c.1924 to 1954. Marks with MADE IN AMERICA under SCAMMELL probably date from c.1924 to c.1935. Marks with U.S.A. under SCAMMELL would date from the 1930s to 1954. This mark was also found with 1938 under U.S.A. indicating that some Scammell marks were dated. The Sterling China Co. continued to use this LAMBERTON CHINA mark after 1954. See p. 135. See also p. 181 for a history of LAMBERTON CHINA.

---

190. E.H. Sebring China Co.
Sebring, OH
1908 – 1929

(c.1908 – c.1920)

This is the earliest as well as the most common mark used by the E.H. Sebring China Co. The quality of the whiteware marked varies from excellent to poor. This mark was used on flow blue ware; however, WINONA is not a flow blue pattern. Other wares also have WINONA. In fact, I don't believe I have seen this mark without WINONA.

E.H.S.C. Co.
S.V.
CHINA

This plain S.V. (Semi-Vitreous) mark could have been used from c.1910 to c.1925 or later; however, I doubt that it was used before c.1915. I've only seen the mark a few times.

BELLVIEW
E.H.S.C.

This mark is from Gates and Ormerod. It is one of 27 marks reprinted from *Historical Archaeology*, Volume 16, Numbers 1 & 2. The mark appears to be dated. The original mark was not clear.

190. E.H. Sebring China Co. (continued)

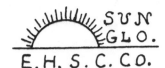

This late 1920s mark was used on ware with a yellow glaze similar to Salem's ANTIQUE IVORY or Crooksville's PROVINCIAL WARE.

191. George A. Sebring

See p. 188.

192. Sebring Pottery Co.

See American Pottery Works on p. 16.

193. Sevres China Co.
East Liverpool, OH
1900 – 1908

Except in name, America's Sevres has nothing to do with the famous French porcelain; however, the Sevres China Co. produced a very good quality semi-porcelain between 1900 and 1908. Unlike most American ware, the quality of their semi-porcelain is extremely consistent. I've seen hundreds of examples of their ware, and in only two cases did the ware show any sign of crazing. Only Maddock's ROYAL PORCELAIN had such consistent quality; however, I've seen fewer examples of ROYAL PORCELAIN. Most SEVRES marked ware has beautiful shapes and decal decorations, thus confusing some dealers.

SÈVRES

The mark at left is by far the most common mark of the Sevres China Co. It comes in black and aquamarine. Also, it is one of the most commonly seen American pottery marks from the early 1900s. The accent above the first *e* of SEVRES may be unclear or completely missing. The toilet and dinner ware marks below are far less commonly seen.

MELTON

BERLIN

GENEVA

Gates and Ormerod say BELMAR was also used on the fleur-de-lis mark of the Sevres China Co.

SÈVRES
HOTEL CHINA

130

194. Sevres China Co. continued
Warner-Keffer China Co.
East Liverpool, OH
1908 – 1911

      Warner-Keffer was a continuation of the Sevres China Co. The following marks are from *The East Liverpool, Ohio, Pottery District* by William C. Gates, Jr. and Dana E. Ormerod. These are three of 27 marks reprinted from *Historical Archaeology,* Volume 16, Numbers 1 & 2. The Gates and Ormerod material was published in *Historical Archaeology.* I've still not seen a Warner-Keffer mark.

195. Shenango China (or Pottery) Co.
New Castle, PA
1901 to the present

      This company had many early problems including a c.1905 reorganization. The name was changed to Shenango Pottery Co. as reflected in the c.1905 to c.1910 marks given below. Many later marks still have *Shenango China* with *New Castle, Pa.* Shenango made hotel and institutional ware even before World War I. I find little Shenango ware at flea markets. I don't think they were terribly productive before the 1930s. See p. 198 for two other, probably early, Shenango marks.

(before c.1904)

(c.1905+)

      The first mark above was used before 1904. The second mark reflects the company's name change c.1905.

MADE BY
SHENANGO POTTERY Co
NEW CASTLE, Pa.

(c.1910)

(c.1915)

195. Shenango China Co. (continued)

SHENANGO CHINA
NEW CASTLE, PA.

(c.1915 – c.1940)

This is a Shenango mark found from time to time at flea markets, etc. It would date from about World War I into the 1930s. U.S.A. was added to the mark c.1930. INCA WARE dates from World War II to the 1950s. A stylized Indian with ANCHOR HOCKING or INTERPACE is frequently found on recent restaurant ware. See final Scammell mark on p. 129 for special Shenago marked railroad ware. Shenango made commemorative Baltimore & Ohio Railroad ware in 1927 and again in 1977. The 1977 ware has a second mark with INTERPACE.

196. Smith, Fife & Co.
Philadelphia, PA
c.1830

They made a porcelain said by most experts to be somewhat inferior to Tucker's. Their mark is SMITH, FIFE & CO. in script. Their ware would be extremely rare.

197. Smith-Phillips China Co.
East Liverpool, OH
1901 – 1929

(c.1901 – c.1910)

Although Gates and Ormerod say this company made only semi-vitreous ware, I found the mark at left on a platter that would certainly be considered ironstone.

(c.1901 – c.1910)

The following three marks are in Barber's 1904 marks book. They date c.1901 to c.1910.

AMERICAN GIRL

FENIX   KOSMO

(c.1901 – c.1923)

The above is the most common mark of Smith-Phillips. It would date c.1901 – c.1923. Two dating systems were used on the mark. See p. 222 for a discussion of their early dating system. MADE IN U.S.A. may have been used as early as 1915. See mark at right.

Gates and Ormerod date the above mark c.1910; but, since it was given in Barber's 1904 marks book, it would date before 1904 to c.1910.

(c.1905)

SMITH PHILLIPS
SEMI PORCELAIN
MADE IN U.S.A.
321

(1921)

197. Smith-Phillips China Co. (continued)

(c.1910 – c.1915)

(c.1910 – c.1915)

The above mark also comes with other pattern or shape names used c.1910 to c.1920.

SMITH-PHILLIPS
ALAMO

(c.1915 – c.1920)
See also p. 198.

(1918)

SMITH-PHILLIPS
IMPERIO

(c.1915)

(1920s)   (1925)

The above mark is noteworthy because it shows a pre-1920 use of MADE IN U.S.A. and a pre-1920 date. Smith-Phillips may have used MADE IN U.S.A. as early as 1915. See p. 222 for their early 1900s dating system.

(late 1920s)

PRINCESS IVORY is probably the last Smith-Phillips mark. It was used in the late 1920s before Smith-Phillips joined the short-lived American Chinaware Corporation.

---

198. Southern Porcelain Co.
Kaolin, SC
1856 – c.1875

Barber said they made a small amount of fine white china and Parian ware between 1856 and 1862. During the Civil War they made brown stoneware telegraph insulators impressed with the mark to the left. Other wares may have been so marked. Ascribe no other marks to this company.

---

199. Southern Potteries, Inc.
Erwin, TN
1920 – 1957

This company began as the Clinchfield Pottery and became Southern Potteries, Inc. in 1920. Hand-painted ware was introduced in the 1930s.

199. Southern Potteries, Inc. (continued)

5-26   (1926)

(1920s)

(1930s)

(1930s)

Blue Ridge
Hand Painted
Underglaze
Southern Potteries, Inc.
MADE IN U.S.A.

Many variations of the mark at left were used in the 1940s and early 1950s. These marks with S.P.I. or ERWIN, TENN. date earlier than the other marks, possibly as early as the late 1930s. Marks with BLUE RIDGE date from World War II and later.

---

200. Standard Pottery Co.
East Liverpool, OH
1886 – 1927

Gates and Ormerod say the Standard Pottery Co. operated from 1886 to 1927. Barber mentioned the company in his 1893 book but does not include them in his 1904 marks book. Gates and Ormerod show one very early mark for the company with an S.C. Co. monogram instead of an S.P. Co. monogram. I believe this mark could be for some other company. See p. 232.

Florence

(c.1905 – c.1915)

I saw this FLORENCE mark on some rather good whiteware. I would date it c.1905 to c.1915. The Modern Stamp Co. has the mark under the Standard Pottery Co. according to Gates and Ormerod.

STANDARD
ESTHER
SEMI-PORCELAIN

(c.1920)

THE *Standard*
MADE IN U.S.A.

7 2 5   (1925)

(c.1915 – c.1927)

The rather common mark at left is usually found dated. Samples found undated were probably from c.1915 to c.1920.

201. Stangl Pottery Co.
Flemington & Trenton, NJ
1930 – 1978

Stangl was a continuation of the Fulper Pottery Co. Evans said they did not use the name Stangl on their ware until c.1946. About this time they began to concentrate on the manufacture of dinnerware rather than the art pottery Fulper was known for making. Stangl ware is probably not really true whiteware; however, since much of it appears to be whiteware, I decided to include them in this book. Stangl was taken over by Pfaltzgraff in 1978.

This mark with slight variations and/or various pattern names was used from the 1950s onward. STANGL/USA was used earlier. See also p. 198.

202. Sterling China Co.
Wellsville, OH*
1917 to the present

Despite its 1917 founding, the Sterling China Co. used no marks before the 1940s with the exception of the first mark given below. Sterling made hotel and restaurant ware primarily. See *The East Liverpool, Ohio, Pottery District* by Gates and Ormerod for many of these marks used in the 1940s and later.

The LAMBERTON mark below shows up once in a while at flea markets and antique shows. Although this particular mark dates from the 1950s and later, LAMBERTON marks have a very long history. See p. 181.

This 1930s mark was found on an ordinary piece of semi-vitreous whiteware. Virtually all Sterling China Co. ware from the 1940s on is vitrified ware. J. L. Pasmantier was a distributor. If this mark is found on vitrified ware, it would date after the 1930s.

(1930s+)

The LAMBERTON-STERLING mark at right was used in the 1950s and later. See p. 181 for a history of this and earlier versions of the LAMBERTON mark.

*Sterling used East Liverpool, Ohio, on some of their marks.

202. Sterling China Co. (continued)

CARIBE (CHINA) was made in Puerto Rico by the Sterling China Co. in the 1950s and later.

---

203. Stetson China Co.
Chicago & Lincoln, IL
c.1933 – c.1965

Stetson began in Chicago c.1933 decorating whiteware made by other companies. According to Jo Cunningham, Stetson decorated much ware made by Mt. Clemens and the Illinois China Co. In 1946 Stetson bought the Illinois China Co. of Lincoln, Ill. The mark below was used in the 1930s and 1940s. See p. 187 for a ROYAL STETSON mark that looks like marks used in the 1950s by Homer Laughlin and the Royal China Co. for more Stetson information and marks see Jo Cunningham's *The Collector's Encyclopedia of American Dinnerware*.

Variations of this Stetson mark were used in the 1930s and 1940s. Marks with HAND-PAINTED date from the late 1940s and the 1950s. Marks that include LINCOLN, ILL. date from c.1950 and later. See p. 189 for another Stetson mark.

---

204. Steubenville Pottery Co.
Steubenville, OH
1879 – 1959

(c.1885 – c.1890)

The mark at right is the earliest Steubenville mark. See p. 190 for more discussion about the mark.

(1880s)

(c.1885 – c.1895)

(1890s+)

This version of the British Coat of Arms mark was used by a number of American companies in the 1890s in imitation of very similar British marks of the 1890s and the early 1900s. See also p. 229.

204. Steubenville Pottery Co. (continued)*

These seven marks are shape or pattern marks used between 1890 and 1895, according to Barber.

DAY is the only one of these seven pattern or shape marks I've seen more than once. I have seen it on whiteware of both very poor and very good quality. One particular set of dishes was of excellent quality — good color, highly vitrified, and absolutely no crazing.

CANTON CHINA

(1890 – c.1904)

(1890 – c.1904)

Barber had some nice things to say about Steubenville's CANTON CHINA in his 1893 book. The CANTON CHINA ware I have seen has been of excellent quality.

Empire China

(c.1910 – c.1920)

EMPIRE CHINA is definitely a Steubenville mark. Jervis first gave it as a c.1915 Steubenville mark. I found it on a bowl that also had the Steubenville mark below.

PORC-GRANITE

(c.1897)

See p. 190 for more about the above mark.

STEUBENVILLE CHINA

(c.1910 – c.1920)

The plain mark at left was used in the 1920s, but with dates. See example on p. 138.

*See p. 189 for a c.1910 Steubenville mark.

204. Steubenville Pottery Co. (continued)

(c.1910 – c.1920)

STEUBENVILLE
CHINA
1 24   (1924)

(1920s)

This mark, without dates, was used before 1920. See p. 137 for this mark.

(late 1920s)

(early 1930s)

The Steubenville stockade mark was used from c.1930 through the 1940s. There are various versions. The mark with ROSE DAWN appears to be a c.1940 mark.

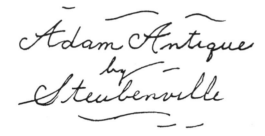

ADAM ANTIQUE was a mark used in the 1940s and 1950s. It may even have been used in the 1960s. For an explanation see the POPE GOSSER BY STEUBENVILLE mark below.

Steubenville's "Woodfield" ware dates from the late 1930s through the 1940s. Their "American Modern" by Russel Wright dates primarily from the 1940s.

SPONSORED BY
BUNDLES FOR BRITAIN, INC.

MFG. BY STEUBENVILLE

(c.1940)

POPE GOSSER
CHINA
MADE IN U.S.A

by
Steubenville

(c.1959 or later)

The mark at left was used c.1959 or even later. In 1958 the Pope-Gosser Co. was absorbed by the Steubenville Pottery Co. About 1959 Steubenville ws taken over by the Canonsburg Pottery where, according to Lehner, the term BY STEUBENVILLE continued to be used. Both Jo Cunningham and Lois Lehner have information about this rather confusing story. See also Pope-Gosser on pp. 118 and 119.

This type of misrepresentation demonstrates the sickness of the U.S. industry in the late 1950s.

205. Summit China Co.
Akron, OH
c.1890 – c.1915

John Ramsay said the company started c.1890. Lehner gives the date as 1901. The company was apparently in Akron, Ohio, until about 1915. Lehner gives a mark that combines Cleveland and Akron that was filed for registration in 1917. Evidently the company continued until c.1930 in Cleveland, Ohio. The mark below is from Ramsay. Lehner gives the same mark as being from the Summit County Historical Society.

For a company that made whiteware for 30 or 40 years, I never saw a single mark for this company until 1989! See p. 170 for a Summit China Co. mark I first saw in 1989. The company was either a small operation or they marked very little of their ware.

 This mark is from John Ramsay. It would date before 1915.

206. Syracuse China Co.   See Onondaga Pottery Co.

207. Syracuse, NY; Robineau Pottery
c.1903 – 1920s

Adelaide Alsop Robineau developed a true hard-paste porcelain of excellent quality. For more about this art porcelain and other early art porcelain see Paul Evans's *Art Pottery of the United States*. Barber stated in his 1904 marks book that Adelaide Robineau decorated hotel ware for the Onondaga Pottery Co. The mark used is given here below. It would date c.1903 or 1904.

A-R

208. Tatler Decorating Co.
Trenton, NJ
c.1876 – c.1904 (or much later; see below)

Elijah Tatler was a famous decorator both in the United States and England. Just before his death in 1876 he established his own decorating business. His wife and his son, W.H. Tatler, continued the business. In 1887 it became the W.H. Tatler Decorating Co. The mark below is the only mark I've seen for this company. I've seen it many times, sometimes on dated pieces; however, the dated pieces have all had a 1904 date! I suspect the mark was used as far back as 1887 but I can't yet prove it. I've found Tatler marked ware decorated with the famous R.S. Prussia "dice players" decal. Up to 1904 Tatler decorated only American whiteware.

The Tatler Co. continued to decorate after 1904, probably contracted to retailers. This later ware may have no Tatler mark. Jenny Derwich and Mary Latos in the *Dictionary Guide to U.S. Pottery and Porcelain* say the Tatler plant in Trenton closed completely in the early 1950s.

208. Tatler Decorating Co. (continued)

Besides Tatler, Barber listed the following decorators as operating in Trenton in 1893: Pope & Lee, Jesse Dean Decorating Co., W.H. Hendrickson, Poole & Stockton. Barber listed the following decorators as operating in Trenton in 1904: Tatler Decorating Co., Jesse Dean, and George Tunnicliffe, whose names are often found on wares they decorated. See p. 190 for a George Tunnicliffe mark. DeLan & McGill were also early Trenton decorators. See p. 173 for their mark.

W. H. TATLER
DECORATING CO

This mark was in use c.1904. Quite possibly it was used from c.1887 to c.1904

---

209. Taylor, Lee & Smith Co.
East Liverpool, OH
1899 – 1901

This company preceded the Taylor, Smith & Taylor Co.

TAYLOR
LEE & SMITH CO.
GRANITE

TAYLOR
LEE & SMITH CO.
PORCELAIN

---

210. Taylor, Smith & Taylor Co.
East Liverpool, OH
1901 – 1972

Taylor, Smith, Taylor is my favorite East Liverpool, Ohio, whiteware company. They were not the leading company in either a creative or business sense; however, they were always a cut above the typical East Liverpool company – never spectacular, but always with a touch of class. Also, they remained to the end basically a true dinnerware company, not resorting to hotel or institutional ware to save themselves. I even find that admirable. Gates and Ormerod say T.S. & T. was taken over by the Anchor Hocking Corporation in 1972. They continued to operate the T.S. & T. plant in Chester, West Virginia, until 1981. Chester is just across the Ohio River from East Liverpool, Ohio.

See next page for the T.S. & T. dating system.

210. Taylor, Smith & Taylor Co. (continued)

The first two marks below were the earliest marks of the Taylor, Smith & Taylor Co. They are the only marks in Barber's 1904 marks book.

(1901 – c.1915+)

VITREOUS

(1901 – c.1915+)

The two marks above were used from 1901 to c.1915 or perhaps c.1920. If the mark includes MADE IN U.S.A. it would date after c.1915. I've not yet seen these marks using the dating system given below. Another version of these marks has TAYLOR, SMITH & TAYLOR CO. under the mark.

CHINA

(1908 – c.1915)

This mark was used on some of Taylor, Smith & Taylor's best ware. Of particular interest to collectors is a series of flora and fauna decals designed by R.K. Beck who designed decals for many companies c.1910. The T.S.T. decals are among Beck's best work. Plates with his corn plant decal are superb! See R.K. Beck on p. 167.

TAYLOR, SMITH & TAYLOR DATING SYSTEM

I spent 6 years recording the numbers under T.S. & T. (or T.S.T.) marks before I was able to decipher their dating system. I believe all, or nearly all, Taylor, Smith & Taylor marks used c.1914 to c.1940 were dated. Marks of the 1940s were seldom dated. In the 1950s some T.S.T. marks were again dated. MADE IN U.S.A. was used as early as 1915, the year after their dating system seems to have been instituted. I believe Taylor, Smith, Taylor and Smith-Phillips were the first companies to use MADE IN U.S.A. on their marks. Both introduced the practice before 1920; however, neither used the phrase frequently. See p. 199 for more about MADE IN U.S.A. See also "American Dating Systems" on p. 208.

In the T.S.T. dating system, some number series begin with a 1 and some do not. I can't explain this.

From 1914 to 1921 the middle digit is the year, if there is a preceding 1.
Sample number series:

	4	3	is 1914
	5	10	is 1915
1	7	10	is 1917
1	8	9	is 1918
1	9	3	is 1919
1	20	7	is 1920
1	20	8	is 1920
1	20		is 1920

210. Taylor, Smith & Taylor Co. (continued)

TAYLOR, SMITH & TAYLOR DATING SYSTEM (continued)

From 1921 to 1929 the final two digits are for the year.

Sample number series:

```
 1  8 21  is 1921
    8 21  is 1921
    1 23  is 1923
    6 23  is 1923
   10 24  is 1924
 1 11 24  is 1924
 1 11 25  is 1925
    1 26  is 1926
 1  7 26  is 1926
    4 27  is 1927
 1 11 27  is 1927
   12 27  is 1927
    3 29  is 1929
```

In the 1930s the date is usually the two middle digits.

Sample number series:

```
 1 30 1  is 1930
11 33 1  is 1933
 3 36 6  is 1936
   39    is 1939
```

Marks of the 1940s were seldom dated. When dated, they probably continued the 1930s system. Marks of the 1950s also continued the 1930s system; however, many 1950s marks are also not dated.

ONE SPECIAL NOTE:

One BELVA CHINA mark seen had PTD under it along with the number dating system. The other BELVA CHINA marks I've seen had 1920s dates (numbers) under them. Perhaps, in imitation of the Knowles, Taylor & Knowles Co., they used letters for dating for a short period of time. Out of dozens of T.S. & T. marks, this was the only one seen with letters under it.

MADE IN U.S.A.:

Taylor, Smith, Taylor used MADE IN THE U.S.A. on their marks as early as 1915; however, the phrase was infrequently used until the 1930s. From the 1930s on most, but not all, marks included MADE IN U.S.A. or just U.S.A.

Shortly after 1900 Taylor, Smith & Taylor began using shape names as marks. The earliest were VERONA, LATONA, and PENNOVA. VERONA was probably introduced first. It was introduced c.1905 or a bit later. LATONA and PENNOVA were introduced c.1910. Up to c.1913 these shape marks were used without a dating system under the mark. Marks after c.1913 will have a dating system under the mark. Marks after c.1914 may include MADE IN U.S.A. Samples of these marks are on the next page.

210. Taylor, Smith & Taylor Co. (continued)

(c.1905 – c.1920)

This VERONA mark was found on a bone dish dating c.1905 or c.1910. I've also found it with various dates from 1915 to 1918. See p. 193 for a discussion about one of these marks.

(c.1910 – c.1920)

<table>
<tr><td>

T. S. T.
LATONA
C H I N A

(c.1910 – c.1920)
</td></tr>
</table>

I've seen the two marks above but once each. In both cases the mark was not dated, indicating a probably pre-1915 date. Jervis gave a c.1915 date for PENNOVA. See p. 186 for another PENNOVA mark that is dated. Lehner claims a 1911 date for LATONA.

(1908 – c.1930)

This mark was used on hotel ware from 1908 to c.1930 according to Gates and Ormerod. Chester, West Virginia, was the location of the Taylor, Smith & Taylor factory. Early marks, probably before c.1915, will not be dated. Later marks will be dated and may have MADE IN U.S.A.

1 20 7

(c.1916 – c.1925)

AVONA was used c.1916 to c.1925. These marks are dated. The mark shown is dated 1920.

Taylor, Smith & Taylor's AVONA marked a shape used by many American and European companies from c.1910 through the 1920s. It was probably the most popular dinnerware shape used in the years after world War I. It was used, with rare exception, on undecorated white dinnerware. See p. 196 for more discussion about the AVONA shape. Included is a picture of the shape.

T. S. T.
-IONA-
China

1 7 2 6

(1926)

IONA is a very plain Taylor, Smith & Taylor shape mark. I've found it dated from 1919 to 1927. I've seen numerous IONA marks and they have all been dated. None has included MADE IN U.S.A.

210. Taylor, Smith & Taylor Co. (continued)

PTD
1 26   (1926)

(1920s)

This is the only T.S.T. mark I've seen with letters under it. Other BELVA CHINA marks seen had only the number dating system under them. They all dated in the 1920s.

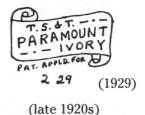

2 29   (1929)

(late 1920s)

PARAMOUNT IVORY dates 1928, 1929 and possibly into the 1930s.

MADE IN U.S.A
6 32 1   (1932)

(c.1930 – c.1935)

3 36 6   (1936)

(c.1935 – 1950s)

This wreath mark was nearly always dated. Various undated wreath marks were used in the 1960s.

CAPITOL IVORY was a mark of the 1930s according to Gates and Ormerod. I still have not seen the mark. Like other 1930s marks, CAPITOL IVORY probably includes a date under it.

(c.1939 – c.1955)

(c.1938 – c.1944)

T. S. T.
Coral Craft
U.S.A.
PAT. PEND.

(1940s)

For many more later Taylor, Smith & Taylor marks see *The East Liverpool, Ohio, Pottery District* by William Gates and Dana Ormerod.

---

211. Tempest, Brockmann & Sampson Pottery Co.

See company no. 30 on p. 24.

212. Thomas China Co.
Lisbon, OH
1902 – 1905

This company made a good quality semi-porcelain dinnerware for just a few years. See *The East Liverpool, Ohio, Pottery District* by Gates and Ormerod for more about the history of this company.

---

213. C.C. Thompson Pottery Co.
East Liverpool, OH
1889 – 1938

I have less confidence about my understanding of this company than any other major American pottery. Likewise, I am uncomfortable with the dating information provided by Gates and Ormerod. In particular, I believe their use of c.1917 as the beginning for semi-vitreous ware for this company has distorted much of their dating. I have considerable evidence indicating an earlier making of semi-porcelain but, as yet, no proof.

Also, although I've seen many C.C. Thompson Pottery Co. marks, all but a few have been variations of just two marks. These two marks are given and discussed below along with many other marks.

This company was called C.C. Thompson & Co. before 1889. See p. 190 for one of these earlier marks.

(c.1890)

(c.1890 – c.1905)

LELAND.   OREGON.

SYDNEY.

(c.1890 – c.1905 for three marks above)

MELROSE
T.

(1890s)

(c.1900 – c.1905)

See p. 146 for a later MELROSE mark.

213. C.C. Thompson Pottery Co. (continued)

DREXEL

(c.1900)

VICTORIA

T.

(c.1905)

SEMI-
VITREOUS

(after c.1905)

The above MELROSE mark is the same mark as the one pictured on the previous page except for SEMI-VITREOUS. Barber had the mark in his 1904 book. SEMI-VITREOUS would have been added when the company introduced semi-porcelain. Gates and Ormerod believe this to be c.1917. I believe it to be at least ten years earlier – thus my date of after c.1905.

WARRANTED

(c.1905 – c.1915)

The above C.C. Thompson mark is the second most common one I've seen. In addition to plain as above, it is found with ELO (for East Liverpool, Ohio) under it, also SYDNEY, PRINCESS and EUREKA. There are probably others. SYDNEY was found on a basin and pitcher of a very good semi-porcelain.

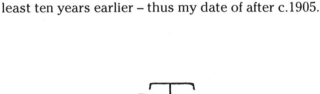

(c.1905 – c.1930)

The above mark is probably the most common Thompson mark. Earlier I found the mark on 1920s or 1930s ware; recently I've seen it on earlier ware including an ironstone type bowl dating from the very early 1900s. The mark may have GLENWOOD, MADISON, SYDNEY, PRINCESS, etc. under the mark. I would date GLENWOOD with the mark c.1910 to c.1915.

Eureka

(c.1910 – c.1915)

Gates and Ormerod show two EUREKA marks. One is under the coat of arms given above. The other is just the word, but in a different style than the one given here. They date EUREKA c.1915. See p. 175 for that EUREKA mark.

THOMPSON
GLENWOOD

(c.1910 – c.1915)

This is another THOMPSON with GLENWOOD mark. Based on one piece seen, I would also date it c.1910 to c.1915.

213. C.C. Thompson Pottery Co. (continued)

(1920s)

CHATHAM

(1930)

1868

𝕯𝕳𝖔𝖒𝖕𝖘𝖔𝖓'𝖘
𝕺𝖑𝖉 𝕷𝖎𝖛𝖊𝖗𝖕𝖔𝖔𝖑
𝖂𝖆𝖗𝖊

(late 1930s)

Gates and Ormerod show a number of other Thompson marks. I've included a couple of these on p. 191. See *The East Liverpool, Ohio, Pottery District* by William Gates and Dana Ormerod for more C.C. Thompson Pottery Co. marks.

---

214. Trenle China Co.
East Liverpool, OH
Ravenswood, WV
c.1910 – 1960s

The Trenle China Co. was a continuation of the East End Pottery Co. For a short time before 1910 the company was called the East End China Co. I found two identical 1910 calendar plates; one was marked E.E.P.Co. (see p. 45); the other was marked E.E.C.Co. (see below). I've also seen a 1911 calendar plate with E.E.P. Co. Probably a backlog of marked but undecorated ware accounts for this belated East End Pottery Co. mark. According to Gates and Ormerod the Trenle Co. moved to Ravenswood, West Virginia, in 1937 where the company continued as the Trenle, Blake China Co. to 1966.

(c.1909, 1910)

Trenle took over the East End China Co. in 1909 but the name wasn't changed until 1910 or 1911.

(c.1909, 1910)

(c.1910 – 1917)

(c.1910 – 1917)

UNDERGLAZE BLUE

(c.1910 – 1917)

The above mark was seen on some rather ordinary flow blue.

214. Trenle China Co. (continued)

TRENLE
CHINA

(c.1917 – c.1937)

Trenle switched from semi-porcelain to vitrified hotel ware in 1917, according to Gates and Ormerod. The mark at left and other marks were used from c.1917 to c.1937. Some of these marks included VITRIFIED CHINA, some did not. For those that don't, the thickness and/or vitrified nature of the whiteware is the key to dating it c.1917 to c.1937.

(c.1940 – c.1960)

TRENLE
BLAKE

(c.1940 – c.1960)

In 1937 Trenle moved to Ravenswood, West Virginia. Within a few years the company was called the Trenle, Blake China Co. The two marks above are from this period.

---

215. Trenton China Co.
Trenton, NJ
1859 – 1891

Barber said they made a fine grade of vitrified china, plain and decorated. Ramsay said they made white granite (ironstone). Whatever the ware, I've yet to see one marked piece for this company, which both Ramsay and Barber date 1859 to 1891. This must have been a very small operation. According to Barber their mark, given below, was impressed on wares.

TRENTON CHINA CO.
TRENTON, N. J.

---

216. Trenton Pottery Co.
Trenton, NJ
1865 – 1870 (for marks)

The complete story of the Trenton Pottery has not been easy to reconstruct. After six years, I believe I've put all the pieces of the puzzle together. The history as given here is a compilation and distillation from many early sources.

Trenton Pottery began in 1852 under Speeler & Taylor. From 1856 to 1859 it was under Taylor, Speeler & Bloor. During this period the manufacture of white granite (ironstone) was introduced.

216. Trenton Pottery Co. (continued)

After William Bloor went to East Liverpool, Ohio, in 1859, the Trenton Pottery was again under Speeler & Taylor, from 1859 to 1865. They also made white granite (ironstone) as did all the following owners.

From 1865 to 1870 Taylor & Co. owned the Trenton Pottery. During this period it was officially called the Trenton Pottery Co. Marks included the T.P. Co. initials. See below.

From 1870 to 1872 Trenton Pottery was under Taylor & Goodwin and the marks included T.P.W. for Trenton Pottery Works. See p. 150.

From 1872 to 1879 the owner was Isaac Davis who continued some of the same marks but substituted I. Davis for T.P.W. In 1879 Davis joined Dale to form the Prospect Hill Pottery. See p. 121 for I. Davis and Dale & Davis marks.

From 1879 to c.1890 or 1893 the Trenton Pottery was under Fell & Thropp. See p. 48 and 49.

Between c.1890 to 1892 or c. 1893 (depending on source used) it was under Thropp & Brewer (J. Hart Brewer).

In 1894 it was under Robert Gruessner who was making only sanitary ware. This was the end of the Trenton Pottery as far as I know.

IRONSTONE CHINA
T.P. Co.

(1865 – 1870)

Although Barber said there were various marks for the Trenton Pottery Co., he pictured only the very plain mark below right. The British Coat of Arms mark at left is a Trenton Pottery Co. mark as is the PARISIAN GRANITE mark below left. See p. 192 for documentation of both these marks.

(1865 – 1870)

T. P. Co.
CHINA

(1865 – 1870)

I've seen the PARISIAN GRANITE mark several times. See p. 192 for more about the mark and another recently seen PARISIAN GRANITE mark.

The above mark is printed in black on white granite (ironstone). Barber gave the same mark for the Trenton Potteries Co. c.1891. This later mark was on porcelain dinner ware.

216. Trenton Pottery Co. (continued)

Between 1870 and 1872 the Trenton Pottery was under Taylor & Goodwin. One mark used T.P.W. for Trenton Pottery Works. After 1872 Isaac Davis continued the use of this mark with I. Davis instead of T.P.W. under the mark. See p. 121.

(1870 – 1872)

(1870 – 1872)

---

217. Trenton Potteries Co.
Trenton, NJ
1892 – c.1960

This company was formed from five (later six) companies of which the Crescent Pottery was the most prominent. Others were Delaware Pottery, Empire Pottery, Enterprise Pottery, and Equitable Pottery. These companies joined Trenton Potteries c.1892. The Ideal Pottery joined in 1897. The Crescent Pottery and Empire Pottery continued to use their own marks, at least for a time, after joining Trenton Potteries. The Trenton Potteries primarily made sanitary ware.

T. P. Co.
CHINA

(1891)

The mark at left was used on vitreous ware, both thick and thin, made at the Crescent plant. See Trenton Pottery Co. for the identical mark used on white granite (ironstone). The 1891 date given by Barber indicates the importance of the Crescent Pottery in starting the Trenton Potteries.

(1892 – c.1904)

(1892 – c.1904)

(1896)

(1892 – c.1904)

The mark at left may also have 3, 4 or 5 in the center. The number indicates the factory. Crescent was number 1 but Barber did not show any marks with a 1 in the center.

217. Trenton Potteries Co. (continued)

(c.1897 – c.1904)

The IDEAL on the mark is for the Ideal Pottery Co. that joined the Trenton Potteries Co. about five years after the first five companies joined. A 6 on the star would also be for the Ideal Co.; however, Barber did not show any marks with a 6. See p. 263 for an IDEAL mark given by Jervis in his 1897 marks book.

(1920s; also earlier and later)

TEPECO was used in the 1920s and probably earlier. It was used later with a circle containing TRENTON POTTERIES CO. around the star. See p. 191 for a discussion and documentation of the TEPECO mark.

---

218. William Ellis Tucker
American China Manufactory
Philadelphia, PA
1820s and 1830s

Tucker was an early maker of true porcelain. His ware is famous and well-documented. There is probably no "unaccounted for" Tucker porcelain to be found. Barber has a great deal of information about Tucker in his 1893 book and in his 1904 marks book.

---

219. Tuxedo Pottery Co.
Phoenixville, PA
1902

Barber said they made semi-granite, colored glaze ware and flow blue. Apparently they did not use any marks.

---

220. Union Porcelain Works
Greenpoint, NY
c.1860 – c.1904

They made true hard porcelain. The owners were Thomas C. Smith and his son. They first marked their porcelain in 1876. Apparently they were making only electrical porcelain c.1904 and later.

(1876,1877)

Impressed on porcelain table ware; printed in green in 1877.

(1878 – c.1900)

Usually printed in green under the glaze.

220. Union Porcelain Works (continued)

The next three marks are decorating shop marks. They are above the glaze – usually in red. Sometimes they are dated.

(1893 – c.1904)

(1879 – 1893)

(1891 – c.1893)

---

221. Union Pottery Co.
Trenton, NJ
1869 – 1889

Barber gave the 1869 to 1889 dates for the company in his 1893 book. These dates were confirmed by John Ramsay. Barber confused the issue by claiming in his 1904 marks book that the New Jersey Pottery Co.'s name was changed to the Union Pottery Co. in 1883. He should have said they joined the Union Pottery in 1883. On p. 239 of his 1893 book he gave 1869 as the incorporation date for the New Jersey Pottery Co., including the list of incorporators – five men in all. On p. 241 of his 1893 book he gave the 1869 – 1889 dates for the Union Pottery Co. He also gave the incorporators for this company. They were a completely different group of men, except for Elias Cook who was on both lists of incorporators. Undoubtedly, the New Jersey Pottery Co. joined the already operating Union Pottery in 1883.

The marks given below are the first ever credited to the Union Pottery Co. of Trenton, New Jersey. I believe they are correct. See p. 192 for discussion and documentation.

(c.1880)

impressed mark

The impressed mark at left could possibly be for the Union Potteries Co. of East Liverpool, Ohio; however, I believe it is for the Union Pottery Co. of Trenton. See p. 192 for documentation.

IRONSTONE CHINA
(probably 1870s)

I first credited this Gates and Ormerod mark to the Union Potteries Co. of East Liverpool, Ohio. See p. 192.

222. Union Potteries Co.

East Liverpool, OH & Pittsburgh, PA
1894 – 1904

These marks were in Barber's 1904 marks book. See also the Union Pottery Co. of Trenton, New Jersey, on the previous page.

The above mark
may say CARNATION
instead of CORINNE.

223. United States Pottery

Bennington, VT
c.1850 – 1858 (for whiteware)

This company made hard-paste porcelain among many other things. They were best known for Parian and Rockingham wares, some made prior to 1850. The earlier marks included Norton, Fenton, Lyman and Bennington, Vermont. Barber said the marks below were used c.1850 or later. The mark on the right was used on porcelain and semi-porcelain; however, most ware was apparently not marked at all.

Barber said the United States Pottery closed in 1858.

 The raised mark at left was used on Parian ware; various numbers are on the mark.

 This mark was impressed on porcelain or semi-porcelain.

224. United States Pottery Co.

East Liverpool, OH
c.1890?

Barber was probably wrong about there being a United States Pottery Co. in East Liverpool, Ohio. He was certainly wrong about it joining the East Liverpool Potteries c.1900. If there was a United States Pottery Co. in East Liverpool, it was well before 1900. I saw the RALEIGH mark below on a chamber pot. It looked like it might be from the 1880s. For this reason I decided not to put these marks from Barber's 1904 marks book with the United States Pottery Co. of Wellsville, Ohio; although, quite possibly they are for that company.

Raleigh   *The Admiral*   *Champion*

225. United States Pottery Co.
Wellsville, OH
1899 – 1900; 1907 – c.1930

This company helped organize the East Liverpool Potteries in 1900. This consolidated company included the United States Pottery, the East Liverpool Pottery, the George C. Murphy Pottery, the Globe Pottery, the Wallace and Chetwynd Pottery and the East End Pottery. The East Liverpool Potteries lost all of its member conpanies in 1903 except the United States Pottery and the Globe Pottery. In 1907 these two split and the East Liverpool Potteries ended; however the mark did not.

Gates and Ormerod indicate that the United States Pottery continued alone until c.1930. They marked their ware as though the East Liverpool Potteries was still a reality. These misleading marks are included here. See also the East Liverpool Potteries Co. on p. 46.

(c.1899)

(1901 – c.1907)

The mark at the left is rather unusual in that it combines THE U.S. POTTERY COMPANY with the EAST LIVERPOOL POTTERIES CO. It would have been used between 1901 and c.1907.

EAST LIVERPOOL
POTTERIES Co.

(c.1907 – c.1920)

(1920s)

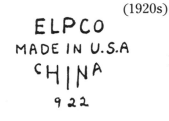

(1922)

I've seen this mark dated as late as 1928.

225. Universal Potteries, Inc.
Cambridge, OH
1934 – c.1960

Universal was noted for its use of the Cat-tail decal in the late 1930s through the 1940s. In her 1982 dinnerware book Jo Cunningham says Universal used the Cat-tail decal on their Camwood shape, their Old Holland shape and Laurelle shape. Much Cat-tail decorated ware was distributed by Sears, Roebuck & Co.

Universal was also known for its Ballerina ware. The BALLERINA mark dates from the late 1940s through the 1950s.

This is a 1940s mark. Jo Cunningham credits it to the Universal Potteries, Inc.

226. Universal Potteries, Inc. (continued)

(late 1940s; 1950s)

BALLERINA is a shape mark of the late 1940s through the 1950s. There are several different BALLERINA marks used on both clear glazed whiteware and whiteware coated with colored glazes. Once in a while a BALLERINA mark will be found with another company name. These marks probably date from the late 1950s.

Marks with the seal of the National Brotherhood of Operative Potters date from c.1940 to c.1955, if the seal says A.F. of L. After c.1955 the seal says A.F.L. – C.I.O. See p. 200 for more about marks with UNION MADE, etc. Some other CAMWOOD IVORY marks date before 1940.

---

227. Vodrey & Brother 1857 – 1896
Vodrey Pottery Co. 1896 – c.1929
East Liverpool, OH

Gates and Ormerod say Vodrey & Brother marks date back to 1876; Barber said 1879.

(1876(1879) – c.1885)

(c.1880 – c.1890)

(c.1885 – c.1895)

(c.1890 – c.1896)

I've found the mark at left on some excellent ironstone ware. The ironstone was of good color without a hint of crazing. The color of the marks seen was aquamarine.

227. Vodrey & Brother; Vodrey Pottery Co. (continued)

IRON STONE CHINA

(c.1890 – c.1896)

GEM SHAPE

(1890 – c.1896)

PALISSY CHINA is a very dense ironstone or semi-porcelain. The pieces I've seen looked like hotel porcelain. The PALISSY CHINA marker is at times impressed. The date may also be impressed in the ware.

(c.1890 – c.1896)

Royal
V. & B.

(c.1890 – c.1896)

(probably 1890s)

Apollo

(probably 1890s)

The marks below were used after the 1896 incorporation of the Vodrey Pottery Co.

(1896 – c.1902)

(c.1903 – c.1920)

The mark at the left is a less sinister version of the mark at far left. It is by far the most common Vodrey mark. I've been able to date it rather accurately through finding it on numerous calendar plates.

(c.1900)

ADMIRAL
V. P. CO.

(1896 – c.1910)

HOTEL
V. P. CO.

(1896 – c.1920)

VERONA
V. P. CO.

(c.1905 – c.1920)

BONITA
V. P. CO.

(c.1905 – c.1920)

VODREY
S – V
CHINA

(after c.1910)

156

228. Walker China Co.
Bedford, OH
1943 – c.1980

The Walker China Co. is a continuation of the Bailey-Walker China Co. See p. 20. At first I had a difficult time with this company beause of the dating system used on the Walker marks. Initially I believed both Bailey Walker and Walker marks were being used at the same time. This is not true. The older Bailey-Walker dating system is a standard system; however, the Walker system is not. You add 22 to the Walker mark number to get the year of manufacture. (I had concluded 20 years; however, Lehner in her 1988 pottery book says 22 for 1922 when the Bailey-Walker China Co. started.) See example below. The dating system on Walker China Co. marks is the only one I know that seems blatantly deceptive. See also Bailey-Walker and Walker dating systems on p. 224.

According to Annise Heaivilin, Walker China Co. was one of the last American makers of ware decorated with tea leaf luster. The Red Cliff Co. used both Hall and Walker blanks for their tea leaf decorations.

(1954)

(1963)

This is a 1930s and/or 1940s mark. Lehner shows a JUS-RITE mark with BAILEY-WALKER above it. That mark undoubtedly dates before 1943. The mark at left may also date before 1943. See p. 20.

229. Wallace & Chetwynd Pottery Co.
East Liverpool, OH
1881 – 1900

230. Wannopee Pottery Co.　　　See New Milford Pottery co. on p. 103.

231. Warner-Keffer China Co.　　　See Sevres China Co. on p. 131.

232. Warwick China Co.
Wheeling, WV
1887 – 1951

(c.1890)

The mark at the left would date c.1890, just prior to the mark given below it. Note the use of TRADE MARK instead of SEMI PORCE-LAIN under the mark.

(1892 – c.1900)

The helmet and crossed swords mark with SEMI PORCELAIN was given by Barber as being used on novelties in semi-porcelain by Warwick c.1892. The helmet and crossed swords mark continued in use through the 1940s; however, slight variations in the mark help to determine the approximate date for the mark. Thorn showed this mark with W.C. Co. instead of Warwick China Co. on the ribbon. I have not seen his version. See A.126 on p. 194.

WARWICK
SEMI
PORCELAIN

(1893 – 1898)

These dates were given in Barber's 1904 marks book.

WARWICK
CHINA

(1898 – c.1910)

The above mark is the most common early Warwick China Co. mark. It was used to mark most Warwick flow blue ware.

(c.1893 – c.1898)

I've seen the mark at left but once. Although not given by Barber, I would date it the same as the above Barber mark.

The IOGA mark at the right is probably the best-known Warwick mark. It dates from c.1900 to c.1915 or a bit later. Note that WARWICK has replaced WARWICK CHINA CO. on the ribbon. An IOGA mark with WARWICK CHINA CO. on the ribbon would date before 1905. I don't know if the helmet mark was ever used without IOGA between c.1900 and c.1920

IOGA

232. Warwick China Co. (continued)

(1920s)

This version of the helmet and crossed swords mark was used in the 1920s and later. In the 1930s MADE IN U.S.A. was added to the mark. Later marks, particularly those from the 1940s, are also dated.

(c.1918)

This mark was found on a nice piece of translucent hotel porcelain. It also had the name of a hotel and was dated 1918. Warwick made much hotel ware from c.1914 to 1951. They also made ware for distributors whose names are on many Warwick marks. See pp. 173, 193 & 194.

---

233. Watt Pottery

See p. 194.

---

234. Weller Pottery
Zanesville, OH
c.1890 – 1948

Apparently Weller made little but art pottery before World War I. Kitchen ware was made from the 1920s on. The word WELLER is on nearly all Weller products. There are numerous books dealing with Weller's art pottery. A good place to begin is Barber's 1904 marks book. See also p. 194.

---

235. Wellsville China Co.

See Pioneer Pottery on p. 116.

---

236. West End Pottery Co.
East Liverpool, OH
1893 – 1938

(1893 – c.1910)

W.E.P.CO.
CHINA

(1893 – c.1910)

I saw the mark at the left on one of the best examples of American semi-porcelain I've yet seen. The whiteware itself, the shape, and the decoration were excellent.

PURITAN
W.E.P.CO.
E.L.O.

(c.1915)

W.E.P.CO.
VITREOUS
HOTEL CHINA

(c.1915)

The two marks at left are from Gates and Ormerod. They are two of 27 marks reprinted from *Historical Archaeology,* Volume 16, Numbers 1 and 2, p. 316.

236. West End Pottery Co. (continued)

WEST END
621   (1921)

(c.1918 – c.1928)

The mark at the left nearly always has numbers under it, indicating a probable dating system. The earliest seen was 1919; the latest 1926.

(1930s)

(1928 – 1938)

Gates and Ormerod show one version of the mark at the left with an O under the mark. These letters possibly indicate a dating system. Gates and Ormerod date the mark 1928 to 1938.

---

237. Western Stoneware Co.
Monmouth, IL
1906 – 1985

Despite its name this company apparently made some whiteware, or a stoneware that looked like whiteware, from the very beginning. See Lois Lehner's *Complete Book of American Kitchen and Dinner Wares* for more about this company.

---

238. Wheeling Pottery Co. 1879 – 1903
Wheeling Potteries Co. 1903 – 1909 or 1910
Wheeling, WV

The La Belle Pottery was formed in 1887 as a part of the Wheeling Pottery Co. The well-known La Belle flow blue was made here.

(1880 – 1886)

The Wheeling Stone China Pottery Co.

(1880 – 1886)

(1880 – 1886)

238. Wheeling Pottery Co./Wheeling Potteries Co. (continued)

(1886 – 1896)

(1896 – c.1904)

See p. 229 for some very similar marks.

The above mark is usually much smaller than shown here. It was drawn larger to show details.

The following five marks were used at the La Belle factory. ADAMANTINE CHINA was made first, from 1888 to 1893. LA BELLE CHINA was made from 1893 to c.1904 or 1905.

(1888 – 1893)

(1888 – 1893)

(1888 – 1893)

LaBelle.
China.

(1893 – c.1904)

LA BELLE
CHINA
(1893 – c.1904)

These LA BELLE CHINA marks were discontinued c.1904 or 1905. A mark with WHEELING POTTERIES CO. and BONITA was used for a short time just before the company ended c.1909. See p. 162.

(1894 – 1904 or c.1909)

THE
WHEELING
POTTERY
CO.

(c.1904 – c.1909)

Although the company's name changed to Wheeling Potteries Co. in 1903, the mark at the left and possibly the mark at the far left were used to c.1909 when the company ended.

238. Wheeling Pottery Co./Wheeling Potteries Co. (continued)

Barber did not date these next four marks; however, he did say they were being used in 1904, the year of his pottery marks book.

The mark at left is a variation of the first mark above. It was seen on a very ornate pitcher. I would date it c.1900, or just about the same as the Barber marks above.

(c.1906 – c.1909)

This Wheeling Potteries Co. mark could have been used as early as 1903 or 1904 when the company's name was changed; however, it was probably used for only a short time just before the company ended in 1909 or 1910. Other marks with Wheeling Pottery Co. continued to be used after 1904.

This mark with BONITA was used on flow blue ware, however, it is not a pattern name. I've seen it on other ware as well. BONITA is probably a shape name.

(c.1903 – c.1909)

Avon was a pottery of Tiltonsville, Ohio, north of Wheeling, West Virginia. In 1902 it was called Vance Faience Co. In 1903 it was taken over by the Wheeling Pottery (now Potteries) Co. Barber said art pottery continued to be made here using the mark at left; however, I saw this mark on a piece of hand painted porcelain or semi-porcelain. The piece was signed E. EARL CHRISTY (spelling uncertain). This isn't traditional art pottery. See Paul Evans's *Art Pottery of the United States* for more about Avon.

239. Whitmore, Robinson & Co.
Akron, OH
1862 – c.1888

They made an imitation whiteware. It was buff-colored ware covered with an opaque white glaze. It was probably not marked.

240. Wick China Co.
Kittanning, PA
1889 – c.1905

This company was an early maker of tea leaf luster ware according to Annise Heaivilin. Wick China Co. became the Pennsylvania China (Pottery) Co. c.1905. See p. 111 for Pennsylvania China Co. marks.

(1890s)

This Pennsylvania Coat of Arms mark was a superior mark artistically; however, it was not stamped well. I could not draw the unclear details. Also, since the word WICK began so far to the right under the coat of arms, I am assuming THE was simply missing from the mark. WICK CHINA CO. was quite clear.

T W C. CO.

(1890s)

Annise Heaivilin showed this mark at left but with KNOBLE above the T.W.C. Co. She had seen the mark on tea leaf luster ironstone ware.

(c.1900)

---

241. Willets Manufacturing Co.
Trenton, NJ
1879 – c.1909

SEMI
W. M. CO.
PORCELAIN

(c.1890 and later)

W. M. CO.

(1879 – c.1884)

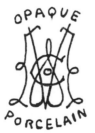

OPAQUE
PORCELAIN

(1884 – c.1890)

The mark at the left is a W.M.Co monogram. It is at times impressed.

There are several variations of the above mark.

(1880s and later)

The ribbon under the mark at the left may say:
1. ARNO
2. ADELAIDE
3. DUCHESS
4. SARATOGA, etc.

WILLETS.

(1890s+)

WILLETS

(1890s+)

Both snake marks were used on decorated and undecorated ware. Some BELLEEK marked ware was factory-decorated, some not.

242. John Wyllie & Co.
Pittsburgh, PA
1870 – 1874

I saw this Pennsylvania Coat of Arms mark on a plain white ironstone platter. It is significant because it is the first mark for John Wyllie & Co. recorded anywhere. Previously it was believed John Wyllie did not mark the ware made while he was in Pittsburgh.

243. John Wyllie & Son
East Liverpool, OH
1874 – c.1893

This company was a continuation of John Wyllie & Co. In 1874 John Wyllie moved from Pittsburgh, Pennsylvania, to East Liverpool, Ohio. He and his son took over the Great Western Pottery Works, refitting it for the manufacture of ironstone (white granite) ware.

(1875 – c.1883)

The mark at the left is from Gates and Ormerod. It is one of 27 marks reprinted from *Historical Archaeology,* Volume 16, Numbers 1 & 2, p. 319.

(1875 – c.1883)

(c.1880 – c.1883)

This mark is an elaboration of the unique two shields (American and English) mark. See p. 200 for a brief history of the mark. The version at the right was probably used after the death of John Wyllie, Sr. in 1882. The G.W.P. Co. is for Great Western Pottery Company.

(c.1883 – c.1888)

244. H.R. Wyllie China Co.
Huntington, WV
c.1910 – c.1929

(c.1910 – c.1920)

This is the earliest, and probably the most common H.R. Wyllie mark. It was used on their "border" flow blue ware. The H.R. Wyllie whiteware I have seen has been a very ordinary semi-porcelain.

(c.1915 – c.1920)

Initially, I believed this mark to be a 1920s mark; however, recently I saw the mark on a plate that looked like a World War I period piece. This mark does not seem to be as common as the mark given above.

H.R.WYLLIE

H.R.Wyllie

(1920s)

These plain marks with various pattern or shape names were used primarily in the 1920s.

---

245. William Young & Sons 1853 – 1870
William Young's Sons 1870 – 1879
Trenton, NJ

W Y S

(c.1870 – 1879)

Barber said this company used an eagle mark in 1858; however, he did not picture the mark. He said they used an English mark (shown here) from 1858 to 1879. The W Y S on the mark at left undoubtedly indicates it was used after 1870. A mark with W.Y. & SONS was most likely used before 1870.

Miscellaneous American Marks

The marks included can be divided into two main categories: 1. Some are marks that for one reason or another need special explanation. These include old American marks whose company of manufacture is in doubt, marks that present unique problems, marks that need special documentation and marks that are questionable in one way or another. 2. The other category consists simply of marks discovered too late to be included in the main section.

A.1

ABINGDON
U.S.A.

1930s; 1940s

The ABINGDON mark is found on an art or craft type pottery made in Abingdon, Illinois, in the 1930s and 1940s. ABINGDON marked wares are rather common at flea markets, etc.

A.2

ALBRIGHT
— • —
• CHINA •
10 8

c.1920

This ALBRIGHT CHINA mark was first seen after the main section of the book had been completed. See p. 14. The numbers under the mark probably indicate an October 1918 or October 1928 date; however, since this is the only mark I've seen for the company, it is quite premature for me to discuss their dating system. See p. 208.

A.3

alice

c.1905 – c.1915

I found this pattern or shape mark on a piece dated 1909. Because the style of the mark is identical to the FLORENCE mark of the Standard Pottery Co. (See p. 134), I believe there is a very good chance this is also a Standard Pottery Co. mark.

A.4

ATLAS
CHINA

1920s and later

The ATLAS CHINA mark at left is definitely for the Atlas China Co. of New York, N.Y. Lehner confirms this on p. 30 of her 1988 pottery book. Although the piece I saw marked was probably a 1920s product, the mark was most likely used well beyond the 1920s.

A.5

MADE IN
U.S.A.
WARRANTED
22 KARAT GOLD
Southern Belle

1930s; 1940s

This is another mark for the Atlas China Co. of New York City. It would date from the 1930s or 1940s.

A.6

This is another version of the AVALON FAIENCE mark of the Chesapeake Pottery of Baltimore, Maryland. See p. 33. A variation of the mark shown here was seen on a majolica type ware. Both AVALON FAIENCE and CLIFTON DECOR marked ware made at Chesapeake Pottery are classified majolica.

A.7

This is a mark dating before 1920. It could be a mark for the Bedford Company that preceded the Bailey-Walker Co. in Bedford, Ohio. See p. 20. It could also be a mark for the Barberton Pottery Co. of Barberton, Ohio.

A.8

c.1910

R.K. Beck was an artist active in the American pottery industry the first decade of the 1900s. Beck designed decals for many American whiteware companies. His signature is incorporated in the decal. Beck is best known for flora and particularly fauna decals. Some are rather ordinary decals produced in large quantities and used by many companies; others are quite special and even spectacular. One series of plant and animal decals designed for Taylor, Smith & Taylor was especially noteworthy.

I saw one hand painted plate with an R.K. Beck signature. It was a winter scene of less than professional quality. I suspect the painting and signature were copied by an amateur artist from a Beck decal. An authentic Beck hand painted piece would be a real find. NOTE: Some dealers may call a decal decorated piece a hand painted piece.

A.9

BENNETT'S
JAN.23,1873.
PATENT.

c.1873

This mark of the Edwin Bennett Pottery was found on a syrup pitcher with pewter lid. Although it was undoubtedly whiteware, except for the handle, the piece had turned the color of tea with cream.

This mark is also listed in price guides as being used on majolica ware. The patent mentioned on the mark refers to the unique way the pewter lid was attached to the pitcher.

A.10 *Bordeaux*
M.C.

c.1900

BORDEAUX is a pattern mark of the Mercer Pottery Co. of Trenton, New Jersey. Most versions of the mark have MERCER under BORDEAUX. See p. 97. The one at left has M.C. under BORDEAUX. Mercer used M.C. on other marks also. BORDEAUX marks are usually quite weak. The word BORDEAUX is often nearly illegible.

A.11

1916

This is a typical example of the BUFFALO POTTERY mark of the Buffalo Pottery Co. of Buffalo, New York. The marks, often dated, were used from 1903 to 1917. Between c. 1910 and 1917 both BUFFALO POTTERY and BUFFALO CHINA marks were in use. See below. BUFFALO POTTERY was marked on semi-vitreous ware. BUFFALO CHINA was used on vitreous institutional wares.

A.12

ALBERT PICK & COMPANY
Vitrified China
CHICAGO
BUFFALO
CHINA
1926

1926

A.13

ALBERT PICK Co., INC.
CHICAGO
BUFFALO
CHINA

1934?

These are two samples of BUFFALO CHINA marks of the Buffalo Pottery Co. of Buffalo, New York. BUFFALO CHINA marks of this style were used from c. 1910 into the 1930s. Many of these marks are dated, as seen on mark A.12. The earliest dated BUFFALO CHINA mark I've seen was 1911; the latest was 1929. The four little circles under mark A.13 may indicate that it dates 1934. I've seen no 1930s BUFFALO CHINA mark with a regular date.

Albert Pick was a Chicago pottery distributor. See p. 115.

A.14

1879 – 1895

This is a Burroughs & Mountford mark found too late to be included in the main section of the book. GRAPEVINE is a pattern mark found on a plate decorated with flow blue grapes. The mark was also in flow blue. See also mark A.15.

A.15   WILD-ROSE
B. & M.

This is another Burroughs & Mountford mark found after the main section of this book had been completed. All Burroughs & Mountford marks date from 1879 to c. 1895. The company was in operation in 1892 but was out of business before 1897 according to Jervis. See pp. 245 and 246.

A.16   GEORGELYN
SUNSET
CANONSBURG
POTTERY CO.

✝

c.1930

At left is a selection of Canonsburg Pottery Co. marks. The first two marks date about 1930. See p. 30 for the same shield mark but with AVON instead of KEYSTONE under the shield.

Marks A.18 and A.19 are later marks. The cannon mark with SIMPLICITY and THE HALLMARK OF QUALITY was found on a 1955 calendar plate. This mark was used in the 1950s and 1960s. See p. 30 for another cannon mark.

I keep finding more Canonsburg Pottery marks dating from the 1940s and later.

A.17

KEYSTONE

c.1930

A.18

CANONSBURG POTTERY
MADE IN U.S.A.

1940s; 1950s

A.19   SIMPLICITY

THE HALLMARK

OF QUALITY

1950s; 1960s

A.20

c.1930 or later

This mark is for the Carr China Co. of Grafton, West Virginia. See p. 30. Based on the style of the mark it probably dates back to c. 1930; however, since the plate found marked was a very plain piece of tan hotel ware, it quite possibly dates well after 1930. Institutional wares are generally very hard to date.

Note that the mark says CRAFTON, W. VA. instead of GRAFTON. Since the mark was quite clear, this was an error in the mark itself, not the result of weak stamping.

A.21

CHELSEA

1930s

This is a Taylor, Smith & Taylor Co. mark from the 1930s. It is sometimes found without T.S.T. initials, making it difficult to identify.

A.22

TRADE MARK

c.1897

This mark first appeared in Jervis' 1897 marks book. See p. 247. I first saw it in Thorn's book. It is a mark of the Cook Pottery Co. of Trenton, New Jersey. Barber said the three feathers (Prince of Wales's Crest) mark was used by the Cook Pottery on belleek ware. He pictured the three feathers mark with just the word ETRURIA on the ribbon. He also pictured it with MELLOR & CO. under the ribbon. See p. 35. Barber did not show BELLEEK on the mark as seen at left. The CH.H.C. initials are for Charles Howell Cook, the president of the company. *Mellor* (a partner of Cook) *& Co.* was used on most ware to prevent confusion with the Cook & Hancock marks of the older Crescent Pottery, which Charles Howell Cook had organized with W.H. Hancock in 1881. The Cook Pottery Co. did use the Cook name on a few "special" products. See mark A.27 on p. 171.

A.23

C - 19

U. S. A.

1919

According to Lehner's 1988 book the Summit China Co. of Akron, Ohio and later Cleveland, Ohio registered a CLEVE-RON mark in 1917. The C-19 under this mark most likely indicates a 1919 date for the mark. Note the rather early use of U.S.A. on the mark. See also p. 139.

A.24

1900 – 1907

This COLONIAL banner mark is one of 27 marks reprinted from *Historical Archaeology*, Vol. 16, Numbers 1& 2, p.197. Gates and Ormerod credit the mark to the McNicol-Smith Co. of East Liverpool, Ohio. They date the mark 1900 to 1907.

A.25

COLONIAL
STERLING
CHINA
PATENTED 1918

AMERICAN MARK?
Mark may read 1919

The true story of COLONIAL STERLING marks remains an enigma. Originally I believed the first COLONIAL STERLING mark shown here to be a mark of the Colonial Co. of East Liverpool, Ohio. See p. 35. Petra Williams in her *Flow Blue, An Aid to Identification* has some information on p. 202 that might indicate that COLONIAL STERLING was an American mark.

A.26

COLONIAL

STERLING
J.&G.MEAKIN
ENGLAND

ENGLISH MARK

Since then I've twice seen the COLONIAL STERLING mark of the J. & G. Meakin Co. of England. See mark A.26 at left. I now believe the first COLONIAL STERLING mark may also be a Meakin mark.

One problem with this theory is that after 1891 the word ENGLAND would have to be a part of J. & G. Meakin marks on wares imported into the United States. Since the mark is rather common I doubt if the ware so marked came indirectly into the country. Perhaps an importer who obtained an American patent didn't have to put the country of origin on the mark. All COLONIAL STERLING marks of type A.25 included PATENTED and a date. NOTE: The final number of the date is usually difficult to read as is true of the mark shown here.

A.27

This mark of the Cook Pottery Co. of Trenton, New Jersey was used on special ware relating to the Spanish American War. This mark is rare in that it used COOK POTTERY CO. instead of MELLOR & CO. MELLOR & CO. was used almost exclusively by Cook until c. 1910. See p. 35.

171

A.28

c.1910

This CORNELL banner mark is one of 27 marks reprinted from *Historical Archaeology,* Vol. 16, Numbers 1 & 2, p. 187. Gates and Ormerod credit the mark to the D. E. McNicol Pottery Co. of East Liverpool, Ohio. They date the mark c.1910.

A.29

c.1863 – c.1870

This Coxon & Co. mark was seen too late to be included in the main section of this book. See Coxon & Co. on p. 36. This is probably the earliest Coxon & Co. mark. Based on the style of the mark and the whiteware marked I would date it c.1863 to c.1870.

A.30

c.1900 – c.1910

I found the DIXIE mark on a portrait plate that would date c.1900 to c.1910. MARQUETTE was recently seen on a plate that would date about the same time. These could be marks for several companies that used C. P. Co. initials; however, the most likely company to have used these marks was the Crown Pottery Co. of Evansville, Indiana.

A.31

c.1900 – c.1910

A.32

c.1925

This is a variation of a mark shown on p. 37. The mark is for the Crescent China Co. of Alliance, Ohio.

A.33

c.1912 and later

A.34

WARWICK CHINA
CRESCENT CHINA CO,
EAST LIVERPOOL, OHIO.

c.1920

I found the mark at left on a 1912 dated plate. Contrary to Lehner's contention, this mark is not for the Crescent China Co. of Alliance, Ohio. The mark is quite possibly for Harry Keffer who was a founder of the Sevres China Co. and the following Warner-Keffer China Co. which ended in 1911. Keffer probably started a decorating and/or distributing company in East Liverpool, Ohio, c.1912. Mark A.34 is a c.1920 mark for the same company. Warwick was the manufacturer; Crescent China Co. was the distributor.

A.35

I included this CRESCENT with UTOPIA mark to show that two American companies, both connected with Charles H. Cook, used registry numbers. See Crescent Pottery on p. 37. See Cook Pottery Co. on pp. 35 and 36. See ELKTON mark on p. 35.

Unlike in England, registry numbers would have no national meaning in this country. Possibly these companies used registry numbers just to make their marks appear to be English. I know of no other American companies which incorporated registry numbers in their marks.

A.36

c.1940 and later

This is a mark of the Cronin China Co. of Minerva, Ohio. It is a sample of the "union" marks used from the 1930s to c.1960. This particular style of mark dates c.1940 to c.1960. See p. 200 for a discussion about union marks. The number under the mark at left might indicate a date.

A.37

DELAN & McGILL
HAND PAINTED
Trenton, N.J.

c.1910 – c.120

DELAN & MCGILL was a decorating concern operating in Trenton, New Jersey c.1910 to c.1920. This mark was found on an ale set with a hand painted Egyptian motif. DeLan had been an important decorator at the Lenox Co. from 1899 to c.1910.

A.38

c.1897

Mark A.38 was used on Delft-type ware made by the Cook Pottery Co. of Trenton, New Jersey. See p. 35. Except for the addition of D.C. this mark is an identical copy of the bottle mark used on Delft ware produced in the 19th century. This mark, without the word Delft, was used many years before but was being used again on Delft ware made in Holland in the middle to late 1800s. Cook was certainly aware of this newer Delft. He was probably trying to make his own form of it. The D.C. could stand for Delft-Cook or possibly a family member who helped him on the project. Barber considered Cook's Delft ware to be the best imitation of Delft made in this country. Although Barber said Cook's Delft was made in 1897, it was made for at least a few years.

A.39

Etruria
Delft
D. O.

c.1897

Mark A.39 was copied from an actual piece of Cook's Delft. Note the use of ETRURIA on this version of the mark. Cook used ETRURIA on several other marks. Note also that the C. of D. C. looks like an O.

A.40

OPAQUE
E
CHINA

c.1885 – c.1890

This is an impressed mark inside an embossed border. The mark is in effect a bas relief inside a raised frame. I believed the mark to be English. This proved not to be true. Barber said the East Trenton Pottery Co. used OPAQUE CHINA as an impressed mark; however he did not picture it in his marks book. The use of OPAQUE CHINA with an *E* in the center strongly suggests the East Trenton Pottery used this mark. Note that this company used a solitary *E* in the shield of one British Coat of Arms mark. See p. 47. I believe the mark would date c.1885 to c.1890.

A.41

before 1900

This mark was seen on several pieces of a very nice toilet set. There was a number under each mark. In every case that number was blurred. It appeared to be 89 or 98, possibly the date of the mark.

The mark is for the East Palestine Pottery Co. Since I keep finding previously unknown E.P.P.Co. marks, I suspect there are still others to be found. See pp. 46 and 47.

A.42

Eureka

c.1915

According to Gates and Ormerod this EUREKA mark was for the C.C. Thompson Pottery Co. of East Liverpool, Ohio. They date the mark c.1915.

A.43

Eureka

c.1905 – c.1915

This EUREKA was included with the C.C. Thompson Pottery Co. of East Liverpool, Ohio. See p. 146. I now believe it was a mark of the Standard Pottery Co., also of East Liverpool. Note the similarity of the style of the mark to that of FLORENCE shown on p. 134. See also ALICE on p. 166. All these marks date c.1905 – c.1915.

A.44

EXCELSIOR ART COMPANY
T. TOMKINSON & SON
EAST LIVERPOOL, OHIO

c.1910

I found the mark for this company on a 1910 calendar plate. This was probably a small decorating company which did not have a long history. Gates and Ormerod, who did extensive research on the pottery industry of East Liverpool, Ohio, did not include this company in their book.

A.45

c.1898 – c.1905

This EXCELSIOR PORCELAIN mark was for the Salem China Co. of Salem, Ohio. Initially I believed the mark to be English, particularly because of the outstanding quality of the whiteware. The piece of EXCELSIOR PORCELAIN seen was a gravy boat of excellent semi-porcelain, light in weight and translucent in its thinner parts. According to Lehner's 1980 kitchen and dinnerware book the Salem China Co. made an "excelsior porcelain" in its earliest years. This information combined with the T.S.C. Co. monogram confirms this as a Salem mark. A few other American companies used THE as a part of their monogram or name. The best example of this is the AURORA CHINA mark of The Wick China Co. See p. 163. See also Salem China Co. on p. 125.

A.46 RAINIER
GEORGE BROS.

before 1909

This mark was found on an old basin with decal decoration. W.S. George and his brother, John, operated a factory in the Canonsburg, Pennsylvania, area sometime before c.1909, perhaps as early as 1905. About 1909 W.S. George took over this company and his brother took over the family's Canonsburg China (now Pottery) Co. See p. 29. See also W.S. George, Canonsburg, Pennsylvania, and W.S. George, East Palestine, Ohio.

A.47

W. S. GEORGE
Iris

c.1910 – c.1920

This IRIS shape mark of the W.S. George Pottery of East Palestine, Ohio, and Canonsburg, Pennsylvania, is identical to a DERWOOD and a QUEEN mark of W.S. George. See p. 53. Note also that an IRIS and a QUEEN mark were used c.1905 to c.1909 by the East Palestine Pottery Co. that preceded the W.S. George Co. in East Palestine, Ohio. See p. 47.

A.48 *W. S. George*

early version

W. S. George

later version*

This plain W.S. George signature mark was used before 1920 to the 1950s. Nearly all the marks used after 1920 included a shape name, other information or numbers along with the signature. I recently saw a plain black version of the mark used on small plates with fruit and flower decals. These plates were from the 1950s but the decals were similar to types used in the early 1900s. The only difference between the signature mark on these plates and the early signature mark is that the later mark is more perfect or "professional" than the early version of the mark.

A.49

(c.1905)

This GLENDORA mark is from Gates and Ormerod. It is one of 27 marks reprinted from *Historical Archaeology,* Vol. 16, Numbers 1 & 2, p. 32. They credit GLENDORA to the Cartwright Bros. Co.

A.50

Golden Maize
Made for
Farberware
—— BY ——
THE SEBRING POTTERY CO.
SEBRING, OHIO
Reg. U.S. Pat. Off. No. 230442

(c.1930)

This is another version of the GOLDEN MAIZE mark of the Sebring Pottery Co. of Sebring, Ohio. See p. 18. This mark dates c.1930. It was found on a serving plate with a Farberware frame. Crooksville's PROVINCIAL WARE was likewise usually inside a chrome frame. See p. 39.

*Later W.S. George signature marks come in several other styles.

176

This Goodwin Pottery Co. mark is in the main section of this book. See p. 58. What makes this mark truly noteworthy is a hidden message. Inside the flower wreath, just to the right of the 1844, is a hidden 93, the actual date for the incorporation of the Goodwin Pottery Co.

This is the kind of thing that makes early American marks so interesting. Some companies used their marks to express humor, to make satirical comment, or to give personal information, as this Goodwin mark does. While wanting to use the date 1844 to recognize the family's earliest attempts at pottery making, they still met their need for historical accuracy by hiding a 93 among the flowers. Not all the versions of this mark have a hidden 93.

A.51

THE GOODWIN POTTERY CO.
SEMI-PORCELAIN

The following is a distillation of many different and sometimes contradictory stories concerning the history of the Greenwood Pottery Co. of Trenton, New Jersey. The early writers gave various dates for the founding of the company. Jervis said the date of incorporation was 1863; however, because of the use of 1862 on mark A.52, it is evident the company considered 1862 their founding date. The 1876 on the mark is the date they developed a new porcelain, later to be called hotel porcelain. They also made art porcelain. See pp. 58 and 59.

In the late 1800s Greenwood began contracting with various New York and Philadelphia retailers to supply them their new porcelain. Greenwood marks of this period and the early 1900s included GREENWOOD CHINA and the retailer's name. These marks continued to be used into the 1920's.

Mark A.52 was an early 1900s mark. In her 1988 pottery book Lehner says the mark's outline was registered in 1910. I've seen the mark on pieces from the 1920s. The company ended c.1930.

A.52

c.1910 – c.1930

A.53

c.1930 or later

I feel sure mark A.53 was used by the Hall China Co., East Liverpool, Ohio; however I can't prove it. I found it marking a small vase with gold decoration so typical of the teapots, etc, Hall made in the 1920s and later. If you are a Hall collector or have had considerable experience with Hall pottery and you see this or similar marks on what you feel certain is Hall ware, I think you, like me, can claim it as a Hall mark; however, if you are not thoroughly knowledgeable with regard to Hall pottery, don't try to ascribe such nondescript marks to them.

A.54

GERMAN MARK

The mark at left must be a German mark. I have previously contended this mark was probably for the Herold Pottery Co. of Golden, Colorado. Herold made chemical and other porcelain. I've seen this mark on mortars with pestles. Other Colorado potteries used arrows in their marks.

Recently I found a mortar and pestle with the H with arrow mark. My initial excitement was dashed when I also discovered an impressed GERMANY with the H and arrow mark.

A.55

HULL POTTERY MARK

A.56

CARROLLTON DESIGN

I first saw mark A.55 many years ago when I began researching American pottery marks. I don't remember much about the piece marked except that it was "craft" type vase or otherwise similar container. I had been hoping to find a more recent example but have thus far failed. An H in a diamond was registered by the Carrollton Pottery Co. of Carrollton, Ohio. See mark A.56. This mark is quite different from A.55. Also the H in a diamond mark of the Carrollton Pottery Co. is really only the center of the total mark. See mark A.57.

Just as the H in a circle mark (see p. 63) is a mark for the Hull Pottery Co. of Crooksville, Ohio, I believe the H in a diamond mark (A.55) is also for that company.

A.57

ACTUAL CARROLLTON MARK

A.58

Inverted arrow

QUESTIONABLE MARK

A.59

H.P. Co. monogram

MONOGRAM ERROR

The inverted arrow mark was first shown in W. Percival Jervis' privately printed *A Book of Pottery Marks* in 1897. See p. 250. The mark was repeated by Spargo, Ramsay, Hartman, Thorn, Kovel and Lehner. Jervis, in a series of articles in the *Pottery, Glass and Brass Salesman*, in the early 1900s repeated the mark.

In its original 1897 publication Jervis' mark was printed with a significant error. The H.P.Co. monogram was partly missing. See A.59, A.60 to the left and see p. 250. Hartman, Thorn, Kovel and Ramsay copied the mark exactly in their books including the printing error! I had thought Ramsay's work was original research, but this proves that, at least in this case, he also was copying. Spargo did draw the mark correctly in his book: Conceivably he got the mark from Jervis' articles in *Pottery, Glass and Brass Salesman*. Here the H.P.Co. monogram was complete.

Edwin AtLee Barber's 1904 *Marks of American Potters* has the mark drawn correctly with the arrow pointing up. See A.61 at left. He does not show the inverted mark!

The truth boils down to choosing between Jervis' or Barber's version of the mark. I have seen Barber's mark many times on various pieces of Harker Pottery Co. ware. I've yet to see Jervis' mark even once! I don't believe it exists.

A.60

CORRECTED MONOGRAM

A. 61

CORRECT MARK
from Barber

A.62

HARVEST

U.S.A.

E 48 N6

c.1948

This is a mark of the Homer Laughlin Co. of East Liverpool, Ohio. It was seen too late to be included in the main section of the book. The mark is dated 1948.

A.63

IMPERIAL
CHINA

c.1902 – c.1912

The first two marks at left, A.63 and A.64, are most likely marks for the Ohio China Co. of East Palestine, Ohio. I previously thought Mark A.63 to be the Owen mark used before 1904. See p. 110. Since then I've discovered their rather rare early mark. Again see p. 110. I've also seen A.63 and A.64 quite a few times, indicating they are not so rare. Because of this I'm rather confident these two IMPERIAL CHINA marks are for the Ohio China Co. They would date c.1902 to c.1912.

Mark A. 63 may have been used only on flow blue ware. I believe I've seen it only on ware with a flow blue border.

Note that mark A.64 is an O.C. Co. monogram.

A.64

c.1902 – c.1912

A.65

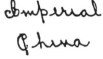

early 1900s

IMPERIAL CHINA mark A.65 may also be a mark for the Ohio China Co. The mark was weak. The I of IMPERIAL and C of CHINA appeared complex and perhaps within these letters is a clue to the origin of the mark. The mark would date c.1915 or earlier.

A.66

IMPERIAL
CHINA

c.1910 – c.1920

IMPERIAL CHINA mark A.66 is probably not a mark of the Ohio China Co. I think there is a fair chance it is a mark of the Limoges China Co. of Sebring, Ohio. It would date c.1910 or a bit later.

A.67

c.1897

The c.1897 mark at left is for the International Pottery Co., Trenton, New Jersey. *Burgess & Campbell* is on many of their marks. See p. 65. The mark was found on a fine piece of flow blue. ROYAL BLUE is marked on most of their flow blue. This mark was very weak.

A.68

c.1935 – c.1941

Gates and Ormerod said JIFFY WARE dates 1935 to 1941. JIFFY WARE was a product of the Limoges China Co. of Sebring, Ohio.

A.69

c.1900 and later

The LAMBERTON CHINA shield mark at left was used c.1900 and for a while after 1900. I've yet to see the mark. This mark was given by Barber in his 1904 marks book. The Maddock Pottery of Trenton, New Jersey, first made LAMBERTON CHINA at the old Lamberton works. Although operated by and partly owned by Thomas Maddock & Sons, the Maddock Pottery Co. was a separate company. At some point a wreath was placed around the shield at left. I've seen this wreath mark but once. I would guess the wreath mark was not adopted until c.1920. The Maddock Pottery Co. became the Scammell China Co. in the middle 1920s. Their LAMBERTON CHINA shield with wreath mark is shown on p. 129. In 1954 the Scammell China was taken over by the Sterling China Co. of East Liverpool, Ohio, (actually Wellsville). They continued to make and mark LAMBERTON CHINA. See p. 135.

Thus the Lamberton China shield mark, with or without the wreath, continued to be used for almost a century.

A.70

1886 – 1889

In his 1904 marks book Barber stated this mark of the Homer Laughlin Co. of East Liverpool, Ohio, was used on a Laughlin china. He did not elaborate and he did not attempt to date it. Gates and Ormerod say the mark was used on both ironstone and porcelain ware only in 1886. Jervis said that for several years Homer Laughlin made a thin, translucent china but, owing to the difficulties of making two entirely distinct products in the same plant, the china was discontinued in 1889 in favor of a high grade of semi-vitreous ware. He also showed the horseshoe mark at left. The mark may be impressed or printed.

A.71

Lebeau Porcelain

c.1907 – c.1920

A.72

La Francaise Porcelain

c.1900

Although I don't have absolute proof that LEBEAU PORCELAIN(E) is a mark for the Saxon China Co. of Sebring, Ohio, I do have considerable circumstantial evidence.

First, I've been able to confirm a very close relationship between Saxon and the French China Co. of Sebring, Ohio.

Second, since the French China Co. used only a LA FRANCAISE mark for 10 years or so, it seems likely the sister Saxon Co. might have done the same. There are no other confirmed Saxon marks used between c. 1907 to c.1920 even though the company was in operation during this period.

Third, both companies made very similar flow blue ware. I've seen various "Dutch scene" decals used on many French China Co. flow blue pieces. I've seen identical decals on flow blue pieces marked LEBEAU PORCELAIN(E). I've not seen these decals used by any other companies.

Fourth, both companies adopted similar plain company initials marks in the 1920s. LA FRANCAISE and LEBEAU PORCELAIN(E) marks were no longer used.

Finally, mark A.72 was seen on a 1900 commemorative plate. This LA FRANCAISE mark was styled like the LEBEAU PORCELAIN(E) mark shown above. This is the only LA FRANCAISE mark of this style I've seen. It does indicates a probable relationship between the two marks. It might also indicate that LEBEAU PORCELAIN(E) was used before 1907 as I have theorized.

NOTE: the LEBEAU PORCELAIN mark usually has a thick upswing on the end that might indicate a final letter *e* giving *porcelain* a French spelling.

A.73

c.1900

This LELAND mark was seen on some fairly good whiteware. Gates and Ormerod say LELAND was a mark of the McNicol-Smith Co. of Wellsville, Ohio. Leland dates c. 1899 to c.1901.

A.74

Thos Maddock's Sons Co. Trenton, N.J.

COMMON MARK

The Thomas Maddock's Sons Co., Trenton, New Jersey, succeeded the Thomas Maddock & Sons Co. in 1902 with the death of Thomas Maddock. In the early 1900s both companies were making chemical porcelain including mortars and pestles. See marks on p. 86. Between 1906 and c.1915 Thomas Maddock's Sons did much decorating of commemorative, Masonic, etc. pieces of whiteware. From 1912 to c.1915 the company used imported (usually German) blanks for decorating. Often the foreign manufacturer's mark is found along with the Thomas Maddock's Sons Co. mark. See mark A.74 at left.

A.75

Tho's Maddock's Son Co.
Trenton, N. J.

POSSIBLE MARK

I found one 1906 dated piece made of an excellent, and probably imported, porcelain. All other pieces decorated between 1906 and 1911 were of ordinary opaque whiteware. What makes this more than just an exception to the rule was that the mark appeared to read Thomas Maddock's Son (not Sons) Co. I don't know if this was the result of an improper marking or if in 1906 only one son was decorating porcelain blanks. See mark A.75 at left.

Since I've seen no Thomas Maddock's Sons decorating marks dating before 1906, it is possible that one son broke away from the company's chemical porcelain making to take up decorating. If true the other son or sons joined the decorating operation almost immediately. I don't know if the whiteware decorated between 1906 and 1911 was made by Thomas Maddock's Sons Co.

A.76

Tho's Maddock's Sons Co.
Trenton, N. J.

Originally I believed mark A.76 was a special mark for flow blue ware decorated by, and possibly made by, the Thomas Maddock's Sons Co.; however, I later saw their regular decorating mark, A.74, on several other flow blue pieces.

A.77

PA

1890s – c.1905

TRIUMPH is an example of a mark used on flow blue ware made at the Mayer Pottery Co. of Beaver Falls, Pennsylvania. The mark was probably used only on flow blue ware. If so, TRIUMPH is most likely a pattern mark. There is at least one more flow blue mark used by J. E. Mayer.

A.78

McNICOL-CORNS
CHINA CO.

Although the McNicol-Corns Co., Wellsville, Ohio, operated between 1907 and 1928, their marks are quite rare. They were probably a small operation. This McNicol-Corns Co. mark was found on a 1913 calendar plate of poor quality whiteware.

A.79

c.1900

This unidentified mark was found on an old basin that would date c.1900 or a bit earlier. I have learned nothing more about the mark.

A.80

Orient
MERCER CHINA
c.1915 – c.1920

This is the only mark for the Mercer Pottery Co., Trenton, New Jersey, I've seen that was not also included in Barber's 1904 marks book. Early Mercer marks are common. Obviously, later ones are not. Based on the style of the whiteware marked and the mark itself, I would date it c.1915 to c.1920.

A.81

MINTON'S

c.1910

This MINTON'S mark was found on several pieces of American flow blue ware. The plates so marked had a border of flow blue with gold stenciling over the blue. Since I found a similarly shaped flow blue plate with identical gold stenciling made by the Carrollton Pottery Co. of Carrollton, Ohio, I am suggesting this might also be a Carrollton mark. It is an American mark dating c.1910.

A.82

C.1885 – c.1895

According to Gates and Ormerod, NAOMI is a mark of the Dresden Pottery (Potters' Cooperative) of East Liverpool, Ohio. I've seen the mark but once. Gates and Ormerod say the mark would date c.1885 – c.1895.

A.83

NASSAU CHINA CO.
TRENTON, N. J.

This mark was found on a very plain white mug of heavy hotel porcelain or semi-porcelain. Lehner says in her 1988 pottery book that the New Jersey City Directory lists a Nassau China Co., Trenton, New Jersey, from 1948 to 1954.

A.84

◇ C. C⁰.

Thorn credited this mark to the Ohio China Co. of East Palestine, Ohio, and well it may be; however, since this isn't a Barber mark, and particularly because the mark is just initials, it could be for another company. There are two prime possibilities: the Oliver China Co. of Sebring, Ohio, or the Owen China Co. of Minerva, Ohio. I've not seen the mark.

A.85

PACIFIC.
4132
MADE IN U.S.A.

1930s

A.85 is a mark of the Pacific Clay Products Co. of Los Angeles, California. In the 1930s they made kitchen and dinnerware. Mark A.85 was found on a pastel green water jug with attached wooden handle. The piece has an art deco look not unlike Manhattan styled depression glass. The water jug also had a paper label. See at left. Pacific Clay Products ware may not have been true whiteware. It is hard to tell when the ware is covered with colored glazes. In earlier years they made stoneware.

The number in the center of mark A.85 may not be accurate.

PAPER LABEL

A.86

PACIFIC CHINA
FINE QUALITY
WARRANTED 22K

C.1941

I found this mark on a plate that also had a 1941 dated Homer Laughlin EGGSHELL NAUTILUS mark. See p. 82. It is obviously a plate made at Homer Laughlin for some distributing or decorating company. The ware looks nothing like the ware made by the Pacific Clay Products Co. It is typical Ohio whiteware complete with a typical decal decoration.

A.87

Papoco
K 31

1931

A.88

Regina
P. C. P. CO.
E 33

1933

In her 1982 dinnerware book Jo Cunningham suggested that PAPOCO was a mark for the Paden City Pottery of Paden City, West Virginia. I am positive she was correct. The PAPOCO mark is identical in style to their REGINA mark. See A.87 and A.88 at left. They even used the same dating system.

A.89

1934

This is a Paden City Pottery Co. mark seen too late to be included in the main section of this book. The mark is dated 1934.

A.90

c.1910 – c.1920

This is another form of the PENNOVA mark of the Taylor, Smith & Taylor Co. of East Liverpool, Ohio. See another PENNOVA mark on p. 142. The number under the mark indicates a 1914 date for the mark. See the Taylor, Smith & Taylor dating system on p. 141. PENNOVA was used between c.1910 and c.1920.

A.91

J. & E.M.

before 1896

This rather questionable mark was first given in Jervis' 1897 marks book. See p. 255. The mark has the identical shape of Knowles, Taylor & Knowles' DAKOTA mark. See p. 72. I suspect Jervis had seen the POTOMAC mark but didn't draw it until later. He probably recognized DAKOTA as being similar to POTOMAC, using its outline for the Mayer Pottery Co. mark. Barber mentioned a POTOMAC mark used before 1896, but he did not picture it. See p. 91. (J.& E. Mayer had a serious fire in 1896 but rebuilt quickly.) I've not seen the Mayer POTOMAC mark.

In 1929 eight companies joined together to form the American Chinaware Corporation. Although the American Chinaware Corporation adopted marks for this company (see p. 16), some of the member companies continued to use their own marks. This was true of Knowles, Taylor & Knowles, the leading company of the A.C.C. In *The Collector's Encyclopedia of American Dinnerware,* Jo Cunningham showed a Pope-Gosser signature mark accompanying an American Chinaware Corporation mark. Other member companies may have continued using their old names. See p. 214. The A.C.C. ended in 1931.

A.92

PRINCETON

1900 – 1907

This PRINCETON banner mark is reprinted from *Historical Archaeology* Vol. 16, Numbers 1 & 2, p. 197. Gates and Ormerod credit the mark to the McNicol-Smith Co. of East Liverpool, Ohio. They date it 1900 to 1907.

A.93

This mark was used on porcelain decorated by hand at the Sinclaire Glass Co. of Corning, New York. The porcelain blanks were European imports. This experiment at decorating porcelain lasted for a short time in the early 1900s. The dates are c.1902 – c1920. The mark is probably rare.

A.94

1950s

1950s

These three 1950s marks are puzzling. One is for the Homer Laughlin China Co. of East Liverpool, Ohio. Another is for the Royal China Co. of Sebring, Ohio. The third is for the Stetson China Co. of Lincoln, Illinois. The mark is a rather common one for the Royal China Co. Why the Stetson Co. and Homer Laughlin used marks virtually identical to it at virtually the same time is a true mystery. The ROYAL STETSON mark might indicate some type of collaboration between the Royal China Co. and Stetson. Note that ROYAL and STETSON seem to to have a hyphen between them, perhaps indicating this collaboration. However, this does not explain the similarity with the Homer Laughlin mark. Note that both the Stetson and Homer Laughlin marks include ROYAL MAYTIME. There is probably an interesting story to explain the duplications. Perhaps there was some type of trade mark challenge involved.

1950s

A.95

THE
"SABINA"
LINE
Warranteed 22 K
Made In U.S.A.

1960s and later

In the early 1960s there was some type of reorganization or takeover of the Sabin Industries of McKeesport, Pennsylvania. SABINA LINE marks were used after that company change. This particular mark was seen on a 1966 dated commemorative plate. See also p. 124.

A.96

c.1920 – c.1925

This Salem China Co. mark usually has MADE IN AMERICA under it. See p. 125. This version, without MADE IN AMERICA, would date a bit earlier than the other. I would date it c.1920 to c.1925.

A.97

PORCELAIN

c.1900

George A. Sebring was the father of five Sebring brothers who were involved with numerous potteries, particularly in eastern Ohio. George A. Sebring had worked in various East Liverpool, Ohio, potteries. Mark A.97 at left indicates that he had his own pottery, at least for a time. This mark was found on an old basin that was not porcelain. It would date c.1900. Note: The final *e* of *George* appeared to be missing.

A.98

possibly 1900 – 1902

A.99

Sterling China

possibly 1900 – 1902

Three STERLING CHINA marks are still mysteries. Marks A.98 and A.99 are rather uncommon. Because of this I believe they are marks for the Sterling China Co. of Sebring, Ohio. This company preceded the Limoges China Co. by about two years. See p. 84. These marks would date 1900 to c.1902 if the above speculation is correct.

A.100

c.1905 – c.1912

Mark A.100 is quite common. It definitely is not a mark for the Sterling China Co. of Sebring, Ohio. I've seen the mark with dates and other information that confirms the mark to have been in use between c.1905 and c.1912, long after the Sterling China Co. of Sebring had become the Limoges China Co. The base of the crown may represent an O. or O.Co. This might indicate that the company's true identity begins with the letter O.

A.101

WILD ROSE
9 KLN

c.1940 – c.1948

In 1940 the Sebring Pottery Co. (originally the American Pottery Works) of Sebring, Ohio, was absorbed by the Limoges China Co. of Sebring. They continued to make and mark whiteware with the Sebring name until 1948. These two marks and similar marks date from this period.

A.102

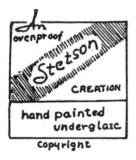

c.1940 – c.1948

A.103

J. F. STEELE

J.F. Steele was a decorator who worked in East Liverpool, Ohio, in the 1880s. His mark may be found alone or accompanied by the mark of the company that made the whiteware.

A.104

late 1950s

This Stetson Co. mark was seen too late to be included in the main section of this book. Stetson was in Chicago, Illinois, and, after 1946, Lincoln, Illinois. See p. 136. This mark is from the late 1950s.

A.105

c.1905 – c.1915

S.P. Co. monogram

This mark is for the Steubenville Pottery Co. of Steubenville, Ohio. This particular mark was found on a 1910 calendar plate of a good quality semiporcelain, comparable to Steubenville's famous CANTON CHINA. See p. 137. This mark is probably for a continuation of that grade of whiteware. It dates c.1905 to c.1915. Note the S.P. Co. monogram under the mark.

189

A.106

1880s

A.107

PORC-GRANITE

before 1897

These two Steubenville Pottery Co. marks are rather interesting. Mark A.106, the earliest Steubenville mark, is designed to resemble the British Coat of Arms in a general way. Two lions hold up a crown; however, the crown is more than it seems. Its central section is sardonically the torch of the Statue of Liberty. Between 1876 and 1886 the stories of the making of the statue by Frederic Auguste Bartholdi, the selecting of a site for it in New York harbor, and the building of the statue's base were frequently in the news. This was obviously the inspiration for this Steubenville Pottery Co. mark.

Early American whiteware manufacturers used considerable creativity in the designing of imitation British marks. While wanting the mark to look superficially British, the Americans' national and personal pride led them to use their marks to satirize the very British marks they were imitating. It is fun trying to discover these devious barbs thrust into the British lion.

Mark A.107 also seems to have an historical connotation. In 1893 Robert E. Peary made his first attempt to reach the North Pole. This mark, in use before Jervis wrote his 1897 marks book, possibly commemorated that failed attempt. The United States flag is at the top of the globe; however the globe is apparently submerged perhaps suggesting the dashed hopes of the Peary expedition.

A.108

I found this mark on a commemorative piece dated 1904. Both W.H. Tatler and George Tunnicliffe were mentioned by Barber as being Trenton, New Jersey, decorators in 1904. Tatler had been in business for a long time. See pp. 139 and 140 for more about the W.H. Tatler Decorating Co. Tunnicliffe was fairly new to the business in 1904. Apparently he had failed as an independent decorator and by 1904 was working for the established Tatler Co. This seems the most plausible explanation for two decorators having marks on a single item.

A.109

c.1905

This c. 1905 TEXAS banner mark is for the Cartwright Brothers of East Liverpool, Ohio. It is reprinted from *Historical Archaeology,* Volume 16, Numbers 1 & 2, p. 32.

A.110

C.C. Thompson & Co. was the name of the C.C. Thompson Pottery Co. before 1889. This mark was found on a badly damaged bowl. The mark was blurred; however the name was legible. The mark would date in the late 1880s.

A.111

c.1920 – c.1935

The C.C. Thompson Pottery Co. of East Liverpool, Ohio, has been one of the most troublesome in terms of dating their marks. Fortunately, Barber has provided quite a few Thompson marks, proving that they were in use in 1904 or earlier. The problems come with the later marks. Gates and Ormerod in their book, *The East Liverpool, Ohio, Pottery District*, provide many later marks for this company including the two marks shown here. The accompanying dates are also from Gates and Ormerod. Both A.111 and A.112 appear to be of an earlier style of mark indicating to me they were in use before 1920. Gates and Ormerod say the Thompson Co. made its first semi-porcelain in 1917. I believe this date is incorrect. 1917 would be very late for a company's instituting the manufacture of semi-porcelain; most did this in the 1890s or early 1900s. If the date is changed to 1907, the dating for these marks might be set back ten years. These marks dated ten years earlier are more in keeping with the style of this earlier period. However, I have not yet seen these two marks and can't prove their use earlier than Gates and Ormerod indicated.

A.112

c.1920 – c.1935

A.113

Mark A.113 probably dates back to World War I or earlier. I found the mark on a piece of whiteware with a moss rose decoration. Generally, American moss rose decorated ware dates c.1860 – 1890. This could not be true for this mark since the Trenton Potteries Co. didn't start until 1892. Neither Barber nor Jervis showed the mark in their early books. The piece I saw marked was one of many moss rose decorated pieces. I failed to note the quality of the whiteware. In her 1982 dinnerware book Jo Cunningham showed this design with THE TRENTON POTTERIES COMPANY in a circle around the star on an ashtray probably dating from the 1930s or later. In her 1988 pottery book Lois Lehner says this same design was used as a mark on art pottery dating in the 1930s or 1940s.

A.114

IRONSTONE CHINA
T. P. Co.
1865 – 1870

This first British Coat of Arms mark looks properly British; however, it has an anomalous central shield. This is seldom true of early British marks. Although the central shield is blurred, it appears to have an eagle in the center. Also, there just isn't any British company with T.P.Co. initials. The mark is in fact for the Trenton Pottery Co. of Trenton, New Jersey. It dates 1865 to 1870. See pp. 148 and 149 for a history of the Trenton Pottery Co.

A.115

1865 – 1870

This PARISIAN GRANITE mark was seen on several pieces that looked quite old for American whiteware. One piece was an attractive rectangular platter that had a British look. It is not a British mark since no British company had the initials T.P. Co. It should also be emphasized the mark isn't for the Trenton Potteries Co. They made a vitreous whiteware while PARISIAN GRANITE marked a type of ironstone ware. The mark is for the Trenton Pottery Co. of Trenton, New Jersey. It would date 1865 to 1870.

A.116

1865 – 1870

This British Coat of Arms mark was seen but once and too late to be included in the main section of the book. The combination of an anomalous central shield and PARISIAN GRANITE on the mark confirms this mark as well as mark A.115 as American. Some details of this marks will not be precise. I made only a rough drawing on the spot. I did note the correct wording and did carefully draw the monogram shown on the central shield. This is also a mark for the Trenton Pottery Co., Trenton, New Jersey.

A.117

c.1880

I found this impressed mark on a soup bowl made of a very porous whiteware decorated with a plain brown transfer design of flowers. I assumed the piece to be for the Union Pottery Co. of East Liverpool, Ohio; however, their product was much later than this piece appeared to be and their whiteware that I've seen was a far superior type of ware. Likewise the coat of arms mark shown on p. 152 didn't ring true as an East Liverpool mark; however, it is very similar to several other early Trenton marks. This and much other empirical evidence convinces me these are marks for the Union Pottery Co. of Trenton, New Jersey.

Since I've not seen the coat of arms mark, I can't be as sure of it as a Trenton mark as I am of the impressed mark at left.

A.118

1900 – 1907

This URSULA banner mark is one of 27 marks reprinted from *Historical Archaeology* Vol. 16, Numbers 1 & 2, p. 197. Gates and Ormerod credit the mark to the McNicol-Smith Co. of East Liverpool, Ohio. They date it 1900 to 1907.

A.119

VASSAR

In *Grandma's Tea Leaf Ironstone*, Annise Heaivilin says VASSAR was a mark of the Buffalo Pottery Co. used on tea leaf decorated ware. A list compiled by Julie Rich and sent to me by Dale Abrams of the Tea Leaf Club International confirms that the Buffalo Pottery did make a tea leaf decorated ware. See p. 241 for the complete list of American potteries that made tea leaf decorated wares.

A.120

MADE IN U.S.A.

5 10

c.1905 – c.1920

This VERONA mark seemed a contradictory mark to me at first. Once I cracked the dating system of the Taylor, Smith & Taylor Co. everything fell into place. The date for the mark is 1915, not 1910 as I had believed. See the T.S.&T. dating system on p. 141. Even dated 1915 it is the earliest use of MADE IN U.S.A. on a mark I've yet been able to verify. See p. 199 for a discussion of *U.S.A.* as used on marks.

A.121

IMPRESSED

VICTOR

probably 1940s

I found this impressed mark on several pieces of thick, white, undecorated hotel porcelain or semi-porcelain. I believed it to be a product of the Pennsylvania China Co. made at the old Ford City China Co. factory. See p. 111. VICTOR had been used as a pattern or shape mark by the Ford China Co. I now believe this may be a false assumption. Lehner shows in her 1988 pottery book that Victor Insulators, Inc. had registered in the 1940s the word VICTOR to be used on dinnerware. This ware, particularly coffee mugs, was made for the company cafeteria and as advertising pieces. Since I've seen these pieces several items, they must have been widely distributed.

A.122

WARWICK CHINA
JOSEPH HORNE CO.,
PITTSBURGH, PA.
COPYRIGHTED

1920s

A.122 and A.123 are samples of marks found on vitreous hotel type ware made by the Warwick China Co. of Wheeling, West Virginia. These two marks date from the 1920s; however, it is very difficult to date institutional ware unless the mark is dated or unless you have some knowledge about the piece marked. Warwick made institutional ware from World War I to c.1950.

A.123

WARWICK CHINA
CRESCENT CHINA CO,
EAST LIVERPOOL, OHIO.

1920s

See information on p. 193.

A.124

before 1940

A.125

1940s; 1950s

Watt Pottery operated in Crooksville, Ohio, from c.1920 to the 1960s. Later pieces appear to be whiteware. Watt is best known for hand painted ware from the 1940s and especially the 1950s. Mark A.124 was found on an undecorated early piece that appeared to be yellow ware or a cream colored ware. The piece was badly stained. Mark A.125 was found on a large "spaghetti" bowl. Like most Watt ware found today it dates from the 1940s or 1950s. Watt marks are large impressed or molded marks. Many marks are circles with just WATT and/or OVEN WARE. Also, there are usually a number and U.S.A. on the mark.

A.126

W. C. CO.

In his 1897 marks book Jervis showed these W.C. Co. initials as being used on Warwick's knight-in-armor mark. See p. 265. Ramsay and Thorn repeated the mark in their books. For a number of rather technical reasons I believe this is a valid mark. I have not seen the mark.

A.127

This is a mark for the Weller Pottery of Zanesville, Ohio. I have generally not included art pottery marks in this book; however, this mark was not on art pottery. It was found on a very typical baby plate. The only difference was the use of a hand painted decoration rather than the usual decal. Although baby plates were in vogue from World War I to the 1950s, this was probably a 1920s piece.

A.128

The Wheelock Pottery began in the late 1800s in Peoria, Illinois, making common utilitarian pottery. I do not know if they ever developed their own whiteware. At some point, probably before 1920, they became importers of foreign wares. This mark is an example of these foreign imports.

A.129   c.1916 – c.1925

169
(1916)

AVONA is a shape mark of the Taylor, Smith & Taylor Co. of East Liverpool, Ohio. This mark was used from c.1916 to c.1925. The shape itself was a very common one used by many potters both in America and Europe from c.1910 to c.1930. I've seen the shape on dinnerware made by various English companies, on German porcelain including Hutschenreuther and on the whiteware of numerous American potteries. It was one of the most widely used shapes for dinnerware, particularly if slight variations of the shape are included. It was so common that it could have been called a fashion. One segment of the shape is given here below. It is the rim of a dish.

A.130

c.1890

This CALIFORNIA mark was seen too late to be included in the main section of the book. It is a mark of the Knowles, Taylor & Knowles Co. of East Liverpool, Ohio. Gates and Ormerod date the mark c.1890.

A.131

1950s

The following information is speculative but is based on considerable empirical evidence. The Crown Potteries (originally Pottery) Co. continued in Evansville, Indiana, until about 1960; however at about the beginning of the 1950s they ceased making pottery and became distributors only. They had pottery made for them at the W.S. George factory until it closed, and at the Canonsburg Pottery Co., both of Canonsburg, Pennsylvania. During this period one name for their ware was ROYAL TUDOR. Another was ROYAL MONARCH. Based on designs from the Quality Stamp Company as shown in Lois Lehner's 1988 pottery book other names were ROYAL WILTON, ROYAL QUEEN & JARDINE. I suspect others. The key to identification is the crown itself. It is identical to the crown used on Crown Potteries Co. marks of the 1930s and 1940s. See p. 40. ROYAL MONARCH also used another style of crown.

A.132

1950s

This 1950s Homer Laughlin mark was found too late to be included in the main section of the book. This mark is usually dated; however, this one was not.

A.133

c.1960

HARMONY HOUSE was a mark used by Sears, Roebuck & Co. on ware made at various American companies including Homer Laughlin. The mark dates from the 1940s to the 1960s. This particular mark is from the 1960s.

A.134

Although Jackson Vitrified China Co. had a rather long history, nearly all the ware found today dates from the 1930s to the 1950s. These marks, particularly A.134, are the marks usually seen at flea markets. ROYAL JACKSON was also used as a mark on a thinner ware dating from about the same period.

A.135

A.136

MADDOX OF CALIF

676

The mark at left was impressed or inscribed on an old looking white spittoon. Although the mark was MADDOX it undoubtedly was supposed to be MADDUX. Lehner said in her 1980 and 1988 books that Maddux of California started in 1938 in Los Angeles. The piece found with the mark at left must have been one of their earliest.

A.137

MAYER
CHINA

A.138

About 1915 or 1916 the Mayer Pottery Co., or J.& E. Mayer, of Beaver Falls, Pennsylvania, switched to making institutional porcelain. The marks used now included MAYER CHINA. Various versions of the mark shown here were used from c.1915 into the 1930s. It was possibly used into the 1950s. Institutional ware is generally difficult to date. Mayer didn't usually date their hotel ware; consequently, it is difficult to be precise in stating when a particular mark was used unless you know something about the hotel, restaurant or business using the mark. For example, mark A.138 could be dated by knowing when the F.F. DeBolt Co. was in business. I believe this oblong mark was used by Mayer in the 1920s and 1930s. Like mark A.137 it may have been used after the 1930s. After c.1970 Mayer incorporated INTERPACE into their marks.

A.139

O.P.CO.
SYRACUSE
CHINA
1-10

1928

These two SYRACUSE CHINA marks were seen too late to be included in the main section of this book. They are marks of the Onondaga Pottery Co. (later Syracuse China Co.) of Syracuse, New York. Marks A.139 and A.140 were both on the same piece. Unlike most makers of hotel ware, the Onondaga Pottery Co. did use a dating system for their marks. See p. 220. The O.P.CO.; SYRACUSE CHINA mark would date 1928. Thus, the other mark would date the same.

A.140

CHINA
SYRACUSE © OF ART MODERNE

1928

A.141

Ostrow
22 KARAT GOLD

c.1930

Sol Ostrow was the founder of the Hopewell China Co., which operated in Hopewell, Virginia, in the 1920s. About 1929 there was some type of reorganization. The company mark became OSTROW or OSTROW CHINA. The design at left is part of a larger mark. I first believed this design was for WESTROW instead of OSTROW. PRINCESS ANNE was also part of the mark.

A.142

RV

This is a mark of the Roseville Pottery of Roseville and Zanesville, Ohio. It was found on a baby plate, not Roseville's usual art pottery. It dates from the 1920s or a bit earlier.

A.143

According to Lois Lehner in her 1988 pottery book, this SHEFFIELD mark was used on ware made by Homer Laughlin for a distributing concern. Apparently they also distributed foreign wares. It is to be hoped that all those with U.S.A. on their marks were American made. This mark would date from the 1960s and possibly 1970s.

A.144

SHENANGO
NEW CASTLE, PA.
CHINA

A.145

I am not sure when these two Shenango marks were used. Mark A.144 was found on a plain white platter that could have been made almost anytime. The other piece with a plain decoration would be equally hard to date. The Shenango Pottery Co. of New Castle, Pennsylvania, made a hotel type porcelain that, like most hotel ware, is difficult to date. From World War I onward the Shenango Pottery used an Indian on most marks. These two marks were probably used before 1920; however, I would have to see more examples to be sure.

A.146

Smith Phillips
Cordova

c.1920

This CORDOVA mark of the Smith-Phillips China Co. of East Liverpool, Ohio, was seen too late to be included in the main section of the book. See p. 133 for similar marks. This mark dates c. 1920.

A.147

Standard
TRENTON

after c.1915

This is a mark for the Standard Sanitary Pottery Co. founded in 1901. Although they made sanitary ware primarily, this mark was found on a mortar with pestle. After 1915 Thomas Maddock's Sons joined Standard. They made mortars and pestles before 1915. This is probably a mark used on their ware after c.1915. It is impressed. See also p. 86.

A.148

Stangl ®
TRENTON, N.J.
CARNIVAL

1950s

This is another version of the Stangl Pottery Co. mark shown on p. 135. This mark was used in the 1950s. Some patterns were used into the 1960s and later.

A.149

c.1905 – c.1910

The inclusion of U.S.A. and particularly MADE IN U.S.A. is a helpful indicator of the age of American marks. U.S.A. was almost never used on marks before 1900. The only exception was U.S.A. used as location, for example: East Liverpool, Ohio, U.S.A. A few companies did this very infrequently in the 1890s and early 1900s. Often this was done to mark wares that might be exported to other countries. Wares entered in foreign pottery competitions were so marked. The only early marks that set U.S.A. apart were two c.1905 – c.1910 marks of the American China Co. of Toronto, Ohio. One of these marks is shown at left. See p. 15 for the other less frequently used one. The Thomas China Co. also used U.S.A. set apart, but, in this case, U.S.A. would still indicate location. See p. 145.

MADE IN U.S.A. was very seldom used on marks before the 1920s. There are a few exceptions. The 1915 mark at left (See Taylor, Smith & Taylor dating system on p. 141.) is the earliest verifiable use of MADE IN U.S.A. I've seen so far; however, Taylor, Smith & Taylor used MADE IN U.S.A. on very few marks before the 1930s. I've seen a few marks of other companies from 1918 and 1919 with MADE IN U.S.A. but, as a general rule, the term was not used until the 1920s. Many companies, Lenox and Edwin M. Knowles for example, did not use MADE IN U.S.A. on marks until the 1930s.

Note: MADE IN AMERICA was used on one c.1900 Wheeling Pottery Co. mark. See p. 161.

A.150

T.S.T.
VERONA
CHINA

MADE IN U.S.A.

5 10

1915

A.151

K.T. & K.
S————V
CHINA.
REH
WARRANTED
18 CARAT GOLD.

1922

18 CARAT (or KARAT) GOLD and 22 KARAT GOLD on marks are helpful indicators of the age of American marks. 18 CARAT GOLD was used as early as 1922 by the Knowles, Taylor & Knowles Co. if my dating system for that company is correct. See p. 214. It was used by quite a few companies by the late 1920s. The use of 22 KARAT GOLD was common on marks of the 1930s. I don't have any examples of it being used before 1930 although a late 1920s use of it would not surprise me. The use of 22 KARAT GOLD on marks continued from the 1930s to the present. Decorating companies frequently used the term. Often the mark itself is in 22 KARAT GOLD. There are numerous but fairly rare variations of 18 CARAT GOLD and 22 KARAT GOLD. None of these date before the use of 18 CARAT GOLD. They include:

12 KARAT GOLD	19 KARAT GOLD
14 CARAT GOLD	22 K GOLD
18 CARAT COIN GOLD	23 KARAT GOLD

There are other variations including PLATINUM instead of GOLD. WARRANTED is often part of the phrase.

A.152

18 CARAT COIN GOLD
ATLAS CHINA COMPANY

A.153

THE
EDWIN M. KNOWLES
IVORY
29-2-11

1929

A.154

CUNNINGHAM
PICKETT DIV.
TROPIC

A.155

K.T.& K.
IVORY

c.1929

A.156

c.1940 – c.1960

A.157

(used in various marks)

This mark for the Edwin M. Knowles Co. is typical of the various IVORY marks used c.1929. The Sebring Pottery Co. (American Pottery Works) was probably the first to use an IVORY mark in the 1920s. Their IVORY PORCELAIN was patented in 1925 and continued to be made through the 1930s and possibly even later. The Cunningham and Pickett under the mark at left were retailers or jobbers. They did not make whiteware. For more about Cunningham and Pickett, see Lehner's *Complete Book of American Kitchen and Dinner Wares.*

By the late 1920s most American whiteware companies had a product they marked IVORY, often given a special name such as ROYAL IVORY, ANTIQUE IVORY, PRINCESS IVORY. Since many companies were dating their marks in the 1920s, the date for a mark can be verified. I have seen hundreds of these IVORY marks. By far, the most common date for them is 1929. Since many companies failed in 1929 or soon after, the IVORY mark was often a death knell. Knowles, Taylor and Knowles' IVORY mark is a prime example of this. For companies that survived the Great Depression, IVORY marks continued well into the 1930s. This is particularly true of those companies that made hotel ware. Some of these companies continued to use IVORY on marks at least to the 1950s.

The American union movement reached its peak in the 1930s, 1940s and 1950s. During this period union power was reflected on some pottery marks. About 1935 UNION MADE appeared on some marks. From c.1940 to c.1960 the seal of the National Brotherhood of Operative Potters was frequently incorporated in pottery marks. See the example at left. After 1955 A.F. of L. was usually replaced by A.F.L.-C.I.O. in the center of the seal.

The double shield mark is my favorite American (and/or British) mark. The left shield is American; the right one is British. In 1878 or 1879 Edward Clarke (Barber correctly spelled it Clarke in his 1893 book but misspelled it Clark in his 1904 book), a potter from Burslem, England, and James Carr from the New York City Pottery jointly organized the Lincoln Pottery Co. at Trenton, New Jersey, in the old Speeler Works, adopting the double shield mark with Carr and Clarke printed under the shields. Carr and Clarke were helped by John Moses of Trenton's Glasgow Pottery and his younger brother, James Moses, from the Mercer Pottery also of Trenton, New Jersey.

A.158

N.Y. City Pottery mark

A.159

A.160

Just a few months later the partnership ended. Edward Clarke went back to England where, from 1880 to 1887, he used the double shield mark at the Churchyard Works, Burslem. His mark was the same as the Mercer Pottery mark (A.160) shown here. Under the mark was Edward Clarke/Burslem, England.* James Carr returned to the New York City Pottery where he used the double shield mark on cream-colored ware. Barber pictured the Carr double shield mark as using only the words TRADE MARK with the shields.

Carr sold his interest in the company to John Moses, who then proceeded to sell his now half-interest in the company to William Burgess and John A. Campbell. With the leaving of Carr and Clarke, the company became the International Pottery Company in 1879. Burgess and Campbell continued to use the double shield mark with Burgess & Campbell printed under the shields. Edward Clarke sold his interest to Burgess and Campbell at some point. James Moses of the Mercer Pottery Co. may or may not have sold his interest; however, he did remain connected with the company in some way. His Mercer Pottery Co. and the International Pottery Co. of Burgess and Campbell worked together for at least a few years. He used two versions of the double shield mark. One is identical to the Burgess & Campbell mark shown at left; the other, shown below, is identical to the English mark used by Edward Clarke. There must have remained some connection between James Moses and Clarke. It seems more than coincidence that they would use identical marks. In any case, there were five companies using the double shield mark and, except for the short-lived Lincoln Pottery Co., the mark was used at about the same time in both America and England.

To add to this already complicated story, John Wyllie & Son of East Liverpool, Ohio, used the double shield as part of some of their marks; however, since it is an elaboration of the original mark it would most certainly date after the other marks. See p. 164. I do not know why this company used the double shield. Perhaps Mr. Wyllie had some connection with one of the other companies. He was originally from England.

*I've seen the Edward Clarke mark with Tunstall instead of Burslem.

A.161

UNDERWOOD'S
HIGH CHAIR BABY PLATE
PAT'D JUNE 11, 1912

This mark was found on a baby plate. The 1912 date is quite early for a baby plate. I know nothing about Underwood.

A.162

The Ovington Brothers Co. was a distributor of whiteware. This c.1910 red mark was seen on an English looking piece of semi-porcelain. Ovington Bros. may have distributed and marked both American and foreign wares.

A.163

A.E.T.CO. LTD.

This is a mark of the American Encaustic Tile Co., which operated in Zanesville, Ohio, between 1879 and c. 1930. The mark was found on a tile with a blue and white Delft-type decoration. The tile would not be whiteware but the decoration made it look like whiteware.

A.164

KIRKHAM
Art Tile
Pottery Co.
BARBERTON, O.

No information available on this company.

A.165

PAUL REVERE POTTERY

This impressed mark was found on a piece of art pottery. It was dated 1935. There are other marks for the Paul Revere Pottery including S.E.G. for Saturday Evening Girls. See also p. 122.

A.166

This mark was found on a set of flow blue dishes. Apparently the mark is not English. I have not been able to determine the maker. The dishes date before 1900.

A.167

XX CENTURY
SEMI
PORCELAIN

I've seen this mark a few times. The last time was on a pitcher with an interesting floral flow blue decoration comparable to the "LA BELLE" flow blue decoration of the Wheeling Pottery Co. I don't know if the mark is English or American. Godden doesn't have it in his definitive marks book. It is probably American, dating from the early 1900s. The mark may have been used on flow blue ware exclusively.

A.168

ᵶARCO
DE SOTO
E. Palestine
O.

This mark was found on a typical piece of Ohio whiteware. The first letter of the initials was blurred. It may be LARCO or CARCO – possibly something else. I have not been able to determine the company of manufacture.

A.169

This decorator's mark was found on a LIDO shaped plate of the W.S. George Co. The George mark was also on the plate. Based on the decoration I would date the mark, and thus the decorating company itself, c.1950. I believe W.S. George's LIDO shape was introduced in the 1930s or very late 1920s. The Dorlexa China Co. was a reorganized S. Alexander & Sons, New York, New York.

A.170

LIDO
W.S. GEORGE
CANARYTONE
MADE IN U.S.A.
I 8 8 A

A.171

This decorating company mark was found on a gold decorated shaving mug that date c.1900 or a bit later.

A.172

THUEMLER MFG.
PITTSBURGH,PA.

This company's mark is found on advertising mugs, etc. of the early 1900s.

A.173

CLARKSBURG,
WEST VIRGINIA

This mark was found on a souvenir plate with various scenic spots of West Virginia highlighted. It appeared to be a 1950s or 1960s product. The ware marked was typical American semi-porcelain. I don't know if the Laurel China Co., Inc. was a manufacturer or a distributor of whiteware. Attempts to obtain information about the company from the Clarksburg, West Virginia, public library have failed. Laurel probably operated in the old McNicol plant. See p. 94.

A.174

SAMPLE MARK

As a general rule the California whiteware industry was a phenomenon of the period 1930 to 1960. Jo Cunningham's *The Collector's Encyclopedia of American Dinnerware* has a concise history and marks of the major California makers of whiteware. Lois Lehner's 1980 and 1988 books also have considerable information.

A.175

ENGLISH MARK

This English Maddock mark is quite similar to one American Maddock mark. The American mark was probably designed to look like the English one. See p. 87 for the American mark. Both the English and American marks were printed in the same brown color – at least in all the examples I've seen. Ironically the American marked ware is generally superior to the British ware so marked.

A.176

ENGLISH MARK

F.B. & Co.
F.

This is an English mark. I included it here because it is the only English mark that fooled me into believing it to be American. I found the mark on a plate in a stack of plates I was checking. They were mostly American – some fairly old. This mark looks like a French Limoges mark, but the plate was ordinary whiteware, not French porcelain. I recorded the mark as American to be researched later. It is, however, a mark of Frank Beardmore & Co. of Fenton, England. Although a 20th century product, the word ENGLAND was not a part of the mark. This mark is not typical of the English marks one usually finds in this country.

A.177

Unidentified Shape or Pattern Marks

I don't know anything about this mark except that it is old. I found it on a toilet set of five or so pieces. Only the larger pieces were marked. I am sure the set would date before 1900. Based on shape and decoration, I would not be surprised if it dated c.1880.

A.178

This unidentified mark would date before 1900.

A.179

This mark would date c. 1900 or a bit earlier.

A.180

This is a c.1900 mark. It is possibly a mark for the Steubenville Pottery Co. See p. 137.

A.181

This c.1900 pottery mark is possibly for the Dresden Pottery Co. (Potters' Cooperative Co.) See p. 43.

A.182

FLORENCE

This impressed mark was found on a plain white gravy boat that could date from the late 1800s or early 1900s.

A.183

This unidentified mark would date c.1900.

A.184

1930S

This unidentified mark dates from the 1930s. Quite possibly this is a mark for the Taylor, Smith & Taylor Co.

A.185

A.186

These two marks from John Ramsay were listed for the New York City Pottery. Ramsay's marks are usually quite simplified. Some seem to be drawn from memory, resulting in inevitable mistakes. This can be seen by comparing marks that both he and Barber included in their books. See p. 104 for Barber's marks for the New York City Pottery.

A.187

(British mark)

Ramsay listed this mark as being for the Anchor Pottery Co. of Trenton, New Jersey. Barber had no marks for this company with A.P. initials. See pp. 18 and 19. However, the Anchor Porcelain Co. of Staffordshire, England, did use initials with their anchor mark. If the ware in question is true porcelain, the mark would undoubtedly be for the English company. If the ware is common whiteware, the mark would likely be for the Anchor Pottery Co. of the United States. Keep in mind Ramsay's marks are usually quite simplified and the actual anchor mark may be more than a little different from this mark.

A.188

John Ramsay listed this mark for the C.C. Thompson Pottery Co. I doubt the validity of this mark but felt that it should at least be included.

A.189

This mark from John Ramsay is a mistake. The mark correctly reads BURGESS & CAMPBELL. There was also a Burroughs & Mountford Co. in Trenton. I am rather sure there was never a collaboration between Burgess and Mountford.

A.190

Ramsay illustrated this mark for Thomas Maddock & Sons. Barber showed a similar mark. This is likely a true, if simplified, Maddock mark. See p. 86. I can find no British company this mark could represent. Any anchor mark with T.M.& S. is probably for Thomas Maddock & Sons Co.

A.191

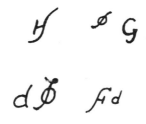

Ramsay illustrated these incised marks for porcelain from the Columbian Art Pottery Co. of Morris and Willmore in Trenton, New Jersey. Since this company made much art pottery, these marks were probably artists' signatures and they may have accompanied the company's shield mark used on belleek ware. See p. 35. These marks may never have been used alone. Barber made no mention of such incised marks for this company.

American Pottery Dating Systems

Many pottery marks incorporate numbers within them, above them, or below them. These numbers can mean many things. Sometimes they represent dates. Often these are the dates for the beginning of the companies. Often such dates are highly exaggerated. Usually they indicate the earliest attempts of the family at pottery making. Such dates are meaningless for determining when pottery marks were used and frequently meaningless for true historical reasons. In the 1880s and 1890s a few companies began to date a few marks. The Mayer Pottery Co. actually began using a dating system in the 1890s. See pp. 218 and 219. Also, a few early marks included a patent date. The mark would date in that year or a few years thereafter. This is true of the Edwin Bennett Pottery Co. and the New York City Pottery. The Sebring Pottery Co. (American Pottery Works) patented their famous IVORY PORCELAIN in 1925 but marks with this date were still being used in the late 1930s and possibly later. However, as a general rule, most pieces with a patent date will have been made soon after the year of the patent.

In the first decade of the twentieth century several companies instituted the use of true dating systems they continued to use for many years. The Mayer Pottery Co., which had instituted their system in the 1890s, quit using it early in the 1900s. The earliest companies to institute dating systems in the 1900s were Knowles, Taylor & Knowles, Edwin M. Knowles China Co., and the Smith-Phillips China Co. The Knowles, Taylor & Knowles Co. was probably the earliest. These and many other American dating systems are discussed in this section. Other than the many old marks included in this book and found nowhere else, this section has the most important, previously unpublished, information. The dating systems included herein are also included individually in the main section of this book accompanying the corresponding company.

1. American Pottery Works or Sebring Pottery Co.

This company generally didn't date their marks; however, they did date the mark shown below.

S. P. Co.
S——V
SEBRING,O.
E 19

(1919)

This S.-V. (for SEMI-VITREOUS) mark was used by many companies in the first three decades of this century. The Knowles, Taylor & Knowles Co. was the first to use and date this mark beginning in 1905. The Sebring Pottery Co. used and dated this mark between c.1919 and c.1930. They used the mark undated between c.1914 and c.1918. See the two dated examples at left. The letter accompanying the number may indicate the month of manufacture.

S. P. Co.
S——V
SEBRING,O.
H 30

(1930)

2. Bailey-Walker China Co.

See Walker China Co. for a discussion of both companies' dating systems.

3. Cleveland China Co./ George H. Bowman Co.

(1922)

Like numerous American companies, Cleveland China dated many of their marks in the 1920s. See example at left. This CLEVELAND CHINA mark was used undated from c.1910 to c.1920.

4. Crooksville China Co.

I have been able to decipher only part of the Crooksville dating puzzle.

IVORA
CROOKSVILLE
CHINA CO,
729

(1929)

Most of the marks used by Crooksville after c.1920 had numbers or two letters under the mark. The numbers indicate a very simple dating system, the last two digits indicating the year. For example: 729 is for 1929 (the earliest I've yet seen); 730 is for 1930; 337 for 1937; 1040 for 1940; 345 for 1945; etc. The first digit or two digits probably represent the month. Marks with two letters under them may also indicate a dating system. See paragraph below. See also p. 39 for more information that might help you to date Crooksville marks.

CROOKSVILLE
CHINA CO,
834

(1934)

My current thinking is that the first letter under the mark (letters A-K seen so far) is the month of manufacture. The second letter (P-X seen so far) is for the year. I believe R is 1926, S – 1927, T – 1928, U – 1929, V – 1930, W – 1931, X – 1932. See two examples below.

CROOKSVILLE
CHINA CO.
345

(1945)

CROOKSVILLE
U.S.A. C-U

(possibly March 1929)

CROOKSVILLE
CHINA CO.
U.S.A. D-S

(possibly April 1927)

5. Crown Pottery Co.

This company did not date its marks until the 1930s and 1940s. See examples of these dated marks on p. 40.

6. Dresden Pottery (Potters' Cooperative Co.)

Like many American companies, this company dated their 1920s marks. They used a variety of marks in the 1920s. See examples of these dated marks on p. 44. They dated a few early marks. See p. 42.

7. Fraunfelter China Co.

This company did not generally date their marks; however, I saw one Fraunfelter mark dated 1938 about the time the company ended.

8. French China Co.

This company used a fleur-de-lis mark with LA FRANCAISE in the early 1900s. The mark usually had a letter and a number under it; however, because the number was almost always blurred, I'm not sure if this was really a dated mark. The company used several plain marks from c.1917 to c.1929. These marks are always dated as shown below. The two digit number on each of these marks is the year the mark was used. For example: 19 is for 1919, 20 is for 1920, 26 is for 1926, etc. This is a simple dating system. Note the inconsistency in the placing of the two digit number. Note also the 6A under the one mark. This is almost certainly 1926; however, this does show the difficulties involved with dating systems that are not always consistent. See the Saxon China Co. dating system on p. 221. The Saxon Co. was a sister company to the French China Co.

F. C. Co. A——18 CHINA (1918)	F. C. Co. 20 3 (1920)	F. C. Co. MARTHA WASHINGTON B 25 (1925)	F. C. Co. MARTHA WASHINGTON 6 A (1926)	F. C. Co. 26-3 (1926)	F. C. Co. 1 27 (1927)

9. W.S. George Pottery Co.

This company used letters and numbers under most of their marks from the 1920s, 1930s and 1940s. Although it seems likely these numbers and letters indicate a dating system, thus far, I've been unable to decipher it. One problem is that very often part of the number and letter series is blurred. On the last page of this chapter is a long list of W.S. George marks with letters and numbers. Perhaps some reader can solve the puzzle of the W.S. George dating system, if, in fact, the company used a coherent dating system. See p. 226.

10. Hall China Co.

MADE IN U.S.A.

633

This company frequently used numbers on their marks. They may or may not indicate a dating system. If it is a dating system, it isn't an obvious one. For example, the 633 under the mark at left does not indicate 1933. Because Hall used some marks for 50 years or more it would be quite helpful to learn their dating system, if they had one. I've not yet made a serious attempt to determine if the numbers on Hall marks do indicate a dating system.

11. Hopewell China Co.

This 1920s company dated most of their marks. See examples of these marks on p. 63.

12. Edwin M. Knowles China Co.

From 1901 to 1909 the vase (or urn) mark shown below will have no numbers or two digits under the mark. The numbers on these early marks are usually blurred. The earliest one that I could read was 83. The 8 was clear, the 3 was not; thus, the second digit may be a letter not a number. From 1910 to 1914 there are three digits under the mark. From 1915 to c.1930 there are three separate numbers under the mark. The first two digits (one before 1910) always indicates the year on an Edwin M. Knowles mark during this period. The following numbers are from actual marks.

83 for 1908
101 for 1910
112 for 1911
133 for 1913
15 1 11 for 1915
16–2–4 for 1916
23–3 6 for 1923
24–1–11 for 1924
30 2–3 for 1930

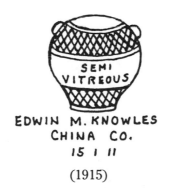

EDWIN M. KNOWLES
CHINA CO.
15 1 11

(1915)

The vase may say VITREOUS or SEMI-VITREOUS. VITREOUS was first used c.1915 or a bit earlier. SEMI-VITREOUS was used from 1901 onward.

About 1925 Knowles began to use other marks. Their IVORY mark dates c.1925 to c.1929. All examples I've seen continued to use the dating system given above. Samples of these IVORY marks are given on the next page.

THE
EDWIN M. KNOWLES
IVORY
26-1-12

(1926)

THE
EDWIN M. KNOWLES
IVORY
29-2-11

(1929)

I believe during the 1930s, except 1930 itself, the vase mark was never used. The mark used was the ship mark given below. There are now two separate numbers under the mark. The first indicates the year; the second indicates the month. The ship mark is said to have been used before the 1930s; so far, I have not seen one.

32–2 1932 (Feb.)
34–12 1934 (Dec.)
35–3 1935 (Mar.)
38–10 1938 (Oct.)

36-4   (1936 – April)

MADE IN U.S.A. was used after 1930.

During the 1930s Knowles introduced a few marks that seldom, if ever, used the dating system. In most cases the ship mark did use the dating system.

During the 1940s the vase mark was again in use; however, it is a bit different from the earlier mark. The cross hatching is wider on the later mark. See comparison below:

EARLY MARK
(bottom of vase)

6 central diamonds

LATER MARK
(bottom of vase)

5 central diamonds

The dating system of the 1940s is the same as the 1930s system.

43–1 1943 (Jan.)
45–8 1945 (Aug.)
46–2 1946 (Feb.)
48–8 1948 (Aug.)

EDWIN M. KNOWLES
CHINA CO.
MADE IN U.S.A.
46-2

MADE IN U.S.A.
was used after 1930.

On some 1948 marks the word KNOWLES is printed across the vase. The numbers under the mark have no relation to the dating system described above. It seems that in 1948 this company abandoned their dating of marks in any consistent way. Some later marks follow the system, many do not.

13. Knowles, Taylor & Knowles Co.

The Knowles, Taylor and Knowles Co. dating system is still tentative. I believe it to be correct; however, I've not yet acquired enough confirming dating information to declare the system absolute. With one possible exception, I have not discovered any information that would invalidate the system.

The Knowles, Taylor & Knowles dating system is probably the oldest in East Liverpool, Ohio. Two K.T. & K. marks I have seen were dated 1904; one may have been dated 1900. Gates and Ormerod show one Smith-Phillips mark dated 1904 in code. See p. 222 for the Smith-Phillips dating system. The following information may need some refinement, particularly before 1905. From 1905 to 1926 the system is probably accurate. After 1926 there are again some unanswered questions.

The following two marks are the only ones used in the Knowles, Taylor and Knowles dating system.

K.T.&K.CO.
326
(1906)

This Eagle mark was used from c.1900 to c.1915. This one dates 1906.

K.T.&K.
S——V
CHINA
145
(1905)

This S.V. mark was used from 1905 to 1926. Letters replace numbers after 1914. See next page. This mark dates 1905.

The following three-digit numbers were found under the Eagle mark above at left. The third digit indicates the year.

334 1904
315 1905

The number 220 was found under one of the two marks shown above. I failed to record which one it was. If it was under the Eagle mark it would most likely indicate 1900. If found under the S.V. mark it would not. The S.V. mark was not used until c.1905.

From 1905 to 1915 the system dated both the Eagle mark and the S.V. mark the same way. From 1905 to 1909 the last of three digits indicate the year. From 1910 to 1915 the last two of four digits indicate the year.

145 — 1905	2210 — 1910
315 — 1905	3410 — 1910
236 — 1906	3012 — 1912
248 — 1908	

The Eagle mark was probably discontinued in 1914. It was used until then with dates. In 1915 the numbers under the mark were replaced with letters. The system now has three letters under the S.V. mark. I've seen no Eagle marks with letters under the mark. If there are, they would be using the same system. The third letter under the mark now indicates the year.

K.T. & K.
S———V
CHINA.
S D F

(1920)

K.T. & K.
S———V
CHINA.
V H L

(1926)

S H A — 1915	R H G — 1921
R G B — 1916	P G H — 1922
– –C — 1917	S H I — 1923
– –D — 1918	R D J — 1924
– –E — 1919	– –K — 1925
S D F — 1920	V H L — 1926

In 1927 the mark became a 27 between two other numbers. For example: 3 27 4

After 1927 the system seems to work as follows: Under the mark is a number, a second number indicating the year, and an A or B.

48A — 1928
39B — 1929
41B — 1931 (?)

K.T. & K.
S———V
IVORY.
49 B

(1929)

Although Knowles, Taylor and Knowles failed in 1929 and became a part of the American Chinaware Corp., it is not unlikely they continued to use their old mark until 1931. See above. In her 1982 book Jo Cunningham shows the Pope-Gosser name on a 1931 American Chinaware Corp. mark. Although Pope-Gosser was a member of the corporation, Knowles, Taylor and Knowles was the leading member and, thus, most likely to continue to use their old mark. All activities ceased in 1931.

NOTE: As originally stated, the K.T. & K. dating system is still tentative.

14. Homer Laughlin China Co.

The Homer Laughlin dating system has been widely publicized. The information is usually given as provided by that company. In my earlier book I tried to combine this company information with my own research. After several more years of research, I can say that the company supplied information is generally reliable with the exception of the first ten years; consequently, contrary to the common consensus, Homer Laughlin was not the first to use a dating system. They were not even the earliest East Liverpool, Ohio, company to date their wares. Knowles, Taylor and Knowles, Edwin M. Knowles, Smith-Phillips and possibly others were ahead of them. The Knowles, Taylor and Knowles Co. was probably first. The Mayer Pottery Co. (J. & E. Mayer) of Beaver Falls, Pennsylvania, had all of the East Liverpool, Ohio, companies beat. See p. 89.

Below are the two versions of the Homer Laughlin monogram and signature mark used from c.1900 to c.1930.

(c.1900 to 1919)   (1920 to c.1930)

The following information will help the collector to quickly distinguish between pre-1920 and post-1920 Homer Laughlin marks without dealing with the dating system. Every pre-1920 mark I have seen conforms to the first sample mark shown above. Every post-1920 mark conforms to the second sample mark shown above. I have studied so many marks that I can say the distinction is absolute. In 7 years I've not seen a single exception! Any exception to the rule would be very rare. Concerning the two marks, note the difference between the first *L*s of the two LAUGHLINS. Also, note the horizontal line connecting the *H* and *C* of the monogram. On the earlier mark the line goes through the left vertical line of the *H* and through the *C* (or right vertical line of the *H*) on the right. It does not on the later mark. Below is given a Homer Laughlin mark used in the 1960s and later. It has the open loop on the first *L* of LAUGHLIN; however, note the different monogram style. Also MADE IN U.S.A. was never used on pre-1920 Homer Laughlin marks.

(1960s and later)

215

MADE IN U.S.A. was not used on Homer Laughlin marks until 1922. The study of hundreds of this company's marks has uncovered only one possible exception to the rule. This mark possibly indicated a 1921 use of MADE U.S.A.

Below are given the details of the Homer Laughlin dating system in reality, not in theory. On p. 225 is given the information as presented in my earlier book.

1900 – 1910:

According to the theory, Homer Laughlin marks during this period had three numbers under the mark. The first indicated the month (1 to 12); the second indicated the year (0 to 9); the third number indicated the factory (1 to 3).

I have not seen even one verifiable dated mark from this period. I have seen some blurred marks that might be from this period. If Homer Laughlin did date these early marks, it was quite infrequently. Personally, I don't believe they dated their 1900 to 1910 marks. I'll have to see a verifiable mark to believe it.

What one does find from this period are monogram with signature marks accompanied by an identifying shape or pattern word. These marks are given below. HUDSON seems to be the most common. It was used from 1903 (from calendar plates) to c.1920 (possibly later). The other marks are less frequently found. If there are no numbers under the mark, it was used before c.1910. If the mark has numbers and a letter under the mark, see the 1910 to 1919 part of the dating system given next page.

HOMER LAUGHLIN
Hudson

(1903 – c.1920)

HOMER LAUGHLIN
The Angelus

(c.1908 – c.1915)

HOMER LAUGHLIN
Colonial

(before 1910)

HOMER LAUGHLIN
Niagara

(c.1909)

Before 1910 these marks will not have the dating system. GENESEE was probably not used in this early period; however, if found without numbers, it would indicate a pre-1910 usage. See next page. Gates and Ormerod also mentioned a KING CHARLES and a REPUBLIC mark. I've not yet seen these marks.

1910 – 1919:

During this period the dating system began to be used in fact, not just in theory. The first number under the mark is the month (1–12) of manufacture. The second single digit number is for the year. The third part is a letter (or letter with number) indicating the factory. They include N, L, and N5.

4 1 L	April 1911	factory L
8 2 N	August 1912	factory N
10 3 N	Oct. 1913	factory N
1 4 L	Jan. 1914	factory L
5 5 N	May 1915	factory N
5 6 L	May 1916	factory L
12 7 N5	Dec. 1917	factory N5
3 8 N	March 1918	factory N
7 9 L	July 1919	factory L

HOMER LAUGHLIN
Genesee
5 6 L

(1916)

The 1911 and 1912 dates given above are simulated. The earliest Homer Laughlin mark with a date that I have seen is 1913.

NOTE: During this period the year is given only as a single digit.

1920 and 1921:

During this period the number for the year (1920 or 1921) is probably always a 20 or 21. The monogram and the signature have changed slightly. See p. 215.

2 20 N5	Feb. 1920	factory N5
3 20 L	March 1920	factory L
8 21 N	Aug. 1921	factory N
12 21 N	Dec. 1921	factory N

HOMER LAUGHLIN
2 20 N5

(1920)

This mark is possibly an exception to the rule above. It is the only Homer Laughlin mark I've found that does not fit the rules as given in this book. This is possibly for Jan. 1921; factory N. If so, it is a very rare exception to the rule. Possibly it is just an incorrect or incomplete mark. It is definitely not a mark for Jan. 1911!

HOMER LAUGHLIN
MADE IN U.S.A.
1 1 N

(1921?)

1922 – 1929:

From 1922 to 1929 the system works as follows: a letter (A to L) has replaced the month number; the single digit number in the middle is the year (1922 to 1929); the factory letter (or letter with number) is last. MADE IN U.S.A. was first used on Homer Laughlin marks in 1922. (See previous page for a possible 1921 use of MADE IN U.S.A.)

L 2 N	Dec. 1922	factory N
B 3 N	Feb. 1923	factory N
K 4 L	Nov. 1924	factory L
D 5 N5	April 1925	factory N5
F 6 L	June 1926	factory L
J 7 N5	Oct. 1927	factory N5
A 8 N	Jan. 1928	factory N
C 9 N	March 1929	factory N

Sample mark:

HOMER LAUGHLIN
MADE IN U.S.A.
K 3 N

(1923)

1930 and later:

From 1930 onward the dating system is quite simple. The middle two digit number is the year.

B 33 N4 is for 1933; D 42 N5 is for 1942; K 55 N5 is for 1955; etc.

Note: From 1930 onward many Homer Laughlin marks were not dated.

15. Limoges China Co.

Like many American companies, this company dated their 1920s and, in this case, some 1930s marks. See examples on p. 85.

16. Mayer Pottery Co.

The Mayer Pottery Co. instituted a dating system in the 1890s. I have not seen enough of their dated marks to determine just when the system started. For example, the mark at right could date 1890 or 1900. The first mark probably dates 1899. On next page is another Mayer mark that is frequently dated.

(probably Aug. 1899)

(April 1900?)

After 1900 the stone china mark given on the previous page was discontinued. The Pennsylvania Coat of Arms mark continued to be used now with IRON STONE CHINA as well as SEMI-VITREOUS above the mark. See p. 90. There are numbers on both sides of these marks. The number on the left is probably the month and the number on the right is probably the year. Again, I have not seen enough of these marks to be positive. Also, I'm not sure how far into the 1900s these marks continued to be used. Be that as it may, the Mayer Pottery Co. was the first American company to institute a regular dating system.

(August 1901?)

(c.1900 – c.1910)

(January 1902?)

(c.1900 – c.1910)

(March 1901?)

(c.1900 – c.1910)

17. D.E. McNicol Pottery Co.

D.E. McNicol used the mark given below from c.1915 (possibly earlier) to c.1929. Before 1920 they used two numbers under the mark. These two numbers probably determine the year of manufacture. I've not yet decoded the dating system used. In 1920 a fourth D.E. McNicol factory opened in East Liverpool, Ohio. From 1920 to 1929 the mark had three letters under it. The first letter indicates one of the East Liverpool factories (V, W, X or Z). The other two letters are probably a dating system. Although I've seen many of these marks, I have not been able to decode the system. In any case, three letters indicate a 1920s mark. D.E. McNicol also had a Clarksburg, West Virginia, factory that dated their 1920s marks in a traditional way. See below.

D. E. McNicol

EAST LIVERPOOL, O.

8 9

(c.1915 – c.1920)

D.E. McNicol

EAST LIVERPOOL, O.

X F S

(c.1920 – c.1929)

D. E. McNicol

CLARKSBURG, W.VA.

10 25

(1925)

18. T.A. McNicol Pottery Co.

Like many American companies, T.A. McNicol dated their 1920s marks. See p. 95.

19. Mount Clemens Pottery

This company dated their early marks particularly those from the 1930s. See p. 99.

20. Onondaga Pottery Co.

Onondaga is said to have used marks with a number in a circle from 1903 to 1911 and a number in a diamond from 1912 to 1919. I've seen no such marks; however, they definitely did date their marks from 1920 to 1959. There is a number and a letter under the mark. Sometimes the number is first; sometimes the letter is first. The letter is for the year of manufacture. The number is probably for the month. After 1945, two letters give the year.

A for 1920	V for 1941		
B for 1921	W for 1942		
C for 1922	X for 1943		
D for 1923	Y for 1944		
E for 1924	Z for 1945		
F for 1925	AA for 1946		
G for 1926	BB for 1947		
H for 1927	CC for 1948		
I for 1928	DD for 1949		
J for 1929	EE for 1950		
K for 1930	FF for 1951		
L for 1931	GG for 1952		
M for 1932	HH for 1953		
N for 1933	II for 1954		
O for 1934	JJ for 1955		
P for 1935	KK for 1956		
Q for 1936	LL for 1957		
R for 1397	MM for 1958		
S for 1938	NN for 1959		
T for 1939			
U for 1940			

O. P. CO.
SYRACUSE
- CHINA -
F-10

(1925)

O. P. CO.
SYRACUSE
CHINA
N - 1

(1933)

O. P. CO.
SYRACUSE
CHINA
1 - 10

(1928)

O. P. CO.
SYRACUSE
CHINA
5 - F

GLENDALE
COPYRIGHTED 1923

(1925)

GLENDALE was found with the 1925 mark above right. COPYRIGHTED 1923 does not determine the date, just the earliest possible date for the mark.

9 - KK
SYRACUSE
China

(1956)

8 - NN
SYRACUSE
China
U.S.A.

(1959)

I have not attempted to date any marks beyond 1959.

21. Edward J. Owen China Co.

Like many American companies, Owen China dated many of their 1920s marks. See p. 110.

22. Paden City Pottery Co.

Paden City dated most of their marks from the 1930s, 1940s and 1950s. The mark usually has a letter and a two digit number. Examples are E 33 for 1933, B 34 for 1934, H 45 for 1945, and G 51 for 1951. The letter is probably for the month. Once in a while, some other dating system seems to be used; however, the simple one given here is far more common. See also p. 111.

23. Wellsville China Co. (originally Pioneer Pottery Co.)

Like many American companies, Wellsville dated many of their 1920s marks. See p. 117.

24. Pope-Gosser China Co.

Pope-Gosser dated their 1920s marks and also some marks of the late teens. See example below. They used this same mark again in the 1940s and again dated the mark at least in the early 1940s. See example below. Pope-Gosser seems to have dated few marks after the early 1940s; however, a wreath mark used in the 1950s was dated once in a while. See pp. 118 and 119 for more information about Pope-Gosser and for a sample wreath mark.

POPE-GOSSER
– . –
· CHINA ·
MADE IN U.S.A.
K 24

(1924)

POPE-GOSSER
– . –
· CHINA ·
MADE IN U.S.A.
ROSE POINT
41

(1941)

25. Royal China Co.

This company dated some of their 1950s marks. I've seen none dated before 1950 or after 1959. See example on p. 123. Royal also dated other marks in the 1950s. Not all marks used in the 1950s were dated.

26. Saxon China Co.

S. C. Co.
───────
MARTHA
WASHINGTON
5 B
(1925)

S.C.Co.
──────
4 A
(1924)

Saxon dated their plain marks from the 1920s. These marks are virtually identical to the plain marks used by Saxon's sister company, the French China Co., in the 1920s. See p. 210 for these more commonly seen French China Co. marks.

27. Smith-Phillips China Co.

The Smith-Phillips Co. used an unusual dating system in the early 1900s. The dates for this system are from *The East Liverpool, Ohio, Pottery District* by Gates and Ormerod. I have seen these Smith-Phillips marks and suspected they indicated a dating system but I would not have known the starting date for them. The earliest mark I've seen and the earliest given by Gates and Ormerod was the 1904 mark given below. Company records indicated that Smith-Phillips used the first mark in 1903. If true, then Smith-Phillips may have instituted a dating system before Knowles, Taylor & Knowles. See p. 213. As of now the earliest dated marks I've seen for both companies are for 1904.

| (1903) | (1904) | (1905) | (1906; early 1907) |

Note: The Smith-Phillips mark shown above was used for many years without the dating ticks under the mark. See p. 132.

The Smith-Phillips China Co. also used a more traditional dating system from c.1915 through the 1920s. See pp. 132 and 133 for samples of this later Smith-Phillips dating system.

28. Southern Potteries, Inc.

Like many American companies, Southern Potteries dated many of their 1920s marks. The mark used by Southern Potteries in the 1920s was called CLINCHFIELD CHINA. See p. 134.

29. Standard Pottery Co.

Like many American companies, the Standard Pottery Co. dated many of their 1920s marks. See p. 134.

30. Steubenville Pottery Co.

The Steubenville Pottery dated their primary 1920s mark. This mark is given on p. 138.

31. Taylor, Smith & Taylor Co.

I spent 6 years recording the numbers under T.S. & T. (or T.S.T.) marks before I was able to decipher their dating system. I believe all, or nearly all, Taylor, Smith & Taylor marks used c.1914 to c.1940 were dated. Marks of the 1940s were seldom dated. In the 1950s some T.S.T. marks were again dated. MADE IN U.S.A. was used as early as 1915, the year after their dating system seems to have been instituted. I believe Taylor, Smith, Taylor and Smith-Phillips were the first companies to use MADE IN U.S.A. on their marks, both introducing the practice before 1920; however, neither used the phrase frequently. Most T.S. & T. marks from the period do not have MADE IN U.S.A. See p. 199 for more about MADE IN U.S.A.

The only confusing thing about the T.S.T. dating system is that some number series begin with a 1 and some do not. I can't explain this.

Sample number series:

From 1914 to 1921 the middle digit (two digits in 1920) is the year, if there is a preceding 1.

4	3	for	1914
5	10	for	1915
1 7	10	for	1917
1 8	9	for	1918
1 9	1	for	1919
1 9	3	for	1919
1 20	7	for	1920
1 20	8	for	1920
1 20		for	1920

Sample number series:

From 1921 to 1929 the final two digits are for the year.

1 8	21	for	1921
8	21	for	1921
1	23	for	1923
6	23	for	1923
10	24	for	1924
1 11	24	for	1924
1 11	25	for	1925
1	26	for	1926
1 7	26	for	1926
4	27	for	1927
1 11	27	for	1927
12	27	for	1927
3	29	for	1929

Sample number series:

In the 1930s the date is usually the two middle digits.

1 30 1	for	1930
11 33 1	for	1933
3 36 6	for	1936
39	for	1939

Marks of the 1940s and 1950s were seldom dated. When dated, they continued the 1930s system.

One Special Note: One BELVA CHINA mark seen had PTD under it along with the number dating system. See p. 144. The other BELVA CHINA marks I've seen had 1920s dates (numbers) under them. Perhaps, in imitation of the Knowles, Taylor & Knowles Co., they used letters for dating for a short period of time. Out of dozens of T.S. & T. marks seen, this was the only one with letters under it.

MADE IN U.S.A.:
Taylor, Smith, Taylor used MADE IN U.S.A. on their marks as early as 1915; however, the phrase was infrequently used until the 1930s. From the 1930s on most marks included MADE IN U.S.A. or just U.S.A.

32. Union Porcelain Works

Some of the decorating shop marks used by this company between 1879 and c. 1904 included a date. See p. 152.

33. United States Pottery Co.

This company continued to use marks of the East Liverpool Potteries Co. into the 1920s. Their ELPCO mark of the 1920s was dated. See p. 154.

34. Walker China Co. (originally Bailey-Walker China Co.)

The Bailey-Walker China Co. that preceded the Walker China Co. dated some of their 1920s marks using a traditional dating system. See first mark below.

The Walker China Co. dating system is unique. It is the only American dating system I know that seems blatantly deceptive. To get the correct date, you add 22 to the number given under the mark. (See p. 157 for an explanation.) For example: 34 is for 1956. See sample Walker marks below.

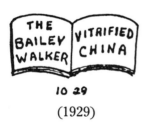

(1929)

(1954)

(1963)

35. Warwick China Co.

This company dated their helmet and crossed swords mark in the 1940s. I don't believe it was dated earlier than this. Other marks were infrequently dated.

36. Wellsville China Co. See p. 221.

37. West End Pottery Co.

Like many American companies, this company dated their 1920s marks. I've seen one 1919 dated West End mark. See p. 160.

Odds and Ends

1. Buffalo Pottery Co.

The Buffalo Pottery Co. was not included in the main part of AMERICAN DATING SYSTEMS because they did not really use a dating system. They simply dated their marks. For example: 1909 is for 1909, 1916 is 1916, etc. See sample marks on p. 168. Although they began production in 1903, the earliest date I've seen on a Buffalo Pottery mark was 1906.

2. Homer Laughlin Dating System

This is basically the dating system provided by the company. This is how I understood Homer Laughlin's system in 1986. Readers may have seen this in other books. It is offered here so the reader can compare it to my original research. The revised system is given in the main section of "American Dating Systems" on pp. 215 to 218.

Homer Laughlin's Dating System (1900 onward) is as follows:

1900–1920   There are three numbers on the mark: the first number (1–12) is for the month of the year; the second number (0–20) represents the year; the final number (from 1910 it's a letter) indicates the factory where the item was made.

1900	(1–12)	0	factory no. (1,2,3)	1910	(1–12)	10	factory letter
1901	(1–12)	1	factory no.	1911	(1–12)	11	factory letter
1902	(1–12)	2	factory no.	1912	(1–12)	12	factory letter
1903	(1–12)	3	factory no.	1913	(1–12)	13	factory letter
1904	(1–12)	4	factory no.	1914	(1–12)	14	factory letter
1905	(1–12)	5	factory no.	1915	(1–12)	15	factory letter
1906	(1–12)	6	factory no.	1916	(1–12)	16	factory letter
1907	(1–12)	7	factory no.	1917	(1–12)	17	factory letter
1908	(1–12)	8	factory no.	1918	(1–12)	18	factory letter
1909	(1–12)	9	factory no.	1919	(1–12)	19	factory letter
				1920	(1–12)	20	

There may be some deviation from the above system. A single digit may be used for the years 1911 to 1919, particularly if the month number has two digits. For example: 11 9 L might be used for Nov. 1919. The L indicates the factory.

1921–1929   A letter (not a number) now indicates the month of the year (A-L); a single digit number indicates the year (1-9); a final letter (or letter and number) still indicates the factory. N5 is a common factory indicator.

1921	(A-L)	1	factory letter	1925	(A-L)	5	factory letter
also	(A-L)	21	factory letter	1926	(A-L)	6	factory letter
1922	(A-L)	2	factory letter	1927	(A-L)	7	factory letter
1923	(A-L)	3	factory letter	1928	(A-L)	8	factory letter
1924	(A-L)	4	factory letter	1929	(A-L)	9	factory letter

From 1930 on, the middle number is the year itself; for example: 32 is used for 1932, 45 is for 1945, etc.

3. W.S. George marks

This is a collection of miscellaneous W.S. George marks. I've been unable to decode their dating system from the numbers and letters under the marks — if, in fact, they do represent a dating system. W.S. George numbers are sometimes blurred; however, most of these numbers will be accurate.

For anybody trying to decipher the system, a few points are in order. DERWOOD is an old shape mark. It was used before 1920; however, all of these DERWOOD marks could date after 1920. See p. 53 for an early DER-WOOD mark. There was a similar early RADDISON mark used before 1920. The WHITE GRANITE marked wares looked like they could date before 1920. LIDO is a shape mark of the 1930s, 1940s, and probably the 1950s. It may have been introduced in the late 1920s. ARGOSY was a fairly early mark; however, when used with IVORY or PINK, it dates from c.1930 to c.1950. See mark on p. 53.

WHITE GRANITE
W. S. GEORGE
1062

WHITE GRANITE
W. S. GEORGE
177B

W. S. GEORGE
EAST PALESTINE
OHIO
MADE IN U.S.A.
014A

DERWOOD
W. S. GEORGE
171 C

DERWOOD
W. S. GEORGE
133B
MADE IN U.S.A.

DERWOOD
W. S. GEORGE
152B

DERWOOD
W. S. GEORGE
1120   (O or C)
MADE IN U.S.A.

Looked pre-1920

DERWOOD
W. S. GEORGE
290B

Looked 1920s

DERWOOD
W. S. GEORGE
152B

RADDISON
W.S.GEORGE
395B

RADDISON
W.S.GEORGE
116A

LIDO
W. S. GEORGE
WHITE
MADE IN U.S.A.
133 A

Looked 1940s; whole set of dishes had same 133 A

LIDO
W.S.GEORGE
WHITE
014A

LIDO
W. S. GEORGE
CANARYTONE
MADE IN U.S.A.
176A

LIDO
W.S.GEORGE
CANARYTONE
196 A

same mark with: 295A, 296A, 396A, 172A.

LIDO
382A

I didn't record any other information.

LIDO
W.S.GEORGE
CANARYTONE
MADE IN U.S.A.
016A

Looked 1940s; also seen with 183A.

Decoration as a Dating Tool

Other than hand painting, there were two main methods of applying decoration to whiteware. One was the copper engraving method. The other was the decalcomanie, or decal, method. Before 1900 nearly all American decorations on whiteware were applied by the copper engraving method. This copper engraving process is described on page 13 of Edwin AtLee Barber's 1893 edition of *The Pottery and Porcelain of the United States*:

> *Decoration may be hand-painted or printed, and both methods may be employed either before or after the ware has been glazed. In the printing process which is used extensively at the present time, the designs are engraved on copper plates and transferred to the surface of the ware. Mineral colors which have been mixed carefully with a prepared printing oil, are used to print the design on linen-tissue paper, which is then laid upon the ware and rubbed with a piece of soft flannel until it adheres evenly and firmly. In a few hours the paper is plucked from the ware and the printed design is then touched up with color by hand, and gold lines are then frequently applied.*

This copper engraving process resulted in a printed decoration of a single color. Sometimes this was the final decoration. Many colors were used. The most unusual I've seen was a "shocking pink" used on a piece of ALBA CHINA made at the Edwin Bennett Pottery Co. of Baltimore, Maryland. Other times, as Barber mentions above, the printed design was "touched up" with hand painted colors. In these cases the printed design, usually of brown or black, served as an outline for hand painting. The color was usually added quickly, resulting in the hand painted parts not quite fitting inside the printed outline. It should be noted that it was possible to use the printing process described by Barber more than once on a particular piece, resulting in two or more printed colors. This was infrequently done in England and almost never in the United States. It was too difficult and expensive. Hand painting over the single colored outline was simpler.

About 1900 the copper engraving decoration method was replaced with the decal method of decorating. Although used for a long time by some European companies, the process was almost never used in the United States before 1900. One exception was the Knowles, Taylor & Knowles Co., which was doing some beautiful decal work in the 1890s, particularly on Masonic and other commemorative items. Here is a description of the decal method given on page 240 of Edwin AtLee Barber's 1893 edition of *The Pottery and Porcelain of the United States*:

> *The American China Company of Trenton produced to a limited extent stone china decorated by the chromolithographic process, which has been employed in Europe for perhaps forty years. This process consists in the application of vitrifiable decalcomanie designs to the surface for the ware, either under or over the glaze, usually the latter. On a plate in my possession, made by the above-named company, is a central design of a crab, with marginal fronds of sea-weed in colors – green, brown, black, and red. The effect is that of the ordinary decalcomanie transfer work, but, having been fired, the designs are permanently affixed, as in the other overglaze decorations. This process has been carried to great perfection, especially by the Doulton factory of Lambeth, England, and by some of the French potters, intricate and artistic designs being produced in delicate coloring which resemble fine hand-painted work, but the transfer printing can be distinguished by the dots and lines of the engraving, which can be readily detected on close inspection.*

It must be noted that the American China Co. of Trenton was never mentioned again by Barber in any of his books. He was possibly talking about the American Crockery Co. The only American China Co. in his 1904 marks book was the American China Co. of Toronto, Ohio. It should also be mentioned that many antique dealers and auctioneers confuse decalcomanie decorated wares with hand painted ones. You will have to ascertain this for yourself.

In conclusion, a copper transfer decoration generally indicates a nineteenth century product, a decal decoration, a twentieth century product. A hand painted item could be from either century.

British Royal Coat of Arms Marks

The British Royal Coat of Arms consists of a lion and a unicorn with a crown-topped shield between them. What Americans call the English or the British Coat of Arms is called the Royal Coat of Arms in Great Britain. Barber sometimes called it simply "the English mark." Whatever the name, it was frequently used as a mark both in this country and in Britain.

It might appear strange that American companies would use this uniquely British mark. The reason was simple economics. The American public, for many reasons, preferred British or other imported wares. To compete, American companies resorted to copying the British Arms. The first commercially successful American company to make whiteware exclusively used only a very proper-looking Royal Arms mark. This was the Jersey City Pottery of Rouse and Turner. Barber pictured only the one Royal Arms mark for this company from the 1850s to c.1880. More than 40 American companies used the British Arms mark, some using two or more versions of the mark. A few companies used a two-lions variant of the mark; others used whimsical or satirical simulations of the Royal Arms mark. Some continued to use the British Royal Coat of Arms to mark whiteware right into the twentieth century.

Another similar practice was using as marks the coats of arms of various American states. The coats of arms of New Jersey and Pennsylvania were most often used. Others included New York, Massachusetts, Maryland and Michigan. See p. 234.

The following several pages show the British Royal Coat of Arms marks used by American companies that did not include company names, initials or other distinguishing words as part of the mark. (If the Arms mark does have the company name, initials or other distinguishing words, use the index to identify it.) Since some British companies also used the Royal Arms as marks without company names or initials, the lack of same does not necessarily indicate an American mark. However, all the Royal Arms marks used by British companies that I have seen have a central shield that is regular.* The first four marks on the following page have regular shields. American potters, on the other hand, frequently used the central shield to display company monograms or initials. Others left them blank. After the British Arms marks is a section on the two-lions coat of arms variant. Also included is a page of American states coats of arms used as marks.

*There was at least one early English company that depicted pastoral scenes in the central shield; however, I've yet to see an English mark with company initials or a monogram inside the shield.

East End Pottery
See no. 74 on p. 45

Wheeling Pottery Co.
See no. 238 on p. 161

Steubenville Pottery Co.
See no. 204 on p. 136

The first two marks are almost identical. The key difference is the star under the Wheeling mark. The crown atop the shield is slightly larger on the Wheeling mark. The Steubenville mark is different in three ways. First, it has a wider border around the shield. Second, there is an *S* and *C* under the shield. Since the mark may be quite small, these letters may be difficult to see. Finding them, however, would confirm the mark as that of the Steubenville Pottery. A third difference is that the horn on the unicorn is longer on the Steubenville mark.

Peoria Pottery Co.
See no. 164 on p. 112

Akron China Co.
See no. 2 on p. 14

American China Co.
See no. 7 on p. 15

The Peoria mark is like the three marks above except that it has *ironstone china*, not *royal ironstone china*, above the shield. Note also that it has a wide border around the shield like the Steubenville mark. The Akron China and the American China marks are virtually identical. There is just a tiny difference between the crowns and a very tiny difference between the unicorns' manes. Note that the initials on the shields are the same.

Peoria Pottery Co.
See no. 164 on p. 112

Peoria Pottery Co.
See no. 164 on p. 112

Ott & Brewer
See no. 157 on p. 108

The marks above are similar but easily distinguished. The Peoria Pottery marks are fairly unique in that they have shields with empty centers. Note the O. & B. monogram on the shield of the Ott & Brewer mark.

L.B. Beerbower & Co.
See no. 20 on p. 20

N.Y. City Pottery
See no. 150 on p. 104

Pioneer Pottery Co.
See no. 170 on p. 116

The three marks above and the one below are dissimilar; but, like all of the marks in this section, they are difficult to identify because there are no distinguishing words or initials above or below the marks. In each case the shield is the key. Note the L.B.B.& Co. on the first shield. Note the J.C. (monogram for James Carr) on the N.Y. City Pottery shield. Note the P.P.Co. on the shield of the Pioneer Pottery mark. Finally, note the G.P.Co. monogram on the Glasgow Pottery mark's shield below.

Glasgow Pottery
See no. 93 on p. 55

Trenton Pottery Co. See A.116 on p. 192.

Gates and Ormerod say this mark is for the Standard Pottery Co. dating 1886 – c.1910. See no. 200 on p. 134.

Burford Bros. Pottery Co. See no. 37 on p. 27.

Dresden Pottery (Potters' Cooperative Co.) See no. 73 on p. 42.

This mark is for the Potters' Cooperative Co. (Dresden Pottery) of East Liverpool, Ohio. The P.C. monogram is for the Potters' Cooperative. This mark may have T.P.C.CO. and/or DRESDEN as part of the mark. See no. 73 on p. 42.

Probably Union Pottery Co. of Trenton, N.J. See no. 221 on p. 152. See also A.117 on p. 192.

For reasons hard to document, I believe this is a mark of John Wyllie & Co. See no. 242 on p. 164. See also p. 232 for similar marks.

National China Co. Gates and Ormerod say this mark was used after 1911. See also no. 143 on p. 101.

This mark is for the National China Co. Gates and Ormerod say it was used after 1911 when the company moved from East Liverpool, Ohio, to Salineville, Ohio.

This mark is for C.C. Thompson Pottery Co. of East Liverpool, Ohio. Gates and Ormerod date it c.1915. E.L.O. may be under the mark.

This mark is for the D.E. McNicol Pottery Co. of East Liverpool, Ohio. It dates c.1900. See p. 93 for the same mark but with the company's initials.

J. Hart Brewer helped to start a new company in Trenton, N.J. c.1894 after the Ott & Brewer Co. ceased operations. By c.1900 the company was in Mr. Brewer's name. He died in December of that year. The mark above could be for his company.

Gates and Ormerod say this two-lions mark is for the Standard Pottery Co. of East Liverpool, Ohio. They date the mark 1886 to c.1910. Because of the S.C.Co. monogram, I am a bit dubious.

I believe this mark is for the William Brunt Pottery Co. dating before 1894. Based upon the style and decoration of the ware marked, it may date back to the 1880's when the company was called William Brunt, Son & Co. See p. 26.

This mark is the quintessence of the American version of the British Royal Coat of Arms mark. It is not a direct copy of any British mark, yet it reflects the spirit of the Royal Arms mark. There are many similar versions of the mark. Gates and Ormerod show one mark identical to this one (except for details of the lion and unicorn) attributing it to the Wallace & Chetwynd Pottery Co. I believe this mark and similar versions were used by many early companies. This mark was found on a c.1870 or 1880 platter. See also bottom left mark on p. 231.

Two-Lions Coats of Arms
(A Variant of the British Coat of Arms)

Anchor Pottery Co.
See no. 13 on p. 18.

Crown Pottery Co.
See no. 66 on p. 40.

Vodrey & Brother
See no. 227 on p. 155.

Except for the monogram in the central shield, these marks above are almost identical. The first monogram is A.P.; the second is C.P.Co.; the third is V.& B. (Brother).

Vodrey & Brother
See no. 227 on p. 156.

Vodrey & Brother
See no. 227 on p. 155.

Steubenville Pottery Co.
See no. 204 on p. 136.

The first mark is like the three marks above except that the position of WARRANTED and IRON STONE CHINA has been reversed. Note the V.& B. (Bro.) monogram on shield. The next two marks are unique. Note the V. & BRO. on the shield of the middle mark. Note the S.P.Co. on the shield of the last mark. See p. 232 for one more two-lions mark.

State Coat of Arms Marks

New Jersey Coat of Arms

This mark is for the Trenton Pottery Works. See no. 216 on p. 150.

Similar marks, including company initials, were used by several other companies. See nos. 54, 79, 83, 98, 124.

The Crescent Pottery used this mark with just IRON STONE CHINA under the mark. See no. 63 on p. 37.

Maryland Coat of Arms

This mark was used only by the Maryland Pottery Co. See no. 125 on p. 89.

Pennsylvania Coat of Arms
See nos. 21, 52, 126, 240, 242.

New York Coat of Arms

This mark was used only by the Onondaga Pottery Co. See no. 156 on p. 106.

Massachusetts Coat of Arms

This mark was used only by the New England Pottery Co. See no. 146 on p. 102.

Hard To Identify American Marks

See no. 23, page 22.

See no. 23, page 23.

E.B.P. Co.
(monogram)

See no. 33, page 26.

See no. 50, page 32.

See no. 66, page 40.

The crown mark at left was used on dinnerware. The crown must look exactly like this. There will be other crown marks with no words. Crowns are common on English and other foreign marks.

See no. 70, page 41.

See no. 78, page 46.

See no. 82, page 48.

See no. 104, page 61.

See no. 121, page 77.

HC

See no. 121, page 83.

M
CHINA
L

See no. 124, page 88.

See no. 125, page 89.

The letter *A* before some of the numbers below indicates that mark as being in the chapter "Miscellaneous American Marks."

See no. 37, page 28.

See no. 104, page 62.

See no. 119, page 71.

See no. 125, page 89.

See no. 132, page 95.

See no. 139, page 99.

See no. 143, page 101.

See no. 210, page 141.

See no. 213, page 147.

(incised)
See A.191, page 207.

See no. 78, page 47.

See no. 130, page 93.

See A.111, page 191.

See A.112, page 191. This T.P.Co. monogram is in the center of a complex shield.

IRON STONE
CHINA
See no. 133, page 96.

See no. 133, page 96.

See no. 141, page 99.

See no. 146, page 102.

See no. 146, page 102.

See no. 146, page 102.

See no. 146, page 102.

See no. 148, page 103.

See no. 148, page 103.

See no. 150, page 104.

See no. 241, page 163.

(with or without circle)
See no. 164, page 112.

See no. 154, page 105.

See no. 157, page 109.

See no. 166, page 113.

See no. 167, page 113.

See no. 227, page 156.

See no. 66, page 40.

See no. 238, page 160.

See no. 238, page 162.

See no. 104, page 61.

See no. 190, page 129.

This E.H.S.C.CO. monogram mark at left is for the E.H. Sebring China Co. Without WINONA it might be difficult to decipher.

See no. 172, page 119.

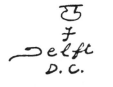

See A.38, page 174.

Etruria
Delft
D. 3.

See A.39, page 174.

(raised mark)
See A.40, page 174.

See A.124, page 194.

See A.142, page 197.

See A.167, page 203.

See no. 143, page 100.

See A.53, page 178.

American Makers of Flow Blue Ware

My study of pottery marks over the past seven years has led to a discovery that far more American companies made flow blue ware than is generally known. Although many of these companies decorated with just a border in flow blue, a surprisingly large number used interesting and intricate flow blue patterns comparable to the much better known English flow blue patterns. Below is a list of American companies that made flow blue ware. Undoubtedly, many others made at least a small amount of flow blue ware.

1. La Belle factory of the Wheeling Pottery Co., Wheeling, WV

2. Wheeling Potteries Co. (continuation of Wheeling Pottery Co.)

3. French China Co., East Liverpool, OH, and Sebring, OH

4. Mercer Pottery Co., Trenton, NJ

5. International Pottery Co. (Burgess & Campbell), Trenton, NJ

6. Warwick China Co., Wheeling, WV

7. New England Pottery Co., East Boston, MA

8. Homer Laughlin China Co., East Liverpool, OH

9. Sebring Pottery Co. (American Pottery Works), East Liverpool, OH, and Sebring, OH

10. Mayer Pottery Co., Beaver Falls, PA

11. Knowles, Taylor and Knowles Co., East Liverpool, OH

12. Chesapeake Pottery, Baltimore, MD

13. Burroughs & Mountford Co., Trenton, NJ

14. Thomas Maddock's Sons Co., Trenton, NJ

15. American China Co., Toronto, OH

16. Cook Pottery Co. (Mellor & Co.), Trenton, NJ

17. Crescent Pottery, Trenton, NJ

18. Buffalo Pottery Co., Buffalo, NY

19. Empire Pottery (impressed Imperial China mark), Trenton, NJ

20. Steubenville Pottery Co., Steubenville, OH

21. Taylor, Smith & Taylor Co., East Liverpool, OH

22. Saxon China Co., Sebring, OH

23. Dresden Pottery (Potters' Cooperative Co.), East Liverpool, OH

24. H.R. Wyllie China Co., Huntington, WV

25. Trenle China Co., East Liverpool, OH

26. E.H. Sebring China Co., Sebring, OH

27. Carrollton Pottery Co., Carrollton, OH

28. Colonial Company, East Liverpool, OH

29. Ohio China Co., East Palestine, OH

30. McNicol-Smith Company, Wellsville, OH

31. Limoges China Co., Sebring, OH

32. French-Saxon China Co., Sebring, OH

33. Paden City Pottery Co., Paden City, WV

34. Sterling China Co., Wellsville, or East Liverpool, OH

35. Sterling China (unknown American company), see p. 188

36. Colonial Sterling China (possible American company), see p. 171

37. XX CENTURY SEMI PORCELAIN (possible American mark), see p. 203

38. Oliver China Co., Sebring, OH

American Makers of Tea Leaf Luster Ware

This list compiled by American Tea Leaf authority Julie Rich was sent to me by Dale Abrams of the Tea Leaf Club International. It is a surprisingly long list. In my seven years of researching pottery marks, I've seen Tea Leaf luster ware made by only a handful of early American companies.

The Mayer Pottery Co. (J. & E. Mayer) was by far the most prolific American maker of the ware. Tea Leaf ware from other early American makers is either rare or very rare today. Annise Doring Heaivilin, author of *Grandma's Tea Leaf Ironstone*, mentioned the C.C. Thompson Pottery Co. as an additional maker of Tea Leaf decorated ware. I've added this name to the list sent by Mr. Abrams.

Early American Tea Leaf Potteries

1. Brockmann Pottery Co., Cincinnati, OH

2. William Brunt & Co., East Liverpool, OH

3. Buffalo Pottery, Buffalo, NY

4. Burford Bros., East Liverpool, OH

5. Cartwright Bros., East Liverpool, OH

6. Crown Pottery Co., Evansville, IN

7. East End Pottery Co., East Liverpool, OH

8. Fell & Thropp Co., Trenton, NJ

9. Ford China Co., Ford City, PA

10. Glasgow Pottery, Trenton, NJ

11. Goodwin Bros., Trenton, NJ

12. Knowles, Taylor & Knowles Co., East Liverpool, OH

13. Mayer Pottery Co. (J.& E. Mayer), Beaver Falls, PA

14. McNicol, Burton & Co., East Liverpool, OH

15. D.E. McNicol Pottery Co., East Liverpool, OH

16. Sebring Pottery Co. (American Pottery Works), East Liverpool, and Sebring, OH

17. Shenango Pottery Co., New Castle, PA

18. Steubenville Pottery Co., Steubenville, OH

19. Dresden Pottery (the Potters' Cooperative Co.), East Liverpool, OH

20. United States Pottery Co., Wellsville, OH

21. Vodrey Pottery, East Liverpool, OH

22. Wheeling Pottery Co., Wheeling, WV

23. Wick China Co., Kittanning, PA

24. C.C. Thompson Pottery Co., East Liverpool, OH

Later Makers and Decorators of Tea Leaf Ware

25. Cumbow China Decorating Co. – a decorating company of Abingdon, Virginia, from 1932 to 1980. They decorated American and English blanks.

26. Red Cliff Co., Chicago, IL – distributed tea leaf decorated ironstone made exclusively for them by the Hall China Co. of East Liverpool, Ohio. See also p. 121.

27. Walker China Co., Bedford, OH – also supplied ware for the Red Cliff Co. See 26 above. See also p. 157.

28. Homer Laughlin Co. – although their mark can be found on tea leaf decorated ware, Annise Heaivilin said it was not decorated at Homer Laughlin.

A Selection of Difficult British Marks

The following marks, if used alone, would be difficult to identify. Remember, these are British marks.

PRINCE OF WALES'S CREST, ICH DIEN may be on a ribbon under the crest. This mark was also used by the Cook Pottery Co. of the United States; however, they used *Etruria* instead of *Ich Dien* on the mark.

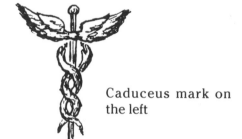

Caduceus mark on the left

A lion rampant (common on British marks)

The above monogram is to be found on several British marks.

The dove mark at right is found with or without TRADE MARK.

DERBY CROWN MARK
1878 – 1890
A D or Derby under crown on various earlier marks

WORCESTER MARK (Later a crown is placed above for ROYAL WORCESTER MARK.) Notice the 51 in center.

A Partial Reprint of Jervis's 1897 Marks Book

The following pages are photocopied from W. Percival Jervis's 1897 marks book. The book had 97 pages. The pages printed here include all the American marks from that book. All other marks were foreign, primarily European, marks. Jervis's book is important because it came out seven years before Edwin AtLee Barber's now-famous 1904 *Marks of American Potters*.

A Book of Pottery Marks

by

W. Percival Jervis

Copyright
W.P. Jervis
Newark, NJ

1897

W. Percival Jervis
62 James Street
Newark, NJ

UNITED STATES.

1-6. EDWIN BENNETT POTTERY CO., Baltimore, Md.—Mr. James Bennett came to this country in 1834, from Woodville, in Derbyshire. After working at the Jersey City Pottery, and afterwards at Troy under James Clews, he established a small pottery at East Liverpool, the first ever founded there. He was joined in 1841 by his brothers, Daniel, Edwin and William, and here they made the first rockingham ware made in America. The difficulties of transportation and the washing away of the banks of the river induced them in 1844 to remove to Pittsburg, Pa., where until 1846 they conducted an increasing business. Edwin and William in this year withdrew from the firm, and the former having found suitable clays at Druid's Hill, Baltimore, built a small works at Canton Avenue, where the business has been continued ever since. Yellow, rockingham, stoneware and majolica were made. In 1851 Mr. Bennett originated the familiar Rebekah teapot. The works were enlarged in 1869 and white ware was added to the products. From 1884 to 1887 both parian and egg-shell china were made, and in 1890 the business was changed to its present form. The marks used up to 1857, consisted of an impressed stamp with the name of the firm. The first mark on white ware was a phœnix, followed in 1873 by a seven-pointed star with the initials E B in the center. Nos. 1-2 were used in 1886; No. 3 in 1890; and Nos. 4, 5, and 6 are the present marks.

7. J. H. Baum, Wellsville, O.—White granite. Closed October, 1897.
8. L. B. Beerbower & Co., Elizabeth, N. J. C. C. ware, etc.
9. Bellmark Pottery Co., Trenton, N. J. Sanitary ware.

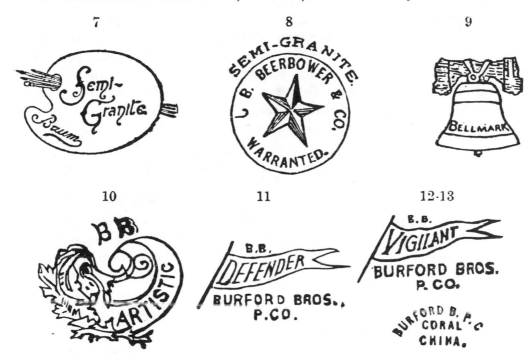

10-13. Burford Bros., East Liverpool, O.—White granite and semi-porcelain, plain and decorated.

14. Brockman Pottery Co., Cincinnati, O.—Established in 1862 by Tempest, Brockman & Co., who were succeeded in 1877 by the present firm. The production of the works is limited to white granite and cream color wares.

15-16. Burroughs & Mountford, Trenton, N. J.—Established in 1879. The character of the designs produced here was excellent, and had a very large influence on American pottery. Whilst partaking of the style of Doulton, they had an individuality of their own impossible to mistake. Unfortunately, the body was sacrificed to the decoration, with the inevitable result. This is much to be regretted, as the production promised much; and had the same care been taken in manufacturing as in decorating and designing, their regretable failure would probably have been averted. The works are now carried on as the Eagle Pottery Co.

CARTLIDGE.—Mr. Chas. Cartlidge, who for a number of years had acted as New York agent for Wm. Ridgway, started a small factory at Greenpoint about 1848 for the manufacture of china, producing at first, principally door furniture of excellent quality, and employing about sixty hands. Later, tableware was made in commercial quantities, at first in bone china, but later in a true hard porcelain. Elijah Tatler, whose son, Mr. W. H. Tatler, now conducts at Trenton one of the most successful decorating works in America, was one of the artists employed. Josiah Jones was the modeler, his figure pieces—busts of prominent men—and plaques being reproduced in parian. Imitation Wedgwood jasper ware was also made. In 1854 or 1854 Mr. Cartlidge, through some outside investment, lost a considerable share of his fortune. The firm was dissolved and reorganized under the style of the American Porcelain Mfg. Co., with Mr. Cartlidge as president; but the new company failed to successfully conduct the concern, and the factory was closed in 1856, the building being afterwards torn down.

CHELSEA
CHINA

18. THE CHELSEA CHINA Co., New Cumberland.—This factory was erected in 1888, but never paid interest on the investment. It was thoroughly equipped, but its capacity was not sufficient to allow the output to yield a fair return for the investment—about $100,000. It was closed down in 1896.

BELLEEK

LENOX

19-20. THE CERAMIC ART Co., Trenton, N. J. —Incorporated under the laws of New Jersey, May 18, 1889—Mr. Jonathan Coxon, president, and Mr. Walter S. Lenox, secretary and treasurer. Mr. Coxon retired in May, 1896, Mr. Lenox purchasing his interest, the present secretary being Mr. H. A. Brown. The product of the Ceramic Art Co. consists of fine china body, decorated in an artistic manner either in the style of Belleek, or with well executed painted subjects, distinguished for their individuality. Mr. Lenox has been fortunate enough to gather around him a staff of artists who share his ambition to make for the products of the Ceramic Art Co. a distinct character of their own, entirely original and entirely independent of any foreign influence. Their treatment of the loving cup, in a dozen different forms, exemplifies this. Painted in monochrome, usually a blue of exceptional softness, an underglaze color is applied on the glaze and then subjected to a glost fire, giving all the durability and softness of an actual underglaze decoration. The process is, however, fraught with peril, as frequently pieces have to undergo this heavy fire five or six times before a satisfactory finish is attained. In vases the variety of shape is very extensive and it is difficult to make a selection where purity of form is such a marked characteristic. The Egyptian lotus leaf has been cleverly adapted as a receptacle for flowers, sometimes with an attendant Cupid, and has proved a popular novelty. It would partake too much of the nature of a catalogue to discuss in detail the large number of novelties produced by this house, but scarcely without exception they bear the evidence of artistic thought, enhanced by intelligent craftmanship and technical execution. Such a combination of qualities is exceptional, and when found is deserving of quick public recognition and appreciation.

| 21 | 22 | 23 | 24 |

CHELSEA KERAMIC
ART WORKS
ROBERTSON & SONS

21-24. THE CHELSEA POTTERY, Dedham, Mass.—Established in 1866 by A. W. Robertson, at Chelsea, Mass. He was joined in 1870 by Hugh C. Robertson, and in 1872 by Jas. Robertson; and they carried on business under the style of the Ceramic Art Works. From 1884 Mr. H. C. Robertson conducted the business alone, making many experiments in the regions of forgotten arts, until 1888, when the factory was closed. In 1891 a company was formed under the style of The Chelsea Pottery, U. S., and later the works were removed to Dedham.

| 25 | 26-27 | 28 |

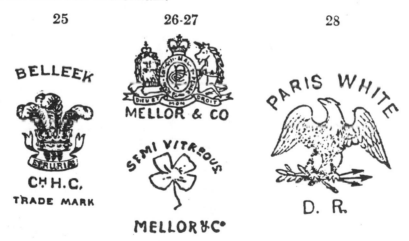

25. COOK POTTERY CO., Trenton, N. J.—This noted old factory was founded in 1863 by an organization composed of three men—Wm. Bloor, Jos. Ott and Thos. Booth—the first two of whom have passed over to the great majority, Mr. Booth being the only survivor of the original firm. In 1864 Mr. Booth retired from the firm, and was succeeded by Garret Schenck Burroughs, and he in turn was succeeded by John Hart Brewer, who entered upon his long career as the active and progressive head of the concern in 1865. Shortly after Mr. Brewer's entrance into the firm Mr. Bloor withdrew his interest, and the firm then became Ott & Brewer, under which name the old pottery was known for many years. Up to 1875 white ware had formed the staple production, but in that year Mr. Brewer engaged the services of

Isaac Broome, a noted sculptor and modeler, who began the preparation of a series of busts and figures in parian for the great Centennial Exhibition of 1876. When the opening took place they had completed a display of artistic work in clay and enamels which came as a revelation to critics and connoisseurs of that period. Encouraged by the success of their first efforts in the creation of artistic work, the firm began the production of the famous Belleek pottery—that delicately beautiful fabric which won for the house a high place in the estimation of the trade and the public. In this production Mr. Brewer had the assistance of Wm. Bromley, who, originally associated with Mr. W. H Goss, of Stoke-upon-Trent, later went to Belleek to assist in its production there. (Messrs. Ott & Brewer's marks on Belleek will be found under their name.) After the much-regretted failure of Ott & Brewer during the financial depression of 1892 and 1893, Mr. Chas. Howell Cook purchased the historic plant, and upon taking possession of the works he announced his purpose of restoring the business to its old-time prestige, and the Etruria works is once again the workshop and repository of much that is best in native ceramics.

28. EAST MORRISANIA CHINA WORKS. 152d Street, New York.— D. Robitzek & Sons, proprietors.

| 29 | 30-31 | 32-33 |

29. FENTON.—See United States Pottery, Bennington, Vt.

30-31. FAIENCE MFG. CO., Greenpoint, L. I.—Founded in 1880. In 1884 Mr. Edward Lycett, a capable potter and decorator, joined the company, and under his able administration much progress was made. He introduced a fine body very nearly approaching china, and in this ware produced many finely painted vases. He also succeeded in reproducing the fine metallic lustres of Spain and Italy, which at that time were despaired of by European potters. It is a fact worthy of mention that the Mexican Indians have long produced these *reflets métalliques*, though in the course of years the lustre fades from exposure to the light. Mr. Lycett severed his connection with the Faience Mfg. Co. in 1890, and two years afterwards the works were closed.

32-33. THE GLOBE POTTERY CO., East Liverpool, O.—The firm now known as above commenced business in 1881 under the style of Frederick,

Shenkle, Allen & Co., making yellow and rockingham ware. In 1888 they were incorporated as above, and at the beginning of the present year added the manufacture of semi-porcelain.

34   35   36

34-36. THE GREENWOOD POTTERY CO., Trenton, N. J.—This company was incorporated in 1863, the first officers being Chas. Brearley, president; Jas. P. Stephens, secretary and treasurer; Jas. Tams, superintendent. Subsequently Mr. Stephens became president and treasurer, Mr. Tams retaining his original position. To-day Mr. Tams is the president and Mr. Stephens the secretary and treasurer, so that practically the works from their inception to the present day have been under the same management. The early days of the factory were days to test the courage of the bravest. Experiment followed experiment, the trials seemed all that could be desired, but the bulk of ware was not satisfactory, and the contents of kiln after kiln were consigned to the rubbish heap. The Greenwood factory may fairly be said to be built on failure, but every failure taught something, and success came at last. It was a success when it came worth waiting for, and made ample amends for all the anxieties of the past. Distinctively an American production, the vitrified earthenware of the Greenwood China Co. was a manifest advance in ceramics. It contains the best properties of both earthenware and china, and the minimum of objectionable qualities of either. It is popularly called "hotel china", but the definition is not sufficiently comprehensive. The firm also make in the same body a line of art pottery, principally with metallic decorations, the prevailing influence in shape being that of Persia and Japan, the forms in most instances being sufficiently modernized to make them adaptable to every-day requirement. A rich ivory glaze considerably enhances their appearance. The stamp on tableware is the name of the firm impressed. No. 34, from 1883 to 1886, on art ware; Nos. 35 and 36, from 1886 to the present time.

37   38   39

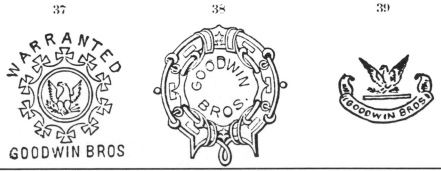

37-39. THE GOODWIN POTTERY CO., East Liverpool, O.—Established in 1844 by John Goodwin, a Burslem potter, who received his training, as did his father before him, at the factory of James Edwards. Rockingham and yellow ware only were made until 1877, two years after his death. Messrs. Speeler and Taylor, the pioneers of the pottery industry at Trenton (1852), were both employes of Mr. Goodwin. In 1877 the manufacture of C. C. was added, soon followed by a decorating department, and under the able and energetic management of his three sons, James H., George S. and Henry J. Goodwin, assumed important proportions. In 1893 the works were incorporated under the present style. Mr. James H. Goodwin, its first president, died in November, 1896.

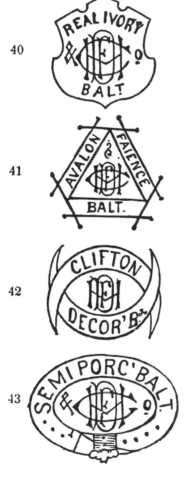

40

41

42

43

40-43. D. F. HAYNES & SON, formerly HAYNES, BENNETT & CO., Baltimore, Md.— For some time no special stamp has been used on the product of this factory, the wares having such an individuality as to render a trade-mark unnecessary. The four given here are old marks formerly used on Clifton and Avalon wares, both of which belong to the majolica family; on ivory, which is a sound, durable body of a soft, ivory tint, produced, not by a stain in the glaze, but by a combination of clays. The remaining one is the mark on semi-porcelain. Mr. D. F. Haynes is to be credited with the leadership in that little coterie of American potters who initiated originality of design as applied to American pottery. The story cannot be fully told here, though it is one of great interest, and affords much food for reflection. Of late years a very considerable trade has been done in clock cases in decorated earthenware.

44

45

44-45. HARKER POTTERY Co., East Liverpool, O.— Benjamin Harker, Sr., established these works in 1840. After operating them for some years he was succeeded by his son, George S. Harker, who carried them on under the style of G. S. Harker & Co., until his death. His widow and two sons continued it under the same style until 1890, in which year it was incorporated as the Harker Pottery Co. Rockingham and yellow ware were made until 1879, in which year their manufacture gave place to white granite.

46-58. THE INTERNATIONAL POTTERY CO., Trenton, N. J.—Organized in 1879, the incorporators being James Moses, John Moses, Edward Clark and Thomas Clark. In September of that year John W. Burgess, Wm. Burgess and John A. Campbell bought out the stock of the above-named gentle men, and became the proprietors of the International Pottery Co. From that date to the present the concern has run under the corporate name, stamping their goods with the trade-mark, Burgess & Campbell. The president of the concern, Mr. Wm. Burgess, served the Government and the interests of the American pottery manufacturers by representing this country in the Pottery district of Great Britain as Consul to Tunstall during President Harrison's administration. In the year 1895, Mr. John Campbell, for fifteen years treasurer of this concern, withdrew, and Mr. E. C. Williamson was elected to fill the vacancy. The present officers are : Wm. Burgess, president ; E. C. Williamson, treasurer ; I. H. Nichol, secretary.

59

60

61

62

63

59-62. THE JERSEY CITY POTTERY CO., Jersey City, N. J.—The Jersey Porcelain and Earthenware Co. was incorporated December 10, 1825, but the venture was not a success, and the production ceased within a year or two. In 1829 it was reopened by David and J. Henderson. In 1833 David Henderson organized the American Pottery Co. Here, for the first time in America, printing on white ware was practiced. They also made a brown earthenware decorated in reliefs and colored enamels. Daniel Greatbatch, a clever modeler, was employed, and here he produced his well-known pitcher with hunting scenes in relief, and the handle in the shape of a hound. In 1845 a change took place, the proprietorship being vested in Wm. Rhodes, Strong and McGerron, who made white and C. C. ware until 1854. In 1855 they sold out to Rouse, Turner, Duncan & Henry, and a little later Rouse and Turner carried it on alone. Some of their shapes were exceedingly good, both in earthenware and parian, and were largely used by decorators. The works were pulled down in; 1892. No. 59 is an impressed mark, about 1830; No. 60 is printed ; No. 61 impressed, about 1840; No. 62 dates from 1840 to 1845.

63. J. E. JEFFORDS & Co., Philadelphia.— Established 1868. Earthenware and colored glaze jardinieres, etc.

252

64-74. THE KNOWLES, TAYLOR & KNOWLES CO. East Liverpool, O.— This concern, now the largest pottery establishment in America, had its beginning in 1853, when ground was broken by Isaac W. Knowles, the founder of the business, who commenced active operations in the following year, 1854. Then the only kiln was used alternately for bisque and glost ware. The power was furnished by a horse. The ware made was yellow ware, known for many years as "Liverpool ware." In 1870 John N. Taylor and Homer S. Knowles, the latter a son of Isaac W. Knowles, associated themselves with

him, the total kiln capacity of the works at this time being two kilns—one for bisque and the other for glost ware. This capacity was then increased to five kilns—a very large institution for those days. The firm, which was then called "Knowles, Taylor & Knowles," began the manufacture of white granite, drawing their first kiln of this improved order of goods on September 5, 1872. This was the first white granite made in East Liverpool. The business grew and the firm put their earnings in the business, enlarged the plant, and extended their manufactures, until to-day they stand one of the best equipped potteries in the world, the works covering six or seven acres of ground and giving employment to about 700 workpeople. In addition to semi-porcelain, white granite and hotel ware, the firm a few years ago produced a number of ornamental pieces they called " Lotus ware ", but the manufacture has never assumed large proportions. In 1891 a corporation was formed, with a paid-in capital of $1,000,000. The officers are as follows: Col. John N. Taylor, president; Isaac W. Knowles (the founder, now in his seventy-eighth year), vice-president; Joseph G. Lee, secretary and treasurer. These, with Edwin M. Knowles, constitute the board of directors.

| 75 | 76 | 77 | 78 |

75-78. THE HOMER LAUGHLIN CHINA CO., East Liverpool, O.—Established in 1874 by Homer and Shakespeare Laughlin, under the title of Laughlin Bros., for the purpose of manufacturing white granite. Shakespeare Laughlin withdrew from the firm in 1879, and from that year until January 1, 1897, when the business was incorporated under the above title, the firm name was Homer Laughlin. For several years a thin, translucent china was produced, but owing to the difficulty of making two entirely distinct products in the same plant, the china was discontinued in 1889, and the product has since been confined to a high grade semi-vitreous earthenware. Mr. Laughlin, realizing the possibilities of his art, has never ceased to study and experiment for better results, and to this indefatigable striving after perfection is in a large measure due the success that has, from the first, followed his efforts. These efforts have been fully appreciated, as witnessed by his steadily increasing trade and by the awards of the Philadelphia, Cincinnati and Chicago exhibitions. Mr. Laughlin seems to have exhausted the possibilities of further improvement in semi-porcelain, and might well rest on the success he has achieved; but I understand that should trade conditions justify it the output of the factory will be changed to a true porcelain exclusively.

| 79 | 80 | 81 | 82 |

79. KEYSTONE POTTERY CO., Trenton, N. J.—Sanitary ware.

80. THE LONHUDA POTTERY CO., Steubenville, O.—The name is derived from the names of the original promoters. Mr. W. A. (Lon)g, Mr. W. H. (Hu)nter, Mr. Alfred (Da)y. The productions are similar to Rookwood, the same beautiful blending of grounds being a noticeable characteristic of both. What has been said of Rookwood may fairly be applied to Lonhuda. Mr. Long may be credited with a distinct success, at least artistically. In 1896 the business was purchased by Mr. S. A. Weller, Zanesville, who is worthily continuing the good work.

81. MARYLAND POTTERY CO., Baltimore, Md.—Formerly made a line of decorated earthenware, but for the last few years have made sanitary ware exclusively.

82. MORRIS & WILLMORE, Trenton, N. J.—The Columbia Art Pottery, as Messrs. Morris & Willmore's works are called, was built in 1892-3. Mr. W. T. Morris was educated at the Worcester Porcelain Works, went afterwards to Belleek, and from there to the Ott and Brewer Works at Trenton, where Mr. Willmore was a decorator. Mr. Morris' training is evidenced by the graceful and artistic designs produced by the firm, both in Belleek effects and in ivory ware for decorators. Some very artistic figure painting on glazed parian is also produced here.

83

84

85

83-85. THE MAYER POTTERY CO., Limited, Beaver Falls, Pa.—Was established in 1881 by Joseph Mayer and Ernest Mayer, who are the sons of the late Joseph Mayer, of the firm of T. J. & J. Mayer, earthenware manufacturers, of the Dale Hall Pottery in Burslem, Staffordshire, England. This latter firm is spoken of in Metyard's "Life of Wedgewood," and also in Jewett's "Ceramic Art of Great Britain." Joseph Mayer, the president of the Mayer Pottery Co., Limited, was one of the Mayer Bros., importers of earthenware in New York; and Ernest Mayer served his apprenticeship in potting with G. W. Turner & Sons, of Tunstall, Staffordshire, after which he was for some time manager of Clementson Bros.' Phœnix and Bell Works, at Hanley, Staffordshire. The Beaver Falls Pottery was originally owned by the "Economy Society," a quaint religious community of Germans, who were at one time very wealthy. The present owners purchased the plant and modernized it. As the name of the town indicates, there is an immense water-power derived from the Falls, and this pottery is probably the only one in the world run entirely by water-power—at any rate, the only one in

America. At first the only production was white granite, but after considerable experiment and adaptation of English methods to American material, a very superior grade of underglaze lustre oand and sprig ware was produced which gave the firm considerable prestige; but the demand for this class of ware was superseded by a call for more modern and artistic decorations, and attention was at once paid to producing a superior grade of underglaze printed dinner and tea ware, and to-day a large portion of the production is confined to this class of goods, although great success has been obtained in producing new and attractive colors in glazes, especially in olive green, which is applied to jardinieres, teapots, parlor cuspidores, etc. The manufactory was completely destroyed by fire in the fall of 1896, but has been rebuilt, and manufacturing has recommenced.

86   87

86. JOHN MADDOCK & SONS. Trenton.—Sanitary ware. Commenced business in 1896.

87. MADDOCK POTTERY CO., Trenton.—Organized in 1893. They purchased the plant formerly operated by the Trenton China Co., and manufacture a full line of thin semi-porcelain dinner and tea ware, and a high grade of toilet ware. Also umbrella stands, pedestals and jardinieres. Much taste is displayed in the decorations, and very rich effects are secured. It speaks volumes for the enterprise of the firm that in the few years they have been in business they should attain the high position unquestionably occupied by them.

88-97. JOHN MOSES & SONS CO., Trenton, N. J.—The Glasgow Pottery was established by John Moses in 1863, and was one of the first ten potteries in Trenton. From a small two-kiln pottery it has gradually developed to its present importance Mr. Moses has catered principally to the wants of the million rather that a select few, producing large quantities of plain and decorated earthenware, and is prominently identified with the history of pottery in Trenton. In 1896, Howard B. Moses was taken into partnership. The marks given are: 88, white granite, 1876; 89, semi-porcelain, 1878; 90, semi-porcelain, 1880; 91, white granite, 1882; 92, same, 1884; 93, vitreous earthenware, 1893 ; 94, C. C., 1894 ; 95, dinner ware, 1895 ; 96, Sappho toilet and dinner ware, 1897. The English arms are still used as a mark on white ware.

THOMAS MADDOCK & SONS, Trenton.—Their works are located on Perry, Ewing, Ogden and Carroll streets, and comprise nearly ten acres of floor space. The chief product of the factory is sanitary earthenware, besides which they manufacture extensively druggists' sundries, dinner and toilet ware, and a number of specialties. The original establishment dates back to 1853, and was the first pottery in America to make sanitary ware. The founders were Millington & Astbury. In 1872 the firm became Millington, Astbury & Maddock ; afterwards Astbury & Maddock, who in turn gave place to Thos. Maddock, who conducted the business until 1882, when the present firm was founded. The mark is an anchor and T M & S.

99. D. E. McNICOL POTTERY CO., East Liverpool, O.

MORRISON & CARR had a pottery in New York from 1853 to 1888.

257

MERCER POTTERY CO., Trenton, N. J.—The Mercer Pottery Co. has since its inception, in 1869, held a prominent position in American ceramics. The past year has seen the production of a rich decoration rivaling in brilliancy the "Old Japan", and executed with a vigor and freedom as remarkable as

it is artistic. Large jardinieres and pedestals of graceful outline, boldly treated in a blue of extreme brilliancy, are equal to anything produced in the old world, and reflect the highest possible credit on the art director of the firm—Mr. John M. Pope. Mr. James Moses has been the president of the company, since 1875, when he purchased the business. M. W. B. Allen is the treasurer and Mr. James Barlow the General Manager.

100-105. NEW ENGLAND POTTERY CO., Boston, Mass.—Founded by F. Meagher in 1854 as a yellow and rockingham factory, and afterwards worked by W. F. Homer, who continued it until 1875, when it was taken by L. W.

Clark and Thomas Gray. In 1886, in addition to white ware, they commenced making a semi-porcelain body, finished and decorated in an effective manner, one of their best efforts being in mazarine blue with decorations in raised gold. This they christened "Rieti" ware, the product consisting principally of chocolate jugs, jardinieres, individual sugars and creams, and such like utilitarian articles. Mr. Thos. H. Copeland, a designer and modeler o much taste, is to be credited with the success achieved by this ware, the manufacture being abandoned on his commencing business as a decorator in Trenton. Marks: No. 100 used on earthenware from 1883 to 1886; No. 101, on C. C. ware; No. 102. on white granite since 1886; No. 103, from 1886 to 1888; No. 104, from 1888 to 1889; No. 105, since 1889.

106   OHIO CHINA CO., East Palestine, O. Commenced business as earthenware manufacturers last year.

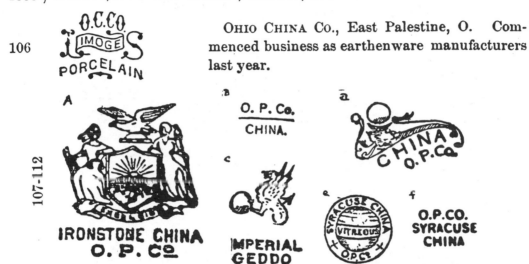

107-112. ONONDAGA POTTERY CO., Syracuse, N. Y.—This company was organized in 1871, and commenced the manufacture of white granite. About 1874 the New York State coat-of-arms was adopted as a trade-mark (107), and was continued on that class of ware until its manufacture was discontinued. In 1886 the manufacture of semi-porcelain was commenced, with the mark 108, the same being still in use. In the fall of 1891 a variety of very pleasing ornamental pieces were made, the mark 109 (c), being confined to them. In the year following, the thin china tableware, which has since grown so popular, and has made for the firm so high a reputation, was introduced. This was stamped with the mark 110, which in 1893 was changed to a globe (111). Last year this was again changed to the present mark (112).

113   114   115   116

BELLEEK.

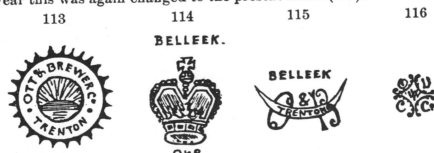

113-115. OTT & BREWER, Trenton, N. J.—(See Cook Pottery Co.)
116. OHIO VALLEY CHINA CO.—Now worked by the Wheeling Pottery Co.

117-124. THE POTTERS' CO-OPERATIVE Co., Dresden Pottery Works East Liverpool.—This pottery was established in 1876 by Brunt, Bloor, Martin & Co., who received a diploma at the Philadelphia Centennial. In 1882 the works were incorporated under their present form. Mr. H. A.

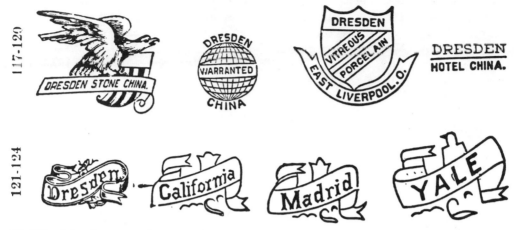

McNicol is the president and treasurer, and Mr. H. A. Keffer, secretary. The last four marks are the names of toilet patterns, some of them seven years old, but which from their merit are still popular in the market.

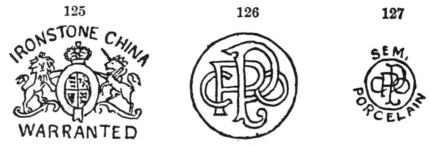

125-127. PEORIA POTTERY Co., Peoria, Ill.—No. 125 is the white granite mark; No. 126 that on C. C., and No. 127 on semi-porcelain.

128-138. ROOKWOOD.—The Rookwood Pottery was founded in 1880 by Mrs. Storer, who had in view the creation of some artistic pottery which should have an individuality all its own. This is not the place to speak of the long years of disappointment and ultimate triumph, which I have dealt with, however imperfectly, in another place. Mr. W. W. Taylor, her partner and valued friend, sustained her by his unswerving faith, and to him, upon her marriage, she turned over her entire interest in the pottery. In 1890 the pottery became a stock company of which Mr. Taylor is the president and Mr. Bellamy Storer vice-president. The marks are as follows:

A. Incised or painted, usually with a date. The most common mark prior to 1882.

B. A variation of above. Stands for "Rookwood Pottery, Cincinnati, Ohio. Maria Longworth Nichols."

C. In relief or stamped. Sometimes in connection with a date. Prior to 1883.

D. Rarely used.

E. Kiln mark, stamped in color on the biscuit, or

F. Impressed in the clay. It also appears in connection with dates.

G. Impressed. Used for a short time only.

H. Impressed. The regular mark from 1882, the date changed each year until 1886.

I. Adopted in 1886.

J. The flame at top indicates 1887.

K. The addition of a flame each year marks the subsequent years.

139. RITTENHOUSE, EVANS & CO., Trenton, N. J.

140. THE SEBRING POTTERY CO., East Liverpool.—This manufactory was founded in the fall of 1887 as a two-kiln plant for white granite. A new plant with eighteen kilns has just been completed, and the production changed from white granite to semi-porcelain. That the production should have been increased nearly ten times in as many years speaks volumes for the enterprise of the firm and the quality of the ware produced.

142-150. THE STEUBENVILLE POTTERY CO., Steubenville, O.—Organized in the fall of 1879; first kiln of white granite drawn February 18,

1881. The capacity was limited, there being only one biscuit and two glost kilns. Business was good, and the demand exceeding the output, two additional kilns were erected in 1884, and the capacity was further increased in 1889, when the plant consisted of three biscuit, four glost, and six decorating kilns. A new body called Canton china—a semi-vitreous earthenware—had

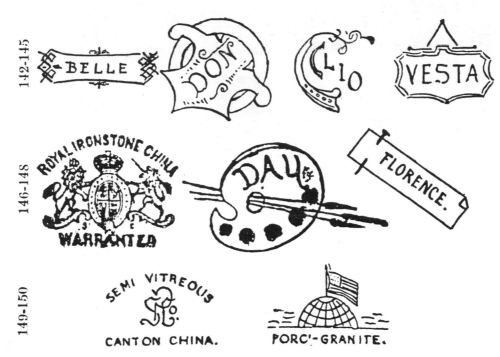

in the meantime been introduced. The capital stock of the company is $100,000, and the officers are: W. B. Donaldson, president and general manager; J. Dunbar, vice-president; Alfred Day, secretary, and these, with Dohrman Sinclair and Thos. Johnson, make up the board of directors.

151 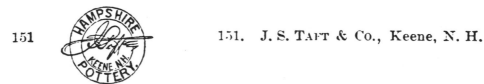 151. J. S. TAFT & Co., Keene, N. H.

141. C. C. THOMPSON POTTERY Co., East Liverpool, O.—Established in 1868 and incorporated in 1889. In 1890 a decorating department was added, the former productions being C. C., rockingham and yellow ware. The works are very extensive.

152-154. THE TRENTON POTTERIES Co., Trenton, N. J.—This company was organized May 27, 1892, for the purchase of the following potteries: Crescent, Delaware, Empire, Enterprise and Equitable. All these potteries were at that time producing sanitary ware, and most of them sanitary ware exclusively. An exception to this was the Crescent pottery, where C. C. of high grade was made. Afterwards the Ideal pottery was built by the company, to enable them to enter into the manufacture of porcelain bath-tubs, laundry tubs, sinks, etc., in which a large trade has been developed. The Trenton Potteries Co., controlling the various factories mentioned above, places them

152   153   154

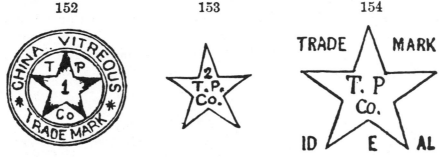

in the position of being the largest manufacturers of sanitary and other clay products in the world. The quality is recognized as being of exceptional merit.

Tucker & Hulme

Philadelphia

1828.

TUCKER & HULME, Philadelphia, Pa.—About 1825 W. Ellis Tucker, who was joined by his brother Thomas in 1828, made tableware, etc., in natural porcelain at the corner of Market, Schuylkill and Front streets. In the latter year Thomas Hulme invested some money in the firm, and pieces were marked in red underglaze "Tucker & Hulme." W. E. Tucker died in 1832, but previous to that Judge Joseph Hemphill was admitted as a partner. They purchased property at the corner of Chestnut and 17th streets, and erected a three-kiln factory there. The venture was not a success and failed for want of support in 1838.

155   156

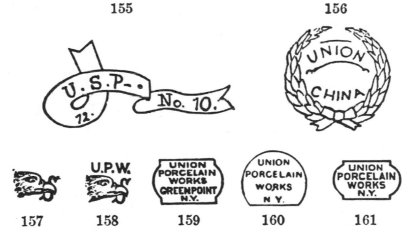

157   158   159   160   161

155. UNITED STATES POTTERY, Bennington, Vt.—A factory was established here about 1846 for the manufacture of yellow, white and rockingham ware, the proprietors being C. W. Fenton, H. D. Hall and J. Norton. The style of the firm then became Lyman & Fenton, and in 1849 the United States Pottery. It is chiefly remarkable from the fact that biscuit figures were made here for the first time in America. It was closed in 1858.

156. UNION POTTERY Co., East Liverpool, O.—Earthenware.

157-161. UNION PORCELAIN WORKS, Brooklyn, N. Y.—Situated in the rthern district of Brooklyn, known as Greenpoint. No. 157, 1876, impressed. In 1877 the same mark was printed in green under the glaze. No. 158, from 1878 to present time, printed in green underglaze; on exhibition pieces the same mark is used as a tablet in relief. No. 159, 1879, decoration mark in red on the glaze. No. 160, 1891, decoration mark. No. 161, 1893 to present time, decoration mark printed on glaze in brown.

162   163   164   165

162-165 —THE VODREY POTTERY CO., East Liverpool. O.—Successors to Vodrey & Bro., who succeeded Woodward, Blakeley & Co. From 1857 to 1875 rockingham and yellow ware only were made, when the manufacture of white granite and semi-porcelain was commenced. No. 162 is the mark used on semi-porcelain; No. 163 on china; No. 164 on white granite, and No. 165 on a special toilet ware shape. The firm was incorporated in 1896. Jabez Vodrey, father of Col. W. H. and James N. Vodrey, made yellow ware in Pittsburg in 1827.

166   167 168   169

166-169. SAMUEL WELLER, Zanesville, O.—Lately Mr. Weller has turned his attention to underglaze decorative paintings on jardinieres, pedestals, etc., somewhat suggestive of Rookwood, but bolder and broader in treatment. It is not inappropriately termed "Dickens Ware".

170   171   172   173

170-173. WILLETS MANUFACTURING CO., Trenton, N. J.—This factory was erected in 1853 by William Young & Son, who made rockingham and C. C. ware. The present proprietors succeeded to the business in 1879, and under their energetic management it has assumed very considerable proportions. William Bromley, after being with Ott & Brewer, went there to introduce the manufacture of Belleek, which is carried on up to the present day with marked success, the designs being selected with special reference to the delicacy of the body in which they are produced.

174   175   176   177

178   179   180

174-176. The Warwick China Co.—The extensive potteries of the Warwick China Co. are situated on the left bank of the Ohio river in the city of Wheeling, W. Va., and are devoted to the manufacture of a superior line of semi-vitreous china, jardinieres, and an extensive line of novelties and art goods in a large assortment of rich and beautiful decorations. The company was organized in September, 1887, with J. R. McCortney, president; and M. N. Cecil, secretary. The board of directors consisted of J. R. McCortney, Henry Stamm, A. J. Clark and O. C. Dewey. In the spring of 1889 Mr. McCortney retired, O. C. Dewey was elected president, and A. T. Young succeeded as director. In November of the same year O. C. Dewey retired from the presidency, and C. W. Franzheim was elected to fill his place, which position he held until February, 1893, when he retired, and Thomas Carr, who at that time was manager, was made president—a position he still holds. Since Mr. Carr assumed the management the product of this factory has made wonderful strides in the favor of both the dealers and the consumers of the entire United States; and as he is never satisfied that the limitations of his art have been reached, further progress may confidently be looked for.

178-179. West End Pottery Co., East Liverpool, O.—The West End Pottery Co. was organized in 1893 by Wm. Burgess, Willis Cunning, Geo. W. Ashbaugh, E. B. Bradshaw, T. R. Bradshaw and Ida O. Bradshaw. The company purchased the bone china works of Burgess & Co., and started the manufacture of ironstone china, in which they have proved very successful. The interests of Ida O. and E. B. Bradshaw and of Mr. Peake have since been bought by the company. In June, 1896, T. R. Bradshaw sold his interest to W. A. Calhoun. The officers of the company at present are Wm. Burgess, manager; Willis Cunning, assistant manager; W. A. Calhoun, secretary, and Geo. W. Ashbaugh, president. These, with the addition of C. C. Ashbaugh form the members of the company.

180. WICK CHINA Co., Kittanning, Pa.

181-185. WELLSVILLE PIONEER POTTERY Co., Wellsville, O.—This business was started by Morley & Co. in 1879. They made white granite and majolica. From 1882 to 1885 the mark 181 was used. In 1885 the concern was incorporated as the Pioneer Pottery Works Co., and the mark 182 was used. From 1888 to 1890 the English arms were used on white granite, and 183 for semi-porcelain. In 1890 the works were burned down, but were rebuilt in the following spring. From that time until September, 1896, 184 was used. On February 1, 1896, the company was organized and incorporated as the Wellsville Pioneer Pottery Co., but 185 was not adopted until September, 1896.

186-193. WHEELING POTTERY Co., Wheeling, W. Va.—Incorporated in 1879, since which time the capacity has been increased fourfold, and practically continues under the same management as originally composed, with Mr. Chas. W. Franzheim as president and general manager. One of their most notable successes has been in rich cobalt decorations, applied not only utilitarian articles, but to jardinieres and other specialties. "Made in America" is no longer a reproach, and the Wheeling Pottery Co., in adopting it as a motto showed the courage of their convictions. The American march of progress is well exemplified here. The first three marks were used from 1880 to 1886, and the next two from 1886 to 1897, on white granite; the two following, since 1893, on semi-porcelain; and the last, since 1894, on C. C. Their latest product is a china body known as cameo china, a thin translucent paste in which some effective decorations, mostly in blue and gold, have been introduced. The eagle and shield mark has been adopted during the present year.

C. P. CO.

CHITTENANGO (N. Y.) POTTERY Co.—This company was organized in 1897, for the manufacture of bone china, but towards the close of the year the manufactory was destroyed by fire and had to be rebuilt. It is now in working order and production has commenced. The officers are F. H. Gates, president; J. R. Eaton, vice president; W. H. Stewart, treasurer; W. J. Logan, secretary. The progress of this company will be watched with interest, as the directors intend competing with the leading English firms. This is an ambitious venture, but with careful workmanship and competent art directorship the chances of success are largely in their favor.

Bibliography

Altman, Seymour and Violet. *The Book of Buffalo Pottery*. New York: Crown Publishers, 1969.

Barber, Edwin AtLee. *The Pottery and Porcelain of the United States*. New York: G.P. Putnam's Sons. Three editions: 1893, 1901, 1909.

Barber, Edwin AtLee. *Marks of American Potters*. Philadelphia: Patterson and White Co, 1904.

Beers, J.H. *The History of Armstrong County, Pennsylvania: Her People Past and Present*. Philadelphia: J.H. Beers & Co., 1914.

Cox, Warren E. *The Book of Pottery and Porcelain*. New York: Crown Publishers, 1944.

Cunningham, Jo. *The Collector's Encyclopedia of American Dinnerware*. Paducah, Ky.: Collector Books, 1982.

Derwich, Jenny B. and Latos, Mary. *Dictionary Guide to U.S. Pottery and Porcelain*. Privately printed, 1984.

Evans, Paul. *Art Pottery of the United States*. New York: Charles Scribner's Sons, 1974.

Gaston, Mary Frank. *The Collector's Encyclopedia of Flow Blue China*. Paducah, Ky.: Collector Books, 1983.

Gates, William C., Jr. and Ormerod, Dana E. *The East Liverpool, Ohio, Pottery District: Identification of Manufacturers and Marks*. Published in book form by the *Journal of the Society for Historical Archaeology* as Volume 16, Numbers 1 & 2, 1982.*

Godden, Geoffrey. *Encyclopedia of British Pottery and Porcelain Marks*. New York: Crown Publishers, 1964.

Hammond, Dorothy. *Confusing Collectibles*. Des Moines, Ia.: Wallace-Homestead Book Co., 1972.

Heaivilin, Annise Doring. *Grandma's Tea Leaf Ironstone*. Des Moines, Ia.: Wallace-Homestead Book Co., 1981.

Jervis, W. Percival. *A Book of Pottery Marks*. Privately printed. 1897, Portions of that book are reprinted in this book. See p. 243.

Lehner, Lois. *Complete Book of American Kitchen and Dinner Wares*. Des Moines, Ia.: Wallace-Homestead Book Co., 1980.

Lehner, Lois. *U.S. Marks on Pottery, Porcelain and Clay*. Paducah, Ky.: Collector Books, 1988.

McCord, William B. *History of Columbiana County*. Chicago: Biographical Publishing Co., 1905.

McKee, Floyd W. *The Second Oldest Profession: A Century of American Dinnerware Manufacture*. Privately printed, 1966.

Newkirk, David A. and Bougie, Stanley J. *Red Wing Dinnerware*. St. Cloud, Minn.: Volkmuth Printers, 1980.

Ramsay, John. *American Potters and Pottery*. New York: Tudor Publishing Co., 1947.

Spargo, John. *Early American Pottery and China*. New York: Garden City Publishing Co., 1926.

Stout, Wilbur. "History of the Clay Industry in Ohio." *Geological Survey of Ohio*, Series 4, Bulletin 26, 1923.

Thorn, C. Jordan. *Handbook of Old Pottery and Porcelain Marks*. New York: Tudor Publishing Co., 1947.

Williams, Petra. *Flow Blue China: An Aid to Identification*. Jeffersontown, Ky.: Fountain House East, 1971.

Williams, Petra. *Flow Blue China II*. Jeffersontown, Ky.: Fountain House East, 1973.

Williams, Petra. *Flow Blue China and Mulberry Ware*. Jeffersontown, Ky.: Fountain House East, 1975.

*Society for Historical Archaeology, P.O. Box 231033, Pleasant Hill, CA 94523-1033.

Index

This index was designed to make possible the easy identification of American whiteware and porcelain marks. Pages 6 through 7 include a step-by-step procedure that will help you to use the index more efficiently. The index includes many British initials. These initials are usually part of a complex mark. British initials used on nineteenth century marks are often in fancy, difficult-to-read script. Initials used on American marks are seldom difficult to read. *Late U.S.* means the term was used after 1930. Marks with these terms are generally not otherwise included in this book.

A.& B. – England
A.& C. – England
A.& Co. – England
A.& M.: 48
A.& S. – England
A.B. – England
A.B. & Co. – England
A B C (or Co.) – late U.S.
Abingdon: 166
A.B.J. & S. (or Sons) – England
A. Bros. – England
A.C. Blair China Studios – U.S. (1940s+)
A.C.Co. (initials or monogram): 14, 15, 16
A.C.Co. on British Coat of Arms: 14, 15
A.C.Co. below British Coat of Arms: 16
Acme Porcelain: 14
Acme Craftware – U.S. (1940s+)
an acorn: 29
Acorn: 29
Adamantine: 161
Adam Antique: 138
Adams (various) – England
Adderly – England
Adelaide: 163
Adler, Jacobi – Germany
Admiral: 156
Admiral, The: 153
A.E. – French Limoges
A.E.T. Co. Ltd.: 202
A.F. & S. – England
A.-G.C.Co.: 19
A.G.H.J. – England
Aich – Germany
Akron China Co.: 14
Akron, Ohio: 14
Akron Revere China: 14
Alamo: 133
Alamo Potteries, Inc. – U.S. (1940s+)
Alaska: 45
Alba China: 22
Albany: 65
Albert Pick: 115, 168
Albion: 23
Albion (Pottery, etc.) – England
Albright China: 14, 166
Alcock (various) – England
Alcora – Spain
Aldridge & Co. – England
Aldwych China – England
Alexander, S., & Sons: 203
Alhambra – Austria
Alfred Meakin – England
Alice: 166
Allerton (& Sons) – England
Alliance: 26
Alliance China Co. – late U.S.
Alliance, O.: 14

Alliance Vitreous China Co.: 14
Allsup, John (or J.) – English retailer
Alma: 40
Alox – late U.S.
Alpha: 37
Alpine China: 26
Aluminia – Denmark
A.M. above an L. – England
Amazon Shape: 90
Amberg – Germany
Amercé (Dinnerware): 16
American Beauty, An: 76, 77
American China: 16, 86, 87, 88
American China Co.: 15, 199
American Chinaware Corp.: 15, 16, 186
American Fine China – U.S. (1960s)
American Girl: 132
American Heritage (Dinnerware) – late U.S. (Stetson): 136
American Limoges: 85
American Modern: 138
American Pottery (Co.): 66
American Pottery Co. (Peoria, Ill.): 112
American Pottery Works: 16, 208
Amstel – Holland
An American Beauty: 76, 77
(Most anchors are for various, often early, European marks.)
an anchor: 18, 19, 86, 207
an anchor and castle (impressed) – England
an anchor and U.S. flag behind a banner: 153
Anchor (Pottery): 18, 19
Anchor Hocking – very late U.S.: 132
Angelus (or Angdus), The: 79
two animals, winged: 58
Annaburg – Germany
Annecy – France
Antique Ivory: 126, 200
A.P. with an anchor: 206
A.P. monogram: 18
A.P.Co. (L.) – England
A.P.M.Co.: 16
Apollo: 156
Apsley, Pellatt & Co. – English retailer
A.Q.W.Co.: 14
A.-R.: 139
Arcadia (China) – England
Arequipa – early U.S. art pottery
Arita – U.S. (1970s)
Ardmore: 97
Argosy: 53
an armor-clad head: 158, 159
Arms (Seal) of Maryland: 89
Arms (Seal) of Massachusetts: 102
Arms of Michigan: 22
Arms of New Jersey: 34, 37, 47, 49, 58, 87, 150
Arms of New York: 106
Arms of Pennsylvania: 21, 33, 90, 91, 163, 164
Arno: 163

(Most arrow marks are European.)
an arrow: 61, 62, 112, 178, 179
Artistic: 27
an artist's palette: 20, 84
an artist's palette with an S in the center: 124
Art Pottery Co. – England
Art Wells Glazes: 82
Art Moderne: 197
Arundel: 33
Asbury – England
Ashby – England
Ashworth – England
Atkinson & Co. – England (very early)
Atlas China: 166
Atlas China Co.: 19
Atlas China above a globe – England
Atlas China under a globe: 166
Atlas-Globe (China Co.): 19
Atona (really Latona): 142, 143
Ato (really Cato) Pattern: 91
Att Are (really Watt Ware): 194
Ault – England
Aurora China: 111, 163
Auxerre – France
Avalon: 31, 33
Avalon China: 33
Avalon Faience: 33, 167
AVCO China: 14
Avisseau – France
Avon: 30, 66, 162
Avon Ware – England
Avona China: 143, 195
Aynsley – England

a B in a complex monogram: 26
B. in a wreath: 167
B.& B. – England
B.& B.Co. monogram: 27
B.& C.: 64, 65
B.& Co. – England
B.& Co. over an L – England
B.& G.: 20, 21
B.& G. (really a C.): 64
B.& G. (Bing & Grondahl) – Denmark
B.& H. – England
B.& K. (L. or Ltd.) – England
B.& L. – England
B.& M. (Co.): 28, 168, 169
B.& P. under a crown – Germany
B.& S. – England
B.& S.H. – England
B.& T. – England
B.& V. (really V.& B.) monogram: 155, 156
B.A. & B. – England
Babbacombe – England
a badge, eagle in center: 36, 57, 71, 116
Baensch – Germany
Baguley (,C.) – England
Bahl Potteries, Inc. – U.S. (c.1940+)
Bailey (various) – England
Bailey-Walker (China Co.): 20, 209, 224
Bailey-Walker, The: 20
Baker (Bros.) – England
Bakerite: 62
Bak-in Ware: 39
Ballerina: 154, 155
a balloon (really a vase): 68, 69
a balloon (a ball): 163
Balmoral: 66

Balt.: 33
Baltimore or Balto.: 33, 89
Baltimore & Ohio Railroad: 129, 132
Barangwka (Baranovka) – Poland (porcelain)
Barker (various) – England
Barratts – England
Barr, Flight (etc.) – England
Barth, L.: 115
Barum – England
Bates, Walker & Co. – England
Batista – Italy
Bauer Pottery Co. – mostly late U.S., California
Baum (,J.H.): 20
Bavaria – Germany
Baye(a)ux – France
B.B.: 27, 28
B.B. on British Coat of Arms: 27
B.B. over a B on shield – England
B.B. (& I. or Co.) – England (Wales)
B.x B.: 162
B.B.M.& Co.: 25
B.- C.: 65
B.C.Co. – England
B.C.G. – England
B.E. & Co. – England
Beardmore, Frank, & Co. – England
Beauty: 28
Beaver Falls, Pa.: 183
Beck, R.K.: 167
Beech & Hancock – England
beehive: 162
other beehives – England, etc.
plain beehive mark – Austria
Beerbower (,L.B.) & Co.: 20
two bees below a hive (B.x B. above): 162
a beetle (scarab): 103
Belfield & Co. – England (Scotland)
a bell: 17, 35
a bell with J.B. or a bell in a wreath – England (Scotland)
two bells, one almost hidden – England
Bell China: 21
Bell Pottery Co., The: 21
Belle: 137
Belleek: 15, 35, 71, 84, 109, 110, 163, 170
Belleek and Co. Fermanagh – famous Irish Belleek
Belleek under hound and harp – famous Irish Belleek
Belle Vue (Pottery) – England
Bellview: 128
Bellvue – France (English-style whiteware)
Belmar: 130
Belmont: 117
Belva China: 142, 144
Benedikt – Germany
Bennett: 23
Bennett, E.: 22
Bennett, E. & W.: 21
Bennett's Patent or Copyright: 22, 167
Bennett, William – England
Bennington: 153
Bentley – England
Berkeley: 55
Berkeley on a clover – late U.S.
Berlin: 19, 73, 130
Berlin (really Oberlin): 73
Beula on map of Ohio: 137
Bevington & Co. – England (Wales)
B.F.B. (or & B.) – England
B.F.(K.) – Belgium
B.G. – England

Cordey China – late U.S. (porcelain)
Cordova: 198
Coreopsis: 33
Corinne: 153
Cork & Edge – England
Corn, W.E. – England
Cornell: 72, 172
Corns China Co.: 95
Corona – England
Cotton, Elijah – England
Cowan – U.S. art pottery (WWI to 1931)
Coxon & Co.: 36, 172
Coxon Belleek: 36
C.P. (really P.C.) monogram: 42
C.P.Co.: 33, 34, 40, 172
C.P.Co. above a cannon: 30
C.P.Co. under a globe: 34
C.P.Co. under N.J. arms: 34
C.P.Co. under a U.S. Shield: 34
C.P.Co. Ltd.: 33
C.P.Co. (Ltd.) with thistle on mark England (Scotland)
Craftsman Dinnerware – U.S. (1930s+)
Creil – France
Cremorne (Opaque Porcelain): 89
a crescent – see moon
Crescent (Pottery): 37
Crescent China (Co.): 37, 172, 173, 194
Crescent China Co., The: 37, 172
Crescent with Utopia: 37, 173
Crest-O-Gold: 124
Crocker – England
Cronin (China Co.): 38, 173
Crooksville (China Co.): 38, 39, 209
a cross (Maltese type): 65, 108, 180
(Crown marks are very common European marks. Crowns are often a part of English marks. Crowns with initials below were common early European marks. The marks below are American.)
a crown: 28, 40, 65, 66
a crown, no words: 40
a crown above a circle: 48, 55, 73, 86, 87, 162, 190
a crown above a circle, fleur-de-lis in center: 162
a crown above a globe: 57
a crown above a G.C.M.& Co. monogram: 99
a crown above an R in circle: 48
a crown above REX: 40
a crown above a shield: 97
a crown in a circle: 45, 65, 66, 147
a crown in an oval: 89
a crown in a wreath: 23
a crown, N.E.P. monogram in center: 102
a crown, Royal Crown, Etruria: 109
a crown, a sword behind crown: 109
a crown with an E in center: 102
a crown with a dragon on top: 156
a crown with a phoenix (bird) on top: 22, 25
Crown: 40
Crown Brand – late U.S.
Crown Chelsea – England
Crown (Dresden) Ware – England
Crown Ducal – England
Crown Hotel Ware: 40
Crown Ovenware: 40
Crown Porcelain: 40
Crown Pottery (or Potteries) Co.: 40, 210
Crown Pottery on circle – England
Crown Semi-porcelain: 40
Crownford Ware – England

C.S. above an A. on a shield – Germany
C.T. under eagle – Germany (porcelain)
C.T.M. (& Sons) – England
Cuban: 159
Cube – England (teapots)
Cumbow China – U.S. (1930s+): 241
Cunningham & Pickett: 18, 41, 200
Cunningham Industries, Inc. – late U.S.
Cupid: 50
C.W. as initials or monogram – England

D.& C. over an L. – England
D.& Co. – French Limoges
D.& D.: 120, 121
Dagoty – France (porcelain)
Dainty: 37
Dakota: 72
Dale & Davis under British Coat of Arms: 120, 121
Dal(l)witz – Austria, now Czech/Slovakia
Daniel (& Sons) – England
Daniell – England (retailer)
Darte Freres – France
Davenport – England
Davis, I. under British Coat of Arms: 120, 121
Davis, I. under shield: 120, 121
Davis, J.H. – England
Dawson – England
Day on artist's palette: 137
Daybreak: 91
Dayton: 30
D.B.& Co. – England
D.C. – England
D.-D.: 120, 121
Deakin (& Son) – England
Dean, Jesse: 140
other Dean – England
DeBolt, F.F.: 197
Deck – France
Decoration: 91
Decoro Pottery – England
Dedham Pottery: 41
a deer (stag) head: 25, 157
a deer (stag) head in circle: 157
two deer standing: 22
Defender: 28
DeLan & McGill: 140, 173
Delaware Pottery: 41
Delft, D.C.: 35, 174
Delft with Etruria: 35, 174
Delphine (China) – England
D.E.McNicol: 93, 94, 219
D.E.McNicol Pottery Co.: 92, 93, 94, 115, 219
D.E.McN.P.Co. (,The): 93
DeMorgan – England (art pottery)
DeMoustiers – France
Denaura: 41
Denby – England
Denver: 41, 52
Denver C.& P. Co.: 41
Depose – French Limoges
Derby: 49
other Derby – England
Derry China Co.: 41, 42
Derwood: 53
De Soto China: 117
DeSoto, E. Palestine, O.: 203
Detroit: 73
Detroit over K.T.K. – U.S. (1920s)

Devon – England
Dewey: 45
D.F.H. (Co.) monogram: 33
D.F. H. (or Hayes) & Co.: 89
Diamond: 65
Diamond China: 23, 99
a diamond: 23, 66, 102, 113
a diamond (baseball?): 103
a diamond with circle inside: 22, 90
a diamond with H inside: 63
a diamond with M inside: 54
a diamond with W inside: 162
a diamond with Warranted Fireproof: 113
Diana: 91
Dicker Ware – England
Dillon – England
Dillwyn (& Co.) – England (Wales)
Dixie: 172
D.L. & Co. (or & Son, or & S.) – England (Scotland)
D.M. & S. – England (Scotland)
Doccia – Italy
Doctor Syntax – England (Clews)
Don: 137
Don, Edward, Co. – U.S. (1940s+)
Don Pottery – England
Doric (China) – England
Doric (U.S.A.): 206
Doris: 91
Dorlexa China Co.: 203
Doulton (,Royal) – England
a dove holding a ribbon or scroll: 38
Dover China: 202
D.P.Co. (Ltd.) – England
D.P.W. monogram: 42
D.R.: 46
a dragon: 58
a dragon atop a crown: 156
a dragon-like figure (over China): 106
a dragon holding a ball: 106
two dragons holding a shield: 58
Dresden: 42, 43, 44
Dresden (Stone) China: 43, 44
Dresden Pottery: 210
Drexel: 146
Dryden – U.S. (1940s+)
Ducal (,Crown) – England
Duchess: 163
Dudson (Bros.) – England
Duesbury – England
Dumonte Fabrique – France
Dunmore – England (Scotland)
Duquesne: 91
Dura-Print: 196
Durham China – England

an E (really N.E.P. monogram) on a crown: 102
an E. in center of raised mark: 174
E.& B. (L.) – England
E.& C.C. – England
E.& G.P. – England
E.& H. – England
E.& W. Bennett: 21
an eagle: 46, 57, 71, 72, 77
an eagle above a circle draped with flags: 155
an eagle above a crown: 22, 25
an eagle above a lion: 76, 77
an eagle above a shield: 54, 93
an eagle above a shield (Arms of Maryland): 89
an eagle above a shield (Arms of New York): 106

an eagle flying, carrying a ribbon with WARRANTED: 102
an eagle holding ribbon in beak: 103, 104
an eagle holding ribbon under a shield and flags: 161
an eagle holding ribbon, U.S. flag behind: 153
an eagle holding ribbon, U.S. shield behind: 43
an eagle head holding an S: 151
an eagle holding U.S. shield: 54, 100
an eagle holding shield, globe behind: 160
an eagle in a circle: 71, 72, 89, 100, 157
an eagle in a wreath: 57
an eagle in a badge, medal, or star: 36, 57, 71, 116
an eagle standing on shield: 100
an eagle with IRON STONE CHINA: 71
East End China Co., The: 147
East End P.Co.: 45
East Liverpool (O.) – common on U.S. marks; can't be used
   to identify marks.
East Liverpool Potteries Co.: 46, 154
Eastwood – England
E.B.: 22
E.B. & B. – England
E.B. & Co. over an F – England
E.B. & J.E.L. over a B – England
E. Bennett: 22, 23
E.B.J.E.L. – England
E.B.P.Co.: 22, 23
E.C. – England
Edge, Malkin & Co. (Ltd.) – England
Edgerton (Handpainted): 115
Edgerton Fine China – late U.S., (Pickard)
Edward Don Co. – U.S. (1940s+)
Edward J. Owen China Co.: 221
Edwards, John or James – England
other Edwards – England
Edwin M. Knowles (China Co.): 67, 68, 69, 70, 211
E.E.C.Co.: 147
E.E.P.Co.: 45
E.F.B. (& Co., or & Son) – England
E.G.& Co. – England
Eggshell (Nautilus, etc.): 82
E.H.S.: 129
E.H.S.C.Co.: 129, 130
E.H.S.C.Co. monogram: 129
E.H. Sebring China Co.: 129, 130
Eighteen (18) carat gold, etc.: 199
E.J.B. (JB joined) D. – England
E.J.D.B. – England
Eichwald – Germany
E.K. & Co. – England
E.K.B. – England
Eland (really Leland): 182
Elbogen – Germany
El Camino China – late U.S.
Electric: 26, 27
Elkin (Knight) & Co. – England
Elkton: 36
ELO: 57
E.L.O. (for East Liverpool, Ohio), common on U.S. marks;
   can't be used to identify marks.
ELPCO: 154
E.L.P.Co. (initials or monogram): 45
Elsmere: 31
Elsmore & Forest (or & Son) – England
E.M.& Co. – England
Emery – England
E.M.K. over C.Co.: 67
Empire China: 137
Empire (Pottery): 48
Empire Ware or Works – England

G.F.B. (B.T.) – England
G.F.S. (Co.) – England
G.G.& Co.– England
G.G.W. – England
G.H.& Co. – England
G.H.B.Co.: 34
Gibson (& Sons) – England
Gien – France
Giesshubel – Germany
Ginder, S., & Co. – England
Ginori – Italy
G.J. as a monogram – England
G.L.A. & Bros. – England
Gladding, McBean & Co. – late U.S.
Gladstone – England
Glasgow China or Pottery Co.: 54, 55, 56
other Glasgow – England (Scotland)
G.L.B.& Co. – England
Glebe Pottery – England
Glendale: 107
Glendora: 176
Glen Rose: 33
Glenwood: 146
Globe China Co., Cambridge, Ohio: 56
Globe (Pottery or China): 56, 57
other Globe Pottery – England
a globe: 43, 56, 57, 96
a globe, half submerged, U.S. flag on top: 137
a globe held by lion and unicorn, an eagle on top: 37
a globe in a circle: 22, 106
a globe in a square: 28
a globe in a wreath: 28
a globe pierced by a sword: 22, 23
a globe under a crown: 57
a globe with CRESCENT across: 37
a globe with IDEAL BB on a ribbon: 27
a globe with a lion on top: 165
a globe with O. WARRANTED B. across: 109
a globe with an eagle holding a shield in front: 160
a globe with bird on top: 34, 174
a globe with WARRANTED across: 43, 96, 109, 152, 192
a globe with WARRANTED around it: 22
a globe with wings: 57
Glo-Tan: 170
G.M. & Son: 98
G.M.B. – late U.S. (Gladding, McBean and Co.)
G.M.C. monogram – England
G.M.T.Co. – U.S. (1940s+)
Godwin (,T. or Thos., or T. & B.) – England
Godwin & Flentke: 57
Gold Medal/ St. Louis: 110
Golden (Col.): 36, 52
Golden Fleece: 77
Golden Gate: 77
Golden Glo – U.S. (1970s)
Golden Maize: 18, 37, 176
Goldscheider – late England, late U.S.
Goldscheider (Wien) – Austria
Gonder – U.S. (1940s+)
Goode – England (retailer)
Goodfellow – England
Goodwin('s): 57, 58
Goodwin (Bros.): 57
Goodwin Pottery (Co.): 57, 58, 177
Goodwin & Harris – England
Gorham – very late U.S.: 83
Goss, W.H. – England
Gosse Bayeux – France
Gotha – Germany

Gouda – Holland
Govan(croft) – England (Scotland)
G.P.: 55
G.P.& Co. – England
G.P.C.: 52
G.P.Co.: 56, 57, 58
G.P.Co. monogram: 55
G.P.Co. – England (Scotland)
G.R.& Co. – England
Grafton China (,Royal) – England
Grainger (various) – England
Grapevine: 168
Gray (Pottery) – England
Green – England
Greenock – England (Scotland)
Greek: 50
Greenwood (China or Pottery): 58, 59, 177
Greenwood Art Pottery: 59
Gresley – England
a griffin (winged lion with eagle's head): 145
a griffin atop "barrels": 141
two griffins: 58
Grimwades – England
Grindley (& Co.) – England (*Grindley exported much early ware to the U.S.*)
Grosvenor (China) – England
Grueby (Faience or Pottery): 59
Grunstadt – Germany
G.S. & Co. – England
G.S. & S. – England
G.S.H. (complex monogram): 113
G.T. & S. – England
G.T.M. – England
Guernsey (Ware): 29
Gustafsberg – Sweden
G.W. (& S. or & Sons) – England
G.W.P. Co.: 164
G.W.T.S. (or & S. or & Sons) – England

an H (impressed on porcelain) – England
an H in a circle: 63
an H in a diamond: 30, 63, 178
an H (really H.L. monogram): 77
an H under an arrow: 178
an H with arrow (monogram): 61
H. & A. – England
H. & B. – England
H. & C. above an F. – England
H. & C. (or Co.)
H. & Co. above an L. – French Limoges
H. & Co. above an S. – Germany
H. & G. – England
H. & K. – England
H. & S. – England
H. & W. – England
H.A. & Co. – England
H.A. & Co. over an L – England
Hackwood – England
Hadley, M.A. – U.S. (1940s+)
Hadley Ware – England
Haeger (Potteries): 59
Haeger, Royal – late U.S.: 59
Haidinger – Germany
Hall (China) – mostly late U.S.: 59, 60
Hall China Co.: 59, 60, 211
Hall in a square – U.S. (1970s+)
Hall Superior Quality – U.S. (1930s+)
Hall, R. – England
Hall (various) – England

Lois: 205
London as part of mark – England (often retailers)
Longpark – England
Longport – England
Longton – England
Longwy – France
Lotta: 205
Lotus: 65, 73
Lotus Ware: 73
Lowe – England
Lowesby – England
L.P.& Co. – England
L.R. & Co. monogram – England
L.S. (& G.) – England
Luna: 73
Luneville – France
Lu-ray Pastels: 144
Luzerne: 97
L.W. – England
L.W. over a P. – Germany
Lygia: 50
Lyman: 153

an M. in "fancy" mark with pattern number – England (Minton)
an M. inside a circle: 54, 55
an M. inside a diamond: 54
M. China L.: 88
an M. on a shield under a crown: 88
M.& A. – England
M.& B. – England
M.& Co.: 99
also M.& Co. – England
M.& E. – England
M.& H. – England
M.& N. – England
M.& S.: 95
M.& S. above an L – England
M.& S. monogram on a shield: 95
Maastricht – Holland
a machete: 159
Macintyre, J., or James (& Co.) – England
Maddock: 86, 87, 88
also Maddock – England
Maddock, John, & Sons (Trenton, N.J.): 88
also Maddock, John, & Sons – England
Maddock's, Thos., Sons Co.: 86, 87, 183
Maddock's American China: 86, 88
Maddock's Lamberton Works: 87, 88
Maddock's Trenton China: 86, 88
Maddox of California: 196
Maddux: 196
MADE IN U.S.A.: 199
Madison: 146
Madrid: 43
Mafra – Portugal
M.A. Hadley – U.S. (1940s+)
Maine: 72
Mainz – Germany
Majestic – early Homer Laughlin mark (c.1910)
Majestic (Wellsville): 117
Majol(l)ica, Morley & Co.: 98
majolica ware marked only with letters and numbers: 114
Maling – England
Malkin – England
a Maltese cross: 65, 108, 180
Mandois – France
Manhattan: 99
Mann & Co. – England

M.A.P. (in oval with Trenton): 97
a map of Ohio: 137
Marcrest – late U.S.
Mare – England
Marine: 92
Marion: 91
Marquette: 172
Marshall, John, & Co. – England (Scotland)
Martha Washington: 51, 127, 133
Martin, Shaw & Cope – England
Mary Louise – U.S. (1940s)
Maryland Coat of Arms: 89
Maryland Pottery: 89
Mason('s) – England
Massachusetts Coat of Arms: 102
Massier – France
Matthews, John – England
Matt Morgan – early U.S. art pottery
Maw (& Co.) – England
Mayer, J.& E.: 89, 90, 91, 92, 183, 218
other Mayer – England
Mayer China: 89, 197
Mayer Pottery Co.: 89, 218
M.B. – England
M.C.: 96, 97, 168
M.C. tiny letters inside a complex monogram: 96
M.C.P.Co. monogram: 99
McCoy: 92
McN.: 93
McN.B.& Co.: 92
McNicol: 93
McNicol China: 94
McNicol-Corns Co.: 95, 183
McNicol, D.E.: 93, 94, 219
McNicol, D.E., Pottery Co.: 92, 93, 94, 115, 219
McNicol, Roloc – late U.S.
McNicol, T.A.: 95, 220
McN.P.Co.(,D.E.): 93
M.C.P. – late U.S.
M.C.P.Co. monogram: 99
M.E.& Co. England
Meakin, Alfred – England
other Meakin – England
a medal (medallion) with an eagle in the center: 36, 57, 71, 116
Meigh, Charles, (& Son) – England
other Meigh – England
Meir (China or Ware) – England
Meissen – Germany
Melba (China or Ware) – England
Mellor & Co.: 35, 36, 170, 171
Mellor, Taylor & Co. – England
Mellor, Venerable & Co. – England
Melloria: 37
Melrose: 145, 146
Melton: 130
two men (or women?) standing on sides of shields (Arms of Maryland): 89
Menelik Co.: 184
Mercer (China): 96, 97, 184
Mercer (Pottery Co.): 96, 97
Methven (& Sons) – England (Scotland)
Metlox – U.S. (1930s+)
Mettlach – Germany
Mexbro – England
M.H.& Co. – England
Michigan Coat of Arms: 22
Middleport Pottery – England
Middlesbro – England